MW01013795

"Are UFOs replacing yesterday's angels? Will flying saucers bring redemption from the sky? What could be the impact of the discovery of extra-terrestrial intelligence on religions? Ted Peters offers some potential answers in this groundbreaking work and a fascinating contribution to the religious and spiritual structures at work in the UFO phenomenon, as well as establishing a new field of research Astrotheology."

— Philippe Ailleris, Unidentified Aerospace Phenomena (UAP) Observations Reporting Scheme, the Netherlands

"Ted Peters brings a much-needed sober voice to topics that can be highly charged. His book examines connections in alternative and traditional belief systems, demonstrating central ideas that buttress our world views are not as disparate as they may seem. It is an important examination that, to me, sheds light on the similarity of our hearts, and our yearning to connect to something greater."

—Alejandro Rojas, editor and writer for *Open Minds Magazine*, and host of Open Minds UFO Radio, *www.openminds.tv/alejandro-rojas*

"This book is a welcome update of Ted Peters' *UFOs: God's Chariots?* It blends historical, cultural, and theological analyses with consideration of the relations today between science and religion, and, importantly, of the nature of human religious longing and experiences. A variety of readers from the general to the scholarly, from the skeptical to the faithful will find this book to be informative, engaging, and thought-provoking."

—Catherine Wessinger, Rev. H. James Yamauchi, S.J. Professor of the History of Religions, Loyola University New Orleans

"*UFOs: God's Chariots?* explores incisively and insightfully the intertwined observer-observed elements of UFO encounters. Peters uses hermeneutical phenomenology to analyze possible symbolic meanings of reported events as he links witnesses (including those claiming to be abductees) to what they perceive; defines a new area of reflective research, Astrotheology; and, rejecting cultural scientism, affirms the religious and spiritual dimensions of human existence. An important contribution to efforts to understand holistically and interpret critically UFO phenomena."

—John Hart, professor of Christian Ethics, Boston University School of Theology; author of *Cosmic Commons*

"Are UFOs best viewed through the eyes of science or religion? In this updated edition of his 1977 classic, Ted Peters says both, and he also adds a third eye, the sociological, noting that UFO 'waves' often come in times of social and political crisis. *UFOs: God's Chariots?* offers a fascinating critical survey of the aerial phenomenon down through the decades since it essentially began in 1947, moved through the era of benign 'space brothers' contacts, and into the often sinister abductions and bizarre medical exams of later decades, and finally provides both problems and data for what Peters calls astrotheology. Highly recommended for reading and reflection."

—Robert Ellwood, University of Southern California

UFOs: God's Chariots?

Spirituality, Ancient Aliens, and Religious
Yearnings in the Age of Extraterrestrials

Ted Peters

New Page Books
A Division of The Career Press, Inc.
Pompton Plains, NJ

UFOs: God's Chariots?
Edited and Typeset by Gina Schenck
Cover design by theBookDesigners
Printed in the U.S.A.

To order this title, please call toll-free 1-800-CAREER-1 (NJ and Canada: 201-848-0310) to order using VISA or MasterCard, or for further information on books from Career Press.

The Career Press, Inc.
220 West Parkway, Unit 12
Pompton Plains, NJ 07444
www.careerpress.com
www.newpagebooks.com

Library of Congress Cataloging-in-Publication Data

Peters, Ted, 1941-
  UFOs--God's chariots? : spirituality, ancient aliens, and religious yearnings in the age of extraterrestrials / by Ted Peters. -- 2 [edition].
     pages cm
  Includes index.
  ISBN 978-1-60163-318-7 -- ISBN 978-1-60163-468-9 (ebook) 1. Unidentified flying objects--Religious aspects. 2. Unidentified flying objects--Miscellanea. I. Title.
  TL789.P439 2014
  001.942--dc23

                                                                    2013046730

This book is dedicated to Kayla Carter, Jessica Carter, David Peters, Nina Frase, Madeline Lulu Peters, Jacqueline Carter, and Lydia Frase, along with Jack Anderson, Will Anderson, and Reynold Anderson—a new generation of sky-watchers.

Contents

Preface

I sat on the floor near the front door. I couldn't wait for my mother and father to arrive home. Along with another couple, my mother and father had driven to Detroit to hear a lecture by George Adamski. I had already read Adamski's first book, *Flying Saucers Have Landed*, a story about how George had met a man from Venus in a California desert. Now, members of my very own family were going to listen to the man who had listened to a space man.

When they arrived at the front door near midnight, they brought with them Adamski's new book, *Inside the Space Ships*. I flipped through it while I listened to the four grown-ups discussing the topics of the evening. On his first encounter Adamski had spoken with a man from Venus, gentle in demeanor with flowing hair—very Jesus like. Now, my family was abuzz about Adamski's new adventures aboard a mother ship orbiting our planet. How thrilling for me as a teenager with a vivid imagination!

Later I concluded that George Adamski was a charlatan. I learned that Venus is covered with an opaque layer of highly reflective clouds of sulfuric acid. The greenhouse effect produces a surface temperature of 860 degrees Fahrenheit and an atmospheric pressure 92 times that of Earth. This means that the Venusian visiting George would not have looked like Jesus. Rather, he would have looked like a burned pancake.

Nevertheless, outer space had entered my inner soul. The nighttime sky glittered like a white-lighted Christmas tree. The daytime sky was no less amazing. I recall one sunny afternoon with my friends at the swimming pool. I was lying back on my towel. My eyes feasted on the dramatic theater of the heavens. Beyond the sun the blue color seemed to go on and on. The unfathomable depth—the incomprehensible infinity—of the heavenly vault buried itself within my soul. It has never been dislodged.

All too soon my daydreaming was interrupted. My burly swimming pool friends said it was time to play water football. We chose teams. For the ball, we selected a diminutive 5-year-old boy. We lined up at scrimmage. The quarterback passed the boy to the half back, who then plunged through the line. When tackled, the little boy found himself smothered under 3 feet of water and under a pile of bodies. He came up sputtering and spitting. But, curiously, he did not complain. We went ahead with second down. Life on Earth goes on, whether or not we're aware of our flyspeck status in this immense universe.

Outer space has been lodged in my soul since my youth. This led me to write the first edition of *UFOs: God's Chariots?* in 1977. In more recent years, I've invested considerable academic energy in the dialogue be-tween science and religion with a special focus on Astrobiology and the search for extraterrestrial intelligence (SETI). One thing I learned is that SETI scientists and UFO researchers do not attend the same barbeques. Rather, they sneer at each other in the other's absence. Each accuses the other of not being scientific enough. I find this curious, but not bor-ing. So, after writing a few treatises on *Astrotheology* and *Astroethics*, I'm returning once again to the UFO question with a focus on the extrater-restrial hypothesis.

As I return, I find today's media right where they were a half century ago. Unfortunately, the media still think that the entire UFO pie can be divided into two slices: people who believe in UFOs and skeptics who do not believe. In order to obtain balance, reporters interview one unbeliever for each believer. Then, they consider their work done. In my judgment, this is too simplistic. When asked by a reporter if I believe in UFOs, I routinely answer: "No. I believe in God. I study UFOs."

The UFO phenomenon is much too textured and complex and nuanced to reduce it to believers versus unbelievers. When I wrote the first edition of *UFOs: God's Chariots?* I tried to show how this is the case. Now as I turn to the revision, it appears that the phenomenon is even more complex that it was three decades ago.

This second edition of *UFOs: God's Chariots?* does two things: First, it offers something toward understanding one of the most intriguing and fascinating mysteries of our post-World War II era, namely, the mystery of unidentified flying objects. Untold hours and incalculable amounts of human energy have been poured into solving this enigma, yet the UFO phenomenon just seems to increase in its mystery. Like trying to catch a greased pig, once we think we have a firm grasp, it squirms out in another direction so that we have to resume the chase. It is one thing to see a daylight disc or a glowing object in the night sky, or even to track an unknown blip on radar. It is another thing to have unknowns follow our aircraft or even land, leaving rings of scorched grass on the ground. It is still another to speak with people who claim that they were abducted by diminutive, gray-skinned entities and taken aboard a flying saucer or, in some cases, even claim to have given birth to hybrid babies that combine heavenly and earthly DNA. What is communicated to abductees, and especially to contactees, is of special interest to me as a scholar. Ufonauts speak of their world among the stars as enjoying a level of peace and love that we on Earth can only envy. When we add up these elements and find an incongruous combination of physical nuts-and-bolts aircraft merged with paranormal experiences such as telepathy and walking through walls, this suggests we have a mysterious phenomenon *extraordinaire.*

The resolution to the mystery in its entirety is well beyond the scope of this book, and, as far as I know, beyond the scope of any scholar working on the problem today. There is a particular contribution I can make, however, which will help to fill out our understanding of at least one important dimension of the UFO phenomenon. This is the religious dimension, the spiritual dimension.

The religious or spiritual qualities of this mystery descending from the sky have, for the most part, been overlooked by UFO researchers during the last 60 years. When the topic of religion has been raised, it has been treated with astonishing naiveté, a naiveté that could be founded only on ignorance, or worse, prejudice against religion. The penchant has been to interpret UFOs from only one perspective, namely, as physical objects whose nature can be discerned through scientific analysis. A form of tunnel vision has been at work. I would like to expand this field of vision. In doing so, I do not wish to add psychic or spiritual facets to an otherwise physical phenomenon; rather, I wish to point out what has been present all along. The religious dimension has been a part of the UFO experience right from the beginning. It will be my task in this book to bring the tools of a scholar of religion and a theologian to bear so that we can see that this is the case.

This brings us to the second task the present book performs; this second task is more indirect than direct. In order to get to the religious domain of the UFO experience, we will have to pass through the land of the scientists. We will have to show the limits of the scientific perspective if we are to open the door to the religious perspective. This will be difficult to do, because the scientific mindset is not the private property of our practicing scientists alone. We all think this way. The scientific way of thinking imbues our culture. It provides us with the horizon and the logic whereby we admit something to our understanding and count it as knowledge. Thus, we will have to go to some lengths to show just how religious or spiritual sensibilities come to symbolic expression in UFO reports. Once this has been accomplished, then we will be ready to make some theological judgments. We will also be ready to offer some advice regarding how UFOs should be understood from the perspective of faith in God. In short, this book is not only about UFOs that descend from the sky. It is about the culture that exists here on Earth. It is a case study of the relationship between science and religion.

In my maturing judgment, I believe the central thesis of the first edition of *UFOs: God's Chariots?* remains sound; namely, the UFO phenomenon exposes a widespread cultural tendency to translate traditional religious or spiritual sensibilities into scientific or materialist language and categories. In short, today's flying saucers replace yesterday's angels. So, this central theme continues to serve as the backbone connecting all the ribs in the second edition. A few new ribs will be added, however.

One new rib has to do with changes taking place in abduction accounts. The early abduction accounts in the 1960s and 1970s tended to look like secularized versions of religious experiences. Abductees, though frightened, roundly considered their experience to be positive, even life-changing. During the late 1980s, however, many abduction reports turned dark, menacing. Abducted women and men claimed to have been abused, even raped by spacelings. Stories of pregnancies and births of hybrid babies were retrieved through hypnotic regression. At first this new dimension to the UFO phenomenon seemed to contradict my thesis regarding ufonauts as celestial saviors. I resolved to look into this matter, to see whether confirmation or disconfirmation of my original thesis might be the implication.

A second new rib is a report on some empirical research of my own, the *Peters ETI Religious Crisis Survey.* I asked people who self-identify as religious or non-religious to answer questions regarding the potential impact of confirmed contact with extraterrestrial intelligence (ETI). I wanted to test the widespread assumption that contact with ETI would precipitate a crisis for religious people, perhaps even destroying traditional religion. I'll share my data and my conclusions.

Overall, this book is an attempt to understand how we understand Unidentified Flying Objects. The big problem almost universally attached to discussions of UFOs is the extraterrestrial hypothesis (ETH): Do UFOs come to us courtesy of intelligent beings from another world in space? This book is not an attempt to answer that question. The arguments for both "yes" and "no" are voluminous. The question is a long way from being resolved. I will attempt as much to suspend judgment on whether the UFO-ETH is true or false.

It is almost irrelevant for our purpose whether or not people see an objective reality that we can name a "UFO" or "flying saucer." Our concern here is how people interpret and understand what they take to be a UFO or flying saucer. It is my parenthetical judgment, however, that there is something real being seen in our skies. Flying saucers are not reducible to an unconscious projection from our imaginations. I base this judgment on the fact that so many people of unquestioned integrity and sanity insist that they have had a UFO experience. Many of these witnesses are competent observers and respected citizens: airplane pilots, astronauts, policemen, Senator Barry Goldwater, former Ohio governor John Gilligan, and former president Jimmy Carter. It would be presumptuous to assume all of these people are hallucinators, kooks, or charlatans. A 2012 National Geographic poll asked: Do you believe in UFOs? The results showed that 36 percent are believers, 48 percent are not sure, and 17 percent are disbelievers.[1] Something has happened that is worthy of investigation.

However, the concern of this book is not to identify with precision just what those poll results saw in its own objective and independent reality. Rather, we will look at how that reality is interpreted, how it is understood. Even if UFOs constitute an objective physical reality in their own right, we may still legitimately be concerned with the complex interpretations that UFOs stimulate in the observers. In his fascinating study comparing UFOs and fairies, Jacques Vallee puts the challenge this way: "Beyond the question of the physical nature of the objects, we should be studying the deeper problem of their impact on our imagination and culture."[2] This is a concern of the present volume.

"Saucer culture is a deeply interrelated web of claims and beliefs, with strands of that web reaching far beyond UFO culture into the nooks and crannies of popular culture and popular religion," writes Gregory Reece.[3] In this volume we will look at the place UFOs occupy in our culture and in our psyches.

TERMS AND DEFINITIONS

As we proceed through this book, let me alert you in advance to some of the vocabulary I plan to employ. Just in case some terms are new to you, I have provided some preliminary definitions.

The terms *UFO* and *flying saucer* I use interchangeably. I recognize that *flying saucer* is the more colloquial of the two, to be sure. And, I would like to emphasize that *UFO* or *unidentified flying object* states that what we are looking at is literally *unidentified*. When this distinction is relevant, I'll say so. Otherwise, the two terms will refer to the same thing.

When it comes to the widely used term *UFO phenomenon*, I will ask for more precision than most others require. A phenomenon deals with both object and subject, both the UFO and the person witnessing the UFO. What happens in human subjectivity is just as important to me as the object perceived. The human mind organizes perceptions by interpreting them, and the strangeness of an unidentified flying object gets interpreted by the human mind.

By *phenomenology,* I mean the method of analyzing and explicating the existing structures of interpretation in the human mind. Our interpretations have identifiable structures, and these structures become my models. The four conceptual models for interpreting otherwise strange and unidentifiable flying objects are reflected in the Table of Contents: Model I: the Interstellar Diplomat; Model II: the Research Scientist; Model III: the Celestial Savior; and Model IV: the Hybridizer.

Human experience in general is organized, and the factors that organize religious or spiritual experience are identifiable. One of the key terms on which I frequently rely is *axis mundi*. This is Latin, and it refers to the center of the Earth. Not the physical center, down under our feet. No; it refers to the center of our world, the center of our worldview. If we compare our worldview to a bicycle wheel, the *axis mundi* would be located at the hub, the axel. All the rest of reality spins around this center. The center is what makes reality real.

The *axis mundi* also marks the point at which heaven and Earth are connected. In pre-modern societies, the center of a city or the center of a worship place would include a tall tower, a church steeple, or the equivalent, to connect Earth with sky. Retreats would be held on mountaintops. Communication between the gods in the heavens and the worshippers on Earth would be located here, at the *axis mundi*.

In Native American tribal life as well as aboriginal life on other continents, it was common for a shaman to emerge as healer or leader. A shaman is a person who travels from Earth to heaven and back, and he or she brings back knowledge that only the gods know. This trip may take place in a dream or vision, frequently on the back of a hawk or an eagle. Bird feathers belong to the shaman's symbolism. Essential here is that previously secret divine knowledge now becomes available to the rest of us. Most often, this secret knowledge is therapeutic. It heals. The shaman becomes the medicine man, the tribe's healer.

One implication is that the shaman can become an incarnate *axis mundi*. Wherever the shaman goes, there is the center of the world. What counts as religion or spirituality consists of keeping ourselves connected with the shaman, orienting ourselves toward the heavenly knowledge now available here on Earth.

One of the points I wish to develop in *UFOs: God's Chariots?* is that these religious or spiritual structures are at work in the UFO phenomenon, but they are disguised. They are hidden behind secular and even scientific language. A flying saucer might be described as a machine, a craft, an object. But it bears a religious valence because, like the ancient shamans, it brings us healing knowledge from the heavens.

The term *gnosticism* refers to the belief that knowledge saves. The term, *gnosis,* is Greek for "knowledge." It refers to special knowledge of invisible realities, especially the path from the darkness of life in the flesh to enlightened life in the spirit above. According to the ancient gnostic redeemer myth, ultimate reality belongs to the unknown divine, bathed in eternal light. Due to a mistake performed by a lesser god, the demiurge, the physical world gets created. Creatures within the physical world can no longer see the glorious light of the divine source of reality. The physical realm is locked in darkness and unreality. The body is less real than the spirit. We human beings would be totally lost except for one thing: buried within our bodies is a divine spark, an ember of the divine fire that lights up heaven above. Despite our darkness, the divine spark lies hidden within each one of us.

Further, according to the myth, a redeemer from above comes down to the realm of darkness to teach us who we really are—that is, to teach us to fan the spark within us into a vigorous flame that rises upward, upward from the realm of flesh into the realm of spirit. If we rise beyond the seven heavens, we will enter the eternal realm of light and there dwell at home with the divine. Or, to put it another way, we are already divine but we need gnostic knowledge to realize the divinity that lies concealed within us.

A question I press throughout this book is: Does today's UFO phenomenon look like the ancient gnostic redeemer myth? Can the roles played by the flying saucer as *axis mundi* and shaman be illuminated by looking through the lens of the gnostic redeemer? Is the ancient myth alive today, hidden beneath secular dress?

Finally, one more term: *Astrotheology.* This is a book about theology. What is theology? Theology is rational reflection on faith. Drew University theologian Catherine Keller provides a fitting definition: "Theology is not the same as faith or belief, but a disciplined and relational reflection upon them."[4] Or, alluding to St. Thomas Aquinas, we can say that theology attempts to explain all of reality in light of the God of grace.

In order to study certain things in reality, of course, we need the help of science. What the scientist can tell us about our cosmic home contributes to our understanding of God's relationship to our cosmic home. "All possible worlds have a common origin and depth in the oneness of God," writes theologian John Haught.[5]

UFOs: God's Chariots?

As we review various expressions of the UFO phenomenon, we will note how alternative theologies are already emerging. We might call them "UFO theologies." In this book we will give special attention to the popular ancient astronaut theology. Those who espouse these UFO theologies do not necessarily use the term *theology*, because they think of themselves as providing a substitute for theology. By substituting UFOs for the gods, they think of themselves as providing an anti-theology or scientized theology.

My own approach will be different. After a phenomenological analysis, I will offer my own constructive response, which will fall under the rubric of Astrotheology. That's *astro* tacked on to the front of *theology*. Here is my working definition: "Astrotheology is that branch of theology which provides a critical analysis of the contemporary space sciences combined with an explication of classic doctrines such as creation and Christology for the purpose of constructing a comprehensive and meaningful understanding of our human situation within an astonishingly immense cosmos." By this term, *Astrotheology*, I will not restrict my work to the interpretation of UFOs alone. I also incorporate analysis and synthesis of the space sciences such as Astrobiology and the Search for Extraterrestrial Intelligence (SETI). But what I have to say on these other scientific topics will have to wait for another book.

I'm well aware that the extraterrestrial hypothesis is not the only hypothesis for explaining the UFO phenomenon. Yet, it is the one that interests me for the purposes of this book. As I see it, space consciousness is built right into the phenomenon. The extraterrestrial interpretation is virtually co-present to any facts or data having to do with flying saucers. The meaning of the UFO is as important to me as any facts associated with the UFO. To a certain degree, *UFOs: God's Chariots?* is a study of human meaning in light of a scientized worldview.

Ted Peters
Berkeley, California
New Year's Day, 2014

1

Chariots, UFOs, and Religious Needs

Is the Bible a garbled interpretation of events long ago that really records visits to Earth by travelers from another world? Is the God worshiped by the Christian religion the supernatural creator of all things or is he really just a super-technological creature living on another planet who is trying to influence affairs here on Earth? These are the kinds of questions being raised by proponents of a developing ancient astronaut theology and by UFO re-interpreters of traditional religion.

In recent years considerable attention has been given to the *ancient astronaut theory*, or *ancient alien theory*. Advocates of this theory believe that the pyramids of Egypt and the giant statues on Easter Island were built by intelligent beings from outer space. They say that when the Old Testament prophet Ezekiel describes his vision of a great cloud with fire flashing forth and a "wheel within a wheel" (Ezekiel 1:4–28) he is really witnessing the landing of a spaceship. Not being a product of our modern space age, Ezekiel could describe what he saw only in primitive religious terms. The theory says also that the Genesis account of God's use of fire and brimstone to destroy the cities of Sodom and Gomorrah is really a description of a nuclear explosion set off by the ancient astronauts. In short, the Christian view of God is a big mistake. The Bible reports experiences of flying saucers with humanoid occupants, reports that have been misinterpreted in order to construct a picture of a spiritual deity.

"Civilization was indeed guided by gods, by a nonhuman, extraterrestrial intelligence," writes Philip Coppens, "though today we would consider this to be the bailiwick of religion, it is not; it is about directly experiencing another reality and contacting this intelligence."[1] Accordingly, the Jewish and Christian belief in primitive "fairy stories" and myths should be replaced with a scientized religion that believes in extraterrestrial intelligence from outer space. Will the ancient astronaut theory put theologians out of work?

Speculation on ancient space visitors is not our only religious concern here. Contemporary experiences with UFOs have strong implications for religious beliefs as well. There are two reasons for this: First, UFOs are obviously associated with the sky. The sky is seen as holy in all primitive cultures. Heaven is in the sky, and heaven is where the gods dwell. And in the modern world, many of the astronauts who have flown into the heavens and back claim to have had religious experiences. The religious character of the sky makes it inevitable that UFOs will pick up religious or spiritual meanings.

The second reason contemporary UFOs exhibit a religious valence is this: There are many individuals who claim to have been contacted personally by the pilots and occupants of UFOs and who describe their experiences in semi-religious terms. The ufonauts are understood as having come from another world in the heavens, often from a society that is not just more advanced than any on Earth, but one that is a utopia as well. Life on the other planets is supposedly lived in truth and love according to God's will. The purpose of coming to Earth is to save us from our sin. The terrestrial sins that primarily concern our visitors from the sky are nuclear war and ecological catastrophe. They seek to save us from self-destruction and deliver us into a new and better life on Earth, a peaceful life equal to their own. Perhaps we could rewrite John 3:16 to read "For God so loved the world that he sent his UFO astronauts to Earth with the message to love one another, and whosoever responds to that message shall not perish but receive life on Earth as it is in heaven."

In a sense, the UFO message is not new. It is the Bible's description of God's law: love God and love your neighbor. It is just that with UFOs the messenger has been updated. Instead of spiritual angels we have physical humanoids. Instead of divine miracles we have quasi-human technology. Instead of supranatural revelation we have natural science. Instead of the incredible we have the credible.

In February 2014 I was invited to address the 23rd International UFO Congress sponsored by Open Minds TV. At one point in the program George Noory, the radio host for "Coast to Coast AM," was speaking. Noory asked the audience: "How many of you believe in UFOs?" Of the 800 in attendance, I estimate 600 raised their hands. Noory immediately followed with another question: "How many of you believe in God?" Only 200 raised their hands. A voice shouted out: "What do you mean by God?" Now I ask: What is going on here? Three times as many people here believe in UFOs as believe in God. Might UFO belief be superseding classical theistic belief? Or, might we see developing here a secularized UFO theology?

UFO-generated theologies seem to be developing, such as ancient alien theology and contactee theology. These are both secular theologies; they belong to no church. UFO theology appeals to those who are Spiritual But Not Religious, the SBNRs. UFO theology does not even look like theology. It looks like science. But here in *UFOs: God's Chariots?* I will try to show that UFO science is actually a vehicle for expressing displaced religious or spiritual hopes.

We ask: why are some people expressing such an interest in the connection of religious doctrines with UFOs? I suggest that the study of UFOs has the appearance of being scientific—hence, it offers the opportunity to discuss religious feelings in seemingly scientific terms. Whether we say it in public or not, many of us believe science is good and religion is bad. Science is for modern, educated people; religion is for old-fashioned, superstitious people. We feel a little embarrassed when we have a religious feeling, as if we were being subverted from within by a pre-civilized emotion. If only we could feel that our religious beliefs had the respectability and credibility of science! Then we could have confidence in what we believe. I suggest that the ancient astronaut theory and other UFO theologies offer us an ostensibly respectable way of talking about our deeper religious needs. Our religious feelings urge us to ponder the ultimate heights and depths of our spiritual reality. If we are compelled to translate our spiritual concerns into naturalistic or scientific terms, then we need nothing short of the infinity of the stars to capture our speculations. A UFO theology can do this for us.

UFOs have a way of drawing out our spiritual sensibilities in masked form, even when we believe ourselves to be no longer religious. Each one of us has a deep spiritual need to be at one with our creator and source of life. Thoughts about self-destruction and death create anxiety. When destruction and death seem inevitable, we begin to ask for God's hand to save us. If we are convinced we are not religious, we may ask the government, the good luck charm, our crystal, the astrologer, or even UFOs to save us.

DICK JACKSON'S LATE NIGHT ENCOUNTER

Around 2 a.m. one morning in late October 1975, Dick Jackson of Fort Myers, Florida, tossed and turned restlessly; his arthritis was bothering him. He got up and went outside. He began walking toward a palm tree that stood some 20 feet from the door of his trailer. He remembers being about halfway to the palm, and then he blacked out.

When he came to, he found himself standing at the foot of a short stairway leading up to the doorway of what he called a "flying saucer." He described the saucer as round and dome-shaped, with a humanoid standing in the doorway. The occupant motioned for Mr. Jackson to come up and enter the craft. As Mr. Jackson climbed the three steps or so to the door, the space being said to him in perfect English, "Do not be alarmed. No harm will come to you. We just want to talk with you."

In my interview with Mr. Jackson, I asked what he meant by "perfect" English. He said that throughout the subsequent conversation the saucer's occupant showed no regional accent and did not use contractions such as "ain't." I noticed that Mr. Jackson was quite articulate and spoke with proper grammar. He seemed qualified to judge good English when he heard it.

When Mr. Jackson walked through the door of the craft he noticed that he did not have to bend to fit. "I am 6 feet 4 1/2 inches," he said, "I know a doorway is tall when I do not risk bumping my head."

As he entered he said he felt as though a suction action were at work over his whole body. He told a local newspaper reporter: "I had the feeling I was being vacuum cleaned—sterilized, I guess. Hell, I'm probably pretty well sterilized anyway. I'm at the age where you're sterilized." Jackson was 55.

Inside the starcraft he saw two space travelers and, though they spoke with each other in a foreign language, only one spoke to Mr. Jackson, and always in English. Mr. Jackson said he was familiar with Spanish and French, but what they spoke to each other was different.

Stressing that the craft's occupants were not monsters or little green men, Jackson told me they looked basically like the Caucasians we know on Earth, although the one who spoke to him had a dark complexion—"like an Italian"—and had a dimple in his chin. He looked like he might be 65 years old, but Jackson was told that he was much older than that. Both were shorter than Jackson. He estimated their height at approximately 5 feet 2 inches. The inside of the cabin was about 24 feet in diameter and very plain, with a control panel on the wall to the left. There was no furniture except a desk or table, behind which sat the host who had beckoned Jackson to come in earlier.

The second occupant stood to Jackson's right, and as Jackson entered he opened and closed a panel in the wall revealing some wires. The panel was part of a cove or rib that circumscribed the craft, and Jackson, noticing that the wire was in the form of field winding (such as one would find in an electric motor), speculated that maybe the whole ship served as an armature. Jackson's first question was to ask how the ship operated. The host responded, "The best I can describe it to you is: This is a generator and battery sitting on top of an electric motor." He also said that the flying saucer occasionally borrowed power from Earth, but did not specify whether or not that power was electricity.

After reassuring Jackson a second time, the space visitor described how, for a number of years, his people had been preparing a presently uninhabited planet for colonization by earthlings. This would not be the home planet of these two visitors; they came from "Planteh," which they spelled out for Jackson. Their own habitat was described as technologically so far advanced beyond the present stage of Earth's evolution that we appear backward in comparison.

The picture of the future abode of earthlings who would choose to emigrate to the new world was a picture, using Jackson's word, of "utopia." On this planet, life for the transplanted earthlings will be new in many ways: There will be plenty of wealth for everybody; competition will be unnecessary. There will be no need for money as we know it, because all things will be shared. Everyone's mental attitude will be different; all will live in peace. There will be no more crime. No more hunger. No work will be required; however, if one feels the need to make a contribution, rewarding work will be made available. No one will get bored.

The spaceman called Dick Jackson by name even though, as Mr. Jackson emphasized to me, they had exchanged no introductions. He has no idea how the spaceman learned his name. The space visitor then asked Jackson if he would serve as a recruiter to encourage colonization of the new planet by earthlings.

Jackson responded by announcing that he was in poor health and would not be a fit recruiter for much longer. In 1971 Jackson had been told by his physician that he had only two years to live. He was suffering from severe arthritis, emphysema, and myocarditis. At that time he was living close to a refinery in Texas; his doctor told him that he might lengthen his life by moving to an area with cleaner air. So Jackson moved to Florida, the state of his birth, and was still living four years later at the time of this encounter.

I asked Jackson if the thought of his imminent death weighed on him continuously. "Oh no!" he quickly responded in a tone of excessive confidence, "I've beaten it now." When I asked him what he meant by the phrase "beaten it," he said he was referring to the fact that he had outlived the doctor's prediction. When I pressed him further, he admitted that he had been very upset when he first received the news, but that now he didn't "think of it at all." I was puzzled. Why did the spaceman's question about recruitment trigger a response about Jackson's health? Did Jackson think more about his poor health than he liked to admit? Or had Jackson suppressed his fear of dying so effectively that he no longer consciously knew that he was afraid?

What the spaceman said in response is fascinating. In return for recruiting, the ufonaut stated, Jackson would be cured of his illnesses and be permitted to join the first group of immigrants to the new world. "He said my perfect *health* would be restored!" Jackson told the spaceman he would be interested.

It was stressed that the emigrating earthlings would not be able to take their possessions on Earth with them. "The people who went would go without anything but the clothes on their back," Jackson explained, "because everything would be furnished there." He said that no metal could be taken, even in the form of buttons, zippers, or jewelry. This theme of forsaking everything in this world in order to enter a new and better world impressed me. It seems I had heard it before. It reminded me of Jesus laying down the requirements of full commitment for entry into the kingdom of God. Jesus said, "Go, sell what you have, and give to the poor, and you will have treasure in heaven." (Mark 10:21)

I asked Jackson about religion. He described himself as a non-religious person. He reported that he had gone to Sunday school as a child and to church as an adult. He said he believed religion is good for children and that ethics are necessary for most people, but he personally did not take religion seriously. He remarked that he could not picture God as most people do. By that he meant as "an old man with a white beard." To a reporter he said he was not superstitious and that he does not "believe in ghosts, because I've never seen one. Show me one and I'll believe in them."

UFOs: God's Chariots?

When the conversations with the space alien were completed, Jackson left the craft and watched it depart. "Then, all of a sudden, *poof*—the ship was accelerating so fast...." Jackson said the spaceman told him he would be contacted at some future date regarding recruitment plans.

I wonder: Did this actually happen as Jackson described it? It was obvious that he was completely sincere and not lying. Could this have been a very vivid dream issuing out of deep, inner desires?

Regardless, Jackson understood his experience with the UFO in at least three ways: First, he understood it in terms of politics, that is, in terms of our experience with such things as war and peace, crime and civility, employment and fiscal exchange. Second, he understood it in scientific and technical terms. He saw "field winding" and was told that the ship's power came from a "generator and battery sitting on top of an electric motor." Third, though in a very disguised way, he understood it religiously. He understood it as the answer to his questions about death and heaven.

Dick Jackson's reported experience gives us much to think about. The new world the Plantehites were preparing for us earthlings sounds a great deal like the new creation mentioned in the Bible, that is, like heaven. Not only will life there be full of peace and joy, but the threats of disease and death will have been conquered. It is tantamount to eternal life. And it can be ours if we do as so many passages of Scripture ask us to do: Give up our attraction to this world and commit ourselves to the better one.

Also, more religious symbolism can be taken out of this experience. The Swiss psychotheorist Carl Jung said the circle is a natural symbol of God because it is the shape of perfection. Perhaps the round, dome-shaped vehicle unconsciously represented the coming of God into Jackson's life. The occupant represented perfection to Jackson as soon as he spoke his first word in "perfect" English.

A bit more obvious, however, is the baptismal rite that prepared Jackson to stand in the presence of the holy. Upon entering the domain of the gods from outer space he said he felt "vacuum cleaned" and "sterilized" all over. The initiation rites of the world's religions routinely include a ritual act of purification, of cleansing, before one enters the presence of religious perfection. Upon entering into the body of Christ, a Christian must be "washed" by the waters of regeneration and don garments "white as snow" in the sacrament of baptism. There is also the message of salvation—the good news that this world is not all there is; there is more, it is great, it is wonderful, and it can be ours almost as a gift from above. Its riches will meet our every need, exactly as it met the particular need of Mr. Jackson for good health.

Note that these religious themes are covert rather than overt. There is nothing patently theological here. There is no mention of spirits, demons, angels, or miracles. Everything is completely natural; nothing is supernatural. It may be a story of fantastic import. It may be difficult to believe. But it is a story that is completely possible according to all our known laws of physics. Even the heavenly chariot is an ordinary electric motor. It does not fly on the wings of supernatural angels.

Mr. Jackson denied his religious feelings because he was convinced he had outgrown the need for religion. He was mature. He had come of age. "Religion is okay for children," he said, but not for him. Similarly, some argue that Western civilization has come of age. We have become so intellectually mature that we may now put aside childish things, such as belief in God. Belief in God is like belief in magic. We moderns believe in science, not magic. Today, we are supposed to know and be able to explain so many things of which our primitive forbearers, who first formulated our religious principles, were ignorant. After all, people in ancient civilizations only used the concept of god to explain things they did not understand. Today, we do understand. Don't we?

Mr. Jackson had no personal belief in superstitious things such as ghosts or God because he had never seen them. "Show me one and I'll believe in them." This is a popularized image of what the scientist does. Scientists supposedly believe only what they can prove through empirical observation or experimentation. To speak of God is to speak of things unseen. To speak of an alien from outer space is to speak of something that, at least in principle, could be seen by anyone with eyes to look.

GRAVEN AND CONCEPTUAL IMAGES

When Moses came down from Mt. Sinai with the two tablets of God's law in his hands, the first and most important of the commandments read: "You shall have no other gods before me. You shall not make for yourself a graven image, or any likeness of anything that is in heaven above." Why were we asked not to make a graven image of God? We make graven images of other important figures. What would the Lincoln Memorial in Washington be without President Lincoln's image in the statue? We commemorate our beloved heroes with statues and portraits. It is a sign of honor and respect. Why would God forbid us to honor him likewise?

The answer is that God is transcendent. *Transcendence* means to rise above, to stand outside or beyond, to exceed the limits or powers of the ordinary world. Our ordinary world is bound by time and space, but the holy God of Israel is eternal and spiritual, not subject to the limits of time and space. The things of this world are finite; God is infinite. Consequently, there is no form on Earth that could possibly portray as a graven image the nature of God. In order to carve the bust or paint the portrait of a dignitary, an artist must see the subject's profile. The transcendent God has no finite profile. Hence, a graven or painted image of God is impossible.

Because God is infinite and transcendent, any image that is finite and "this-worldly" would necessarily be an image of something other than God. And, if one were to worship such an image instead of God himself, it would be idolatry. Recall how the first commandment begins: "You shall have no other gods before me."

The very nature of God makes imaging or imagining the divine extremely difficult. The commandment against graven images applies to all images: engraved, carved, painted, drawn, holographed, and even conceived. Can we picture God in our minds? No, not exactly. Our minds are informed only by our experiences in this finite world, and God by nature transcends this finite world. All of our conceptions are conditioned by finite time and space. To think of God, then, means we must be open-minded and open to truths that we cannot even conceive of.

Recognizing God's transcendence leads to a certain amount of frustration. Everything we picture in our minds is finite. So whenever we think of God we risk committing idolatry. C.S. Lewis tells how when he was a little boy his mother explained the first commandment to him. He tried and tried to think of God without limiting God to the bounds of finite images. He said that in his mind God came to him as a great massive sea of gray tapioca. Our minds inevitably think in this-worldly terms. What are we to do when it comes to understanding God?

The answer given by religion is to think in terms of symbols. Rather than thinking about God directly, we think through symbols of God. A religious symbol is always two-sided; it is open-ended. On the one hand, it is an ordinary thing of this world. On the other hand it represents a sacred and holy reality that transcends this world. The Bible is printed on paper just as any ordinary book is. If we read the Bible online, it's still ordinary. But the Bible is simultaneously much more when it symbolically conveys the presence of God's Spirit.

The preeminent symbol of the Christian faith is the cross. It is ordinary in the sense that it was made of wood and was commonly used by the Roman government for punishment of serious crimes. But it is also symbolic. It represents the presence of the transcendent God in human affairs. God was in Christ. We do not actually see God in the cross; our eyes see only a cross. But our minds and thoughts go beyond to recognize that God is there. To avoid idolatry, we must remember that a symbol is always a symbol and not to be confused with God himself.

What happens when we stop believing in transcendence? If we come to believe that the ordinary things of this world are completely and totally just that—ordinary—then they lose their symbolic power. They are closed off from anything beyond and are no longer able to communicate transcendence. We moderns live in a world without windows, without a vision of what transcends us. We live in a mental or conceptual climate dominated by a naturalistic or scientific understanding of reality.

UFOs: God's Chariots?

According to this modern view, all that exists is a large universe of finite things, every one of which is governed by the laws of nature. These laws of nature never go on a holiday. They are in effect night and day. For example, we have faith that the law of gravity will always keep us safe on the surface of the Earth. We have faith that it will not stop working for a moment and let us drift out into space, or worse, stop for a moment to let us drift, then re-engage, slamming us back down.

Nature is not capricious. It is consistent. We implicitly believe there are no deities or angels who willfully act in such a way as to break a law of nature. In other words, absolutely everything is the same. It is ordinary. You can't go anywhere to find a reality fundamentally different from what it is on Earth. Our way of thinking about and understanding everything in terms of nature has closed the windows of our minds to transcendence.

Perhaps this is why some would like to believe in UFOs as a substitute for the divine. UFOs come from another world, from the heavens, just as God did. But UFOs in principle obey all the laws of nature. In that sense they are ordinary. They are not symbolic because they do not open us toward a transcendent dimension beyond them. Rather, the UFOs become the object of our concern. They fit our worldview. They are finite. We can make images of them, both graven and conceptual. Can they become idols?

Note what Mr. Jackson replied when I asked him about his religion. He said he could not believe God is an old man with a white beard. Was he thinking about the God of Moses on Mt. Sinai or was he thinking about Santa Claus? One can have a graven image of Santa Claus. We see countless images in the department stores every year. Certainly there is nothing in the first commandment that would define the transcendent God as an old man with a white beard. If Mr. Jackson thinks he is rejecting God, he must be mistaken. At best he is rejecting one idol, Santa Claus, and substituting another idol, the flying saucer.

Mr. Jackson says he is not superstitious and will not believe in ghosts unless he sees one. All of us in the modern world are dominated by the worldview of science: We do not want to believe in supernatural things such as ghosts that transcend the laws of nature as we understand them. It is natural to see and to be seen. If the ghost can be seen, the ghost must be natural and, therefore, real. What does not fit our naturalistic framework of understanding is, *ipso facto*, not real. God and ghosts are, therefore, not real.

But, like all of us, Dick Jackson has deep spiritual needs that this world alone cannot fulfill. In particular, he desires a much better world and he needs relief from his fear of death and the eternal dark oblivion of the grave. For many people in times past, orthodox Christian faith met this need with the promise of resurrection to God's kingdom of heaven. But resurrection and heaven are no longer part of our naturalistic framework for understanding reality. The God who promised salvation in Jesus Christ is so difficult to believe in because he is *supranatural*, beyond nature. Would it not be wonderful if we could receive the gifts of salvation from someone we can understand and believe in?

Perhaps—and how we wish it to be true!—natural creatures from another world could, by technological means, answer our deepest inner needs and desires.

CONCLUSION

People almost always interpret UFOs in terms of some familiar model or common category. The four models I intend to discuss in this book are politics, science, religion, and a composite hybridizing. These models do not sit side by side, contiguously. They overlap. Even more subtly, the religious dimension underlies the others.

I will suggest that the religious or spiritual way of interpreting UFOs can include many of the dimensions of the political and the scientific, and perhaps even the hybridizing models. I will also suggest that the religious interpretation of the alleged UFO occupants as celestial saviors goes unrecognized for what it is, namely, a naturalized or scientized theology of salvation. The religious dimension is almost hidden. Certainly Dick Jackson would be reluctant to say he had a religious experience when taken aboard the flying saucer. The religious dimensions of the experience were sublimated, that is, unconsciously redirected away from a superstitious belief in a God who saves and toward a much more acceptable belief in a natural universe where technology saves. Are we not all tempted, at least a little, to believe and hope with Dick Jackson?

2

Model I: The Interstellar Diplomat

UFOs provoke concern in the world of politics. The former prime minister of Grenada (West Indies), Sir Eric M. Gairy, addressing the 31st session of the General Assembly of the United Nations on October 7, 1976, urged that the U.N. make a concerted effort toward solving the UFO enigma. It was the prime minister's plan to create a United Nations department or agency to coordinate research on the problem. Other interested parties were also pressing for the establishment of such a U.N. agency, to be called Project UNUFO. "It is my firm conviction," said Gairy, "that the world is ready, willing and ripe enough to accept these phenomena in relation to man and his existence on the planet Earth, and in relation to the planet Earth and life in outer space."

Whatever UFOs are in themselves, they are understood by society as having political significance. We operate with an imaginary picture or model of flying saucers that includes an important geopolitical dimension. This has given rise to exopolitics. Michael Salla explains that "exopolitics focuses on the implications of the available evidence confirming the presence of extraterrestrial visitors to our planet."[1] What are those implications? Some implications are scientific, others religious, and still others political.

All knowledge is interpretation. When confronted with a new or unusual experience, the process of understanding that experience is the process of integrating it with what we already know. One thing we already know is how politics works, and this influences the way we interpret elements within the UFO experience. Before we examine the political dimension directly, let us look first at the nature of the UFO phenomenon and also at the role that models play in the general dynamics of human understanding.

THE UFO PHENOMENON

What we are talking about is best called the *UFO phenomenon*. When we use the word *phenomenon* here we are referring to the whole complex of what is seen plus the person who sees it. The word comes from the Greek verb, *phaino,* which, in the active voice, means "to bring to light," "to make appear," or "to reveal." In the passive it means to come to light or to be seen. Coincidently, it is related to the noun, *phainon,* meaning "planet," that is, "the shining one."

Whenever the subject of UFOs is examined, the tension in the relationship between what is perceived and the perceiver is ever present. This is evident in the very mission of the UFO field investigator whose first responsibility is, if possible, to turn a UFO into an IFO, that is, to convert an *unidentified* flying object into an *identified* flying object. What may be unidentified to the original witness may, after investigation, become identified as the mistaken perception of an airplane, helicopter, weather balloon, shooting star, satellite, lenticular cloud, and so on. The uncovering of a hoax also counts in making an identification.

On August 19, 2013, astronaut Chris Cassidy spotted a UFO outside the window of the International Space Station. It looked manufactured, not natural. It was an exciting moment. He took a video. A NASA official on the ground identified the object as the Zvezda service module antenna cover. In other words, it was a piece of space junk just floating in the neighborhood of the space station. This UFO became an IFO, as many do.

Model I: The Interstellar Diplomat

For the most part, research efforts have yielded considerable success at turning UFOs into IFOs. Project Bluebook of the U.S. Air Force, which operated from 1952 to 1969, claimed it could explain 80 percent of its reports, leaving only 20 percent as unknowns. The Center for UFO Studies, the private research organization founded by the late J. Allen Hynek, did much better. It was able to turn around 90 to 95 percent of UFO reports into IFOs. What is of decisive importance, of course, is the residuum of 5 to 10 percent, which remain unknown even after careful investigation. And when we find ourselves dealing with nearly 100,000 or so such reports, this residuum becomes a rather significant number.

The tensile relationship between the perceiver and what he or she perceives is built right into the very categories by which we organize UFO sightings. They are distinctively observational categories. They do not presume to know what UFOs are. The point is this: Despite the fact that we observe them, the unidentified objects remain unidentified even after observation.

We will call the first set of observations "relatively distant sightings." This set can be broken down into three subsets: Nocturnal Lights (NL); Daylight Discs (DD); and combination Radar-Visual (RV). The second set is made up of "relatively close sightings," which refers to objects seen from a distance of 500 feet or less. The subsets here are Close Encounters of the First Kind (CE-I), wherein the witness can see considerable detail. Close Encounters of the Second Kind (CE-II) have to do with physical effects. This includes landing trace cases, where we might find a burned ring in the grass, broken tree limbs, and so on. It also includes electromagnetic effects, such as interference with electrical circuits in our cars and airplanes. Then there are the Close Encounters of the Third Kind (CE-III), in which living beings of some kind are confronted. This interpretive structure is the brainchild of J. Alan Hynek.[2] Others have added to Hynek's categories Close Encounters of the Fourth Kind (CE-IV). The CE-IV refers to the kind of abduction cases we will later discuss under Model IV: the Hybridizer (a model that combines the scientific and religious, although I believe the category of CE-III suffices for the hybridizer as well).

What is significant about these categories of observation is that they are designed to preserve the integrity of the phenomenon. They permit us to retain the relationship between what is seen and the individual who sees.[3] If the phrase *unidentified flying object* is to retain its meaning, then we need to be able to discuss something that remains *unidentified* even while we discuss it. This is important for the present book. What we are after here is greater understanding of how we earthlings deal with mystery; how we process confrontations with the strange; and how we translate what is alien into a language we think we can understand—in short, how we interpret our experience.

UNDERSTANDING AND PRE-UNDERSTANDING

We can never understand something that is absolutely new, that is radically different from anything we have experienced prior. The process of coming to understand something new or unusual involves comparing it with things that are familiar and already understood. To explain means to take something cloudy or mysterious and interpret it into familiar terms so that it becomes clear.

Scientists tell us that this is true even at the level of fundamental perception, including the act of seeing. We understand what we see in terms of a pre-existing "perceptual set," in terms of what we expect to see.[4] In addition to perceptual sets, we also operate with conceptual sets. What people know and believe is organized into elaborate "conceptual sets" or "systems of belief." Each one of us has a system of belief, the content of which is the product of everything taught to us by our culture, parents, and peers, plus the accumulation of our own personal experiences. Consequently, our respective systems of belief are, in part, public (shared with others around us), and, in part, private (a product of our own individual fears and hopes).

Jacques Vallée provides us with a thought-experiment, a hypothetical story that provides an excellent example of our urge to explain anomalous phenomena in terms of one's system of belief.[5] Let us suppose that a giant bomber from the Strategic Air Command suddenly finds itself projected backward in time. It is now rushing through the skies of medieval Europe and is witnessed by thousands of farmers, soldiers, and monks. Because none of them has ever witnessed anything of this kind before, they will describe their respective sightings in terms that are familiar to them. Most of the daytime witnesses, who are pious Roman Catholic Christians, will say they have seen a flying crucifix and heard the roaring cries of Jesus jolting the horizon. They will certainly make reports to the archbishop, who will immediately perceive that this information is of very high value to the Church. Sermons will be preached on it throughout the land, some warning that it is perhaps a trick of the devil, and others postulating that it is a divine manifestation with a special message for all to repent and renew their faith.

We understand new and unusual phenomena in terms of prior systems of belief. This principle certainly applies to UFOs. The close encounter, abduction, and contactee cases examined in this book seem to fall loosely into four basic belief subsystems—or explanatory models—through which UFOs are brought into our understanding. They are: the Interstellar Diplomat (a political model); the Research Scientist (a scientific model); the Celestial Savior (a religious model); and the Hybridizer (a model that combines the scientific and the religious).

Granted, all four of these models are part and parcel of a larger single belief system shared by all of us in Western culture, but each model adds a bit more precision and internal consistency to our understanding of UFOs. However, I am not saying all UFOs fit precisely into these four models. Many UFO reports have not yet been admitted into any coherent system of understanding, and hence keep their status as strictly "unidentified." Many close encounter, abduction, and contactee cases, however, involve elaborate perceptions and theoretical interpretation. These are the ones that fit the explanatory models best. And because they do so, they have the greatest impact on our consciousness.

UFOs: God's Chariots?

The first of the four models is the *Interstellar Diplomat*. When we consider the possibility of an encounter between our own civilization and that of an alien world, we do so with centuries of political wars and international diplomacy contributing to our experience. This experience influences our approach to the questions surrounding extraterrestrials. Geopolitics has modeled exopolitics.

The second model or conceptual set is the *Research Scientist*. Our own envoys into space went to the moon to collect rocks and soil samples. What they collected they brought back to analyze in the laboratories. Could we not expect the aliens from space to study Earth in a similar fashion?

The third model is the *Celestial Savior*. Here the space alien is a messianic messenger from a "heavenly" civilization where there is peace and no more war. In this spiritual or religious model, we believe that the reason for the alien mission to Earth is to help us achieve the same utopian level of existence that the aliens have. Even though I use the term "savior" here, the descent of the UFO with saving knowledge better fits the ancient gnostic redeemer myth. That is, the ufonauts teach us to save ourselves rather than do it for us.

The fourth model is the *Hybridizer*. Some abductions, especially those reported after 1985, resemble reports from earlier in that decade of childhood sexual abuse and Satanic ritual abuse. The narratives in both abuse and UFO abductions are obtained by the same method, namely, hypnotic regression and retrieval of forgotten memories. In some narratives the abductee reports multiple incidents of rape or in vitro fertilization, and the birth of hybrid babies.

The importance of studying the UFO phenomenon in terms of these models is that the models reveal a great deal about our own belief system or conceptual set. In the case of the Celestial Savior in particular, the model probably tells us much more about ourselves than it does about UFOs. We on Earth have hopes that our history of warfare will not also be our future. We hope for change, for redemption. Will UFOs bring redemption from the sky?

Model I: The Interstellar Diplomat

JUMPING JULY 1952

The model of the interstellar diplomat presupposes that UFOs are piloted by extraterrestrial beings, and it represents one form of speculation regarding the purposes for the visits. One need not necessarily cite any specific cases from which the image of political encounters emerged. Rather, the simple, widespread recognition that UFOs appear to be spacecraft capable of flying feats far superior to those of any of our aircraft gives rise to the extraterrestrial hypothesis. Cold War anxieties of the 1950s, which included the fear that the United States might be outdone by Soviet weapons technology, were particularly aroused when flying saucers buzzed the White House in July 1952.

Let us look briefly at this period in time. July was the high point of a near year-long flap. (UFOs sometimes come in "flaps" or "waves," that is, numerous reported sightings in a relatively short period of time.) 1,501 sightings were reported to U.S. Air Force officials in 1952, a huge jump from only 169 the year before. Of these reports, 536 were filed for the month of July alone. The government-sponsored "Scientific Study of UFOs" at the University of Colorado from 1967 to 1969, headed by Professor Edward U. Condon, said that there may be 8 to 10 sightings for every one report that is filed.[6]

On the night of July 14, 1952, a Pan American World Airways DC-4 was traveling from New York to Miami. The night was clear with unlimited visibility. The pilots, First Officer William B. Nash and Second Officer William H. Fortenberry, watched six reddish-orange circular objects of about 100 feet in diameter fly underneath them in a narrow echelon formation. They suddenly changed direction, acutely and abruptly, making a 150-degree turn. The only descriptive comparison the pilots could offer was of a ball ricocheting off a wall.

Two more objects joined them, making a total of eight. Then they flew off and disappeared. Using a chart for reference, the pilots calculated that the objects had covered 50 miles in 12 to 15 seconds. This means they were traveling at least 12,000 miles per hour.

UFOs: God's Chariots?

On July 18, Captain E. J. Ruppelt, head of Project Blue Book, released a statement from Wright-Patterson Air Force Base in Dayton, Ohio. He stated that unidentified aerial objects had been tracked by ground radar at speeds up to 2,000 miles per hour. This compares with the record speed at that time of 1,238 miles per hour attained by a rocket-powered Navy plane. Here we were confronted with flying machines in our skies able to fly faster and with better maneuverability than our best defensive aircraft. Is there someone technologically and militarily superior to us? Are they friend or foe?

Then, for a period of 10 days, sightings of flying saucers seemed to explode over the nation's capital. There were multiple sightings on July 19–20, 23, 26–27, 28, and 29. Saucers were seen visually by airplane pilots and by dozens of people on the ground. They were tracked on radar, usually at speeds between 100 and 130 miles per hour, with one reported at more than 7,000 miles per hour.

On the nights of July 19–20 and 26–27, unidentified flying objects appeared on the radar scopes of the Air Route Traffic Control Center at Washington National Airport. F-94 jet fighters were scrambled from the base at New Castle to intercept them and to protect the capital from attack by air. What ensued was a game of tag. Each time the fighter jets were able to get close enough to the targets for observation, the objects sped away. Some pilots saw luminated objects; others did not.

One pilot found himself surrounded by the lights and nervously asked the ground controllers what to do. Shortly after that the lights left the vicinity of his plane; no harm done. The Washington flying saucers made sensational headlines in newspapers all across the country, in many cases eclipsing the otherwise front-page news of the Democratic National Convention. Some news commentators asked the alarming question: could these saucers be a Soviet intelligence device now marking key American targets for later attack?

Government offices and the White House were bombarded with telephone calls and other inquiries. President Truman asked Brigadier General Landry to call Captain Ruppelt at Wright-Patterson AFB to find out what was going on.

Model 1: The Interstellar Diplomat

On July 29 the Air Force held the longest and largest press conference since the end of World War II. The principal spokesperson was Major General John A. Samford, who made two basic points: First, no matter what it was people had seen and pilots had chased, it was the judgment of the U.S. Air Force that it represented no threat to the security of our nation. "There is nothing in them that is associated with material or vehicles or missiles that are directed against the United States."[7] Second, the sightings were natural phenomena, probably explained by a temperature inversion effect on radar beams and light rays. The radar had picked up what is called "anomalous propagation."[8]

At the news conference one reporter who had earlier interviewed the radar operators at Washington National Airport pressed General Samford. He argued that two separate radars picked up one of the objects located 3 miles north of Riverdale. The same blip remained for 30 seconds and simultaneously disappeared from both sets. He asked if that would not count as evidence against the anomalous propagation explanation. Samford in turn diverted the question into an argument over the definition of "simultaneous," and the reporter felt outmaneuvered. Nevertheless, many remained uneasy about the official Air Force explanation.

In response to the incident, the CIA convened the "Scientific Panel on Unidentified Flying Objects" from January 14 to 17 in 1953. Headed by physicist E.P. Robertson from Cal Tech, it became known as the Robertson Panel. Its conclusion was the same as Samford's: Flying saucers pose no threat to national security, and, further, receiving reports of unidentified flying objects might so clutter governmental communication channels as to divert attention from genuine security matters. The Robertson Panel added a recommendation: the government should engage in "debunking" UFO reports to discourage clogging communication channels.

More than a decade and a half later, the Condon Report concurred with General Samford.[9] It concluded that the Washington radar trackings were probably due to anomalous propagation caused by atmospheric conditions, and that the visible objects were probably meteors and scintillating stars.

UFOs: God's Chariots?

Looking back, we might say that the Samford press conference marks a watershed event in UFO history. Like the casting director for a wannabe blockbuster, the key roles were identified at this time: the believer, the debunker, and the government. The believers included Donald Keyhoe and his pro-UFO followers. The debunkers included Harvard's Donald Menzel, and later added the authors of the Condon Report and other skeptics. The government would be represented primarily by the United States Air Force, although from time to time the C.I.A. and the White House became involved. Keith Thompson calls this the "triangular" controversy. "The UFO Phenomenon had reached its first real turning point, with a recognizable plot focused around recognizable conflicts in place. At the debate's present pitch, one of two outcomes seemed inevitable. Either tensions would rise to a point where the air force felt obliged to release its complete UFO file to the public, or else the three-way debate would continue until it exhausted itself on the shores of public disinterest."[10]

Thompson's observation about a turning point in 1952 is correct, in my judgment. But, even with the Condon Report in 1969, the UFO controversy did not shipwreck on "the shores of public disinterest." What happened is that the UFO controversy became embedded in politics, where it has remained, stirring up acerbity to the present day.

SCHIRMER'S SHUDDER

One early abduction case that has strong implications for the political model took place on December 3, 1967. Around 1 a.m., Patrolman Herbert Schirmer of Ashland, Nebraska, was alerted to dogs barking and cattle thrashing on farms near the edge of town. About 2 or 2:30 a.m. he spotted some red lights near the intersection of highways 6 and 63. Presuming it to be a truck in trouble, he investigated.

Upon a closer look he saw the red lights blinking, not from a truck, but from what he described as the windows of a saucer-shaped flying object, hovering 6 to 8 feet above the highway. It was angled about 15 degrees past horizontal. The object glowed brilliantly and started rising, emitting a siren-like sound. Sticking his head out the window of his

42

patrol car, Schirmer watched the object climb to directly overhead and then shoot off out of sight.

Schirmer said he drove directly back to the police station, arriving at 3 a.m. There he wrote in the logbook: "Saw a flying saucer at the junction of highways 6 and 63. Believe it or not!"

However, he realized he should have been back earlier than 3 a.m. The UFO experience had lasted only a few moments. As he considered the matter, Schirmer became convinced that at least 20 minutes of time were lost to his consciousness. What had happened to him during this time?

The Condon Committee invited Herbert Schirmer to Boulder, Colorado, for an interview. Along with the other details, Schirmer mentioned his missing 20 minutes. He also reported that he had a feeling of paralysis at the time of the sighting, and that he felt strange, weak, sick, and nervous when he returned to the trooper barracks. The Condon Committee accepted the testimony of Schirmer's superior officer, who said that the trooper had been given a lie-detector test by an experienced polygraph operator at an official agency. The polygraph reportedly showed no indications that Schirmer was being anything but truthful. Nevertheless, the Condon Committee concluded, "evaluation of psychological assessment tests, the lack of any evidence, and interviews with the patrolman, left project staff with no confidence that the trooper's reported UFO experience was physically real."[11]

I wonder if this negative evaluation could have been sufficiently discouraging to influence the events following Schirmer's experience. Schirmer still felt restless so he contacted Eric Norman, who had written articles about UFOs, and Norman made arrangements for Schirmer to undergo hypnosis. On June 8, 1968, a professional hypnotist, Loring G. Williams, helped Schirmer regress back to the predawn hours of December 3, 1967.[12]

Under hypnosis Schirmer told an incredible story. During the lost 20 minutes, beings emerged from the hovering object, approached the patrol car, paralyzed Schirmer, and took him aboard the ship. The ship's occupants were 4 1/2 to 5 feet tall, wearing close-fitting, silvery gray uniforms with an emblem of a winged serpent on the left side of the chest. (The winged serpent is the symbol of Quetzalcoatl, and is still an emblem used in Mexico today.) Their thin heads were helmeted with an antenna on the left side. Their flesh was gray-white, nose flat, and the mouth, a mere slit that did not move.

He spent 15 minutes aboard the flying saucer in conversation with the aliens. They announced that they came from another galaxy and that they have bases on Venus and beneath the ocean off the coast of Florida. (Could he be referring to the Bermuda Triangle?) The purpose of the craft they were in was reconnaissance and surveillance. Schirmer described the walk of his hosts as stiff. They had a military posture that reminded him of men who have been in the armed service for a long time. The crew leader pressed a button on a viewing screen. Three spacecraft of a different shape appeared to be flying in formation against a background of stars that included the Big Dipper. Schirmer was told that these were "warships" flying in outer space.

The hypnotist asked Schirmer how long aliens had been watching us. The following is taken from the account given by Ralph and Judy Blum.

Schirmer: They have been observing us for a long period of time and they think that if they slowly, slowly put out reports and have their contacts state the truth it will help them.... They have no pattern for contacting people. It is by pure chance so the government cannot determine any patterns about them. There will be a lot more contacts...to a certain extent they want to puzzle people. They know they are being seen too frequently and they are trying to confuse the public's mind. He is telling me they want everyone to believe some in them so we will be open to their invasion and...

Williams: Think carefully now. Did he use the word invasion?

Schirmer: Yes.

Williams: Then this would mean they are operating to conquer the world?

Model I: The Interstellar Diplomat

Schirmer (emphatically): Oh no, no, no. He used the word "invasion" but meant it in a friendly way. He said it would be the showing of themselves completely. The public should consider in their minds that they should have no fear of these beings because they are not hostile.[13]

Dr. Leo Sprinkle, a psychologist at the University of Wyoming, had given Schirmer some psychological tests on behalf of the Condon Committee. Writing for APRO (the Aerial Phenomena Research Organization), he says, "The writer is unable to state absolutely whether Herb Schirmer experienced a UFO sighting or not; however, the writer believes that Herb Schirmer is convinced of his experience."[14] Whether or not the later account given to Loring Williams is an embellishment, Sprinkle considers Schirmer's original report to have been honest.

The space visitors also explained to Schirmer that they borrow electricity from our high-power lines. The Blums took this opportunity to note that UFOs were sighted near high-tension wires in the Niagara Falls and New York City areas during the night of the great northeast blackout in 1965.[15] Could the blackout have been on purpose? Could it have been a test of the effectiveness of their equipment? Could it have been an experiment to see how we react when our normal lives are disrupted? Or could it be that one of the aliens accidentally threw the wrong switch?

Schirmer's shudder fits the first model, the interstellar diplomat. To learn that space visitors have intelligence-gathering devices and that warships can be seen flying in our planet's vicinity make this a matter of national security or, better, planetary security. We can only hope that Schirmer is right in his judgment: "The public should consider in their minds that they should have no fear of these beings because they are not hostile."

MOODY, MOVIES, AND THE POLITICAL MOOD

The abduction case of Air Force Staff Sgt. Charles L. Moody during September 1975 near Alamogordo, New Mexico, resembles Herb

Schirmer's experience in many ways. At about 1:30 a.m., alone out in the country in order to watch a meteor shower, Sergeant Moody saw a brightly lighted, oval-shaped spacecraft about 50 feet long drop out of the sky and hover at 25 to 50 feet above the ground. It then flew away and the frightened Moody drove home.

And, like Schirmer, Moody discovered he had lost conscious track of about 20 minutes' time during the incident. Gradually, strange images of alien beings popped into his mind, and eventually his memory recovered what he had apparently lost. Two of the saucer's crew had glided out and took Moody back aboard the craft. The aliens had disproportionately large craniums, frail, slender bodies, whitish-gray skin, and were about 5 feet tall and wearing skin-tight, white suits.

Speaking "perfect English" but with no lip movements, they asked Moody if he was well. Moody relaxed as the ufonauts explained that the saucer was a small observation craft, and that they actually traveled between solar systems in much larger and faster starships. They are presently studying us prior to considering full contact between our respective civilizations. Our fighter aircraft and guided missiles frighten them because their observation ships are vulnerable to our explosives. If we put them in a corner under attack, they warned, they will retaliate with force. The aliens explained that they belonged to a league of extraterrestrial civilizations and implied that they were considering whether or not Earth would be invited to join their "league of races." One alien made it clear: "It is not whether you accept us—it is whether we accept you."

Moody passed a lie-detector test on a Psychological Stress Evaluator (PSE), and his base supervisor, Technical Sgt. Arthur Wright, said, "Moody is a reliable, trustworthy man. I have never known him to tell a lie. His word can be believed."[16]

In the Moody case, the interstellar diplomat gives us a warning: cease and desist deploying weapons of mass destruction. It seems we've heard this warning before. Where? At the movies.

Model I: The Interstellar Diplomat

The Day the Earth Stood Still (1951)

In 1951, a year prior to the Washington barrage, Hollywood released the first of many movies that capitalized on the public interest in flying saucers, *The Day the Earth Stood Still*. In this movie, a spacecraft lands on the Washington Monument lawn. Its occupant is an emissary named Klaatu from an extrasolar interplanetary confederacy. He seeks to negotiate with the heads of state of every nation on Earth. The issues are grave. The negotiations could determine whether or not planet Earth will continue to exist or be eliminated.

According to the story of the space visitor landing in Washington D.C., Klaatu fails to convince our political leaders of the urgency to meet together to negotiate world peace. In fact, myopic political leaders will not even give Klaatu a hearing. Only scientists take the celestial diplomat seriously. On the question of terrestrial peace, our politicians cannot deliver. Can the scientists deliver?

An important theme in this movie is that Earth's political leaders are unable to transcend their petty nationalisms in order to muster a unified approach to the interstellar diplomat. The political machinery of the post–World War II era had broken down. It was non-functional. But what our petty politicians could not do, the scientists could. An international congress of scientists might be able to provide the united planetary counterpart to the interstellar diplomat. When we lose hope in our politicians, we ask the scientists to do our politics for us.

Klaatu turns from the political establishment to the scientific establishment. He explains to aging physicist Professor Barnhart that his extraterrestrial *confrères* are aware that earthlings have discovered a rudimentary kind of atomic energy and are also experimenting with rockets. Up until this point the interplanetary confederation had not concerned itself with the wars on Earth. As long as earthlings fought with primitive tanks and aircraft they would only kill one another. But soon we would attach a nuclear weapon to a rocket, and that would create a threat to the peace and security of the other planets in the universe.

To negotiate a peaceful stalemate was the purpose for which Klaatu was sent to Earth. In the event that all the peoples of the Earth could not cooperate and enter into a peaceful agreement, then it would be necessary to have Earth "eliminated." He assures Professor Barnhart and the world that the power to do so exists in the hands of the space people.

The concluding scene of the movie is a dramatic speech delivered by Klaatu to an audience of scientists at the foot of his flying saucer. The scientists listening come from a variety of nations and cultures, demonstrating that science is international and global even if politics is not. Klaatu says:

> The universe grows smaller every day, and the threat of aggression by any group anywhere can no longer be tolerated. There must be security for all or no one is secure. Now this does not mean giving up any freedom, except the freedom to act irresponsibly. Your ancestors knew this when they made laws to govern themselves and hired policemen to enforce them. We of the other planets have long accepted this principle. We have an organization for the mutual protection of all planets and for the complete elimination of aggression. The result is we live in peace, without arms or armies, secure in the knowledge that we are free from aggression and war, free to pursue more profitable enterprises.... If you threaten to extend your violence, this Earth of yours will be reduced to a burnt-out cinder. Your choice is simple. Join us and live in peace, or pursue your present course and face obliteration. We shall be waiting for your answer. The decision rests with you.

With this, the interstellar statesman reenters his spacecraft and the ship disappears into the stars.

The movie, along with the flying saucer controversy, was on the minds of many during the time of anti-Communist hearings in Washington, the Korean War, news releases of new developments in atomic weaponry, and a fear of the other great superpower, the Soviet Union. The Cold War consciousness had considerable effect on the speculative image of flying saucers held by many people. The flying saucer drove a wedge between our understanding of what politics could accomplish and what we hoped science could accomplish.

In Klaatu's challenging speech, note how his extraterrestrial confederacy has evolved beyond where we are. The extraterrestrials have progressed to a stage in evolution where war is not an issue. The extraterrestrials bring peace as an option for Earth, and we can choose either peace or obliteration. What the extraterrestrials bring is scientific advancement combined with moral advancement. This is the foundation of the ETI myth in general, and the UFO myth in particular.

What is reflected in the 1951 version of the film is the UFO myth, a variant of the more comprehensive ETI myth. The ETI myth begins with the assumption that science is savior. But, because earthly science has "known sin" by letting loose the nuclear arms race and putting the entire planet at risk, only a terrestrial science augmented by an extraterrestrial science can accomplish salvation. Salvation will come in the form of world peace. Extraterrestrials are able to do for us what we can almost do for ourselves, namely, establish security through a system of global arms control. Perhaps the more highly evolved ufonauts can save us from destroying ourselves. Perhaps flying saucers will become our celestial saviors.

Many scholars acknowledge that the primary context of the 1951 movie is the Cold War, and the secondary context is public interest in flying saucers. What is frequently missed, I think, is the subtle but influential tension over the morality of science. Does science save? Or does science kill?

This tension is best illustrated by the triumphant yet sad career of the second-most revered physicist of the era, atomic bomb–maker J. Robert Oppenheimer. This University of California physicist directed the Manhattan Project, which invented the atomic bombs dropped on Hiroshima and Nagasaki.

The frequently repeated phrase connecting science with sin derives from Oppenheimer. "The physicists have known sin; and this is a knowledge which they cannot lose," wrote Oppenheimer in 1948 in *Technology Review* and *Time* magazine.[17] Once Pandora's box had been opened and nuclear weapons knowledge spread, Oppenheimer sought to slam the lid down again through internationalizing atomic oversight. He proposed in the *New York Times Magazine* "that *in the field of atomic energy* there be set up a world government. That *in this field* there be a renunciation of sovereignty...to protect the world against the use of atomic weapons and provide it with the benefits of atomic energy."[18] He pressed his case in the White House and the United Nations, but his efforts failed. Then President Harry Truman led America into the dizzying arms race of the Cold War. Science, despite is knowledge and power, could not save us.

In their biography of the bomb-maker, Kai Bird and Martin Sherwin comment, "After Einstein, Oppenheimer was undoubtedly the most renowned scientist in the country—and this at a time when scientists were suddenly regarded as paragons of wisdom. His advice was eagerly sought in and out of government." Oppenheimer's advice was sought, but not taken. Citing Freman Dyson, Bird and Sherwin aver that Oppenheimer tried to become "the savior of humanity at the same time."[19] However, this attempt at terrestrial salvation through science failed. Could an extraterrestrial science accomplish it?

The UFO myth that took form in the early 1950s includes impatience and disgust with the government, especially the U.S. government. Everyone saw that politicians could not deliver global peace. Could the scientists give us peace even though they gave us nuclear sin? Shall we hope that there exists an extraterrestrial science that is beyond sin? This tension pervaded global consciousness during the late 1940s and early 1950s; the growth of the UFO myth was nourished by this difficult-to-articulate tension.

THE DAY THE EARTH STOOD STILL *(2008)*

The punch of the original film is lost in the 2008 remake. The pitting of politics against science—where politics emphasizes nationalism and

Model I: The Interstellar Diplomat

science emphasizes internationalism—is so muted it passes by without the viewer's notice. No longer is the threat of nuclear war the source of our anxiety; it is now eco-catastrophe. The health of our planet is a noble cause, to be sure, but the new film disregards the concern for peace that was so prominent in the earlier one. The 2008 version exploits guns firing and bombs exploding and military macho.

Even with these changes, the 2008 film could have been rescued had it maintained the logic of the first version. In both cases we find humanity locked into near hopeless patterns of self-destruction—what theologians would call "original sin"—and both versions leave us in the human race with one more Pelagian chance to make the right decisions and to choose a healing future. Yet, the 2008 version leaves us without the equivalent of a church—that is, without a prophetic fraternity of scientists within terrestrial society to carry on the mission of advocating ecological health, let alone global peace. In 1951, the worldwide fraternity of scientists was ordained with this mission. In 2008, no one was so commissioned. In sum, we have less hope in 2008 than we did in 1951.

Between 1951 and 2008 something happened in both the wider culture and in the UFO phenomenon. The mid-20th century anxiety over the threat of nuclear self-destruction was replaced with an early-21st century anxiety over the threat of environmental self-destruction. Awareness of the anthropogenic causes of global warming along with fear of uncontrolled population growth, pollution growth, and loss of natural resources has palled our new generation with a foreboding. In John Mack's reporting of UFO abduction accounts in the late 1980s and early 1990s, ecology became a big theme: "Emotions of awe, respect for the mystery of nature, and a heightened sense of the sacredness of the natural world are experienced along with a deep sadness about the apparent hopelessness of Earth's environmental crisis."[20] Mack adds, "I was astonished to discover that, in case after case, powerful messages about the human threat to the Earth's ecology were being conveyed to the experiencers in vivid, unmistakable words and images."[21] Whether from nuclear weapons or from ecological degradation, our emissaries from space offer Earth a chance at redemption.

"Klaatu beratta nikto."

EXOPOLITICS

In 1947, Klaatu had not yet landed, but some of us were anticipating it. Among those were two leading physicists, Albert Einstein and Robert Oppenheimer. In a secret letter, they wrote about their hope for interstellar diplomacy:

> On every question of whether the United States will continue testing of fission bombs and develop fusion devices (hydrogen bombs), or reach an agreement to disarm...[until such] an agreement has been reached, the lamentations of philosophers, the efforts of politicians, and the conferences of diplomats have been doomed to failure and have accomplished nothing.... The use of the atomic bomb combined with space vehicles poses a threat on a scale which makes it absolutely necessary to come to an agreement in this area. With the appearance of unidentified space vehicles (opinions are sharply divided as to their origin) over the skies of Europe and the United States has sustained an ineradical fear, an anxiety about security, that is driving the great powers to make an effort to find a solution to the threat.[22]

A few years later some began to imagine that an interstellar envoy like Klaatu may already have landed and approached the heads of state incognito. There is a widely held theory among UFO believers that extraterrestrial diplomats have already made contact secretly with the president of the United States, and that the government plans to release the information gradually to reduce the possibility of widespread panic. This is part of the theory of Donald Keyhoe and NICAP (National Investigations Committee on Aerial Phenomena), who in the 1950s and 1960s accused the U.S. government of conspiring to withhold knowledge about aliens in our midst. In recent decades the charge has been led by Stanton Friedman and Steven Greer of MUFON.[23] We will take up the matter of government secrecy in the next chapter.

It is important to see how strange events regarding lights in the sky evoke within us the thought that we might need to appoint a terrestrial diplomat to confer with an extraterrestrial diplomat. "UFOs are real," says Steven Greer, "they are of extraterrestrial origin; they have been around for decades (if not centuries); there is no evidence that they are hostile; there is probably more than one type of life form visiting us; and aspects of the government have known this for 50 years, at least."[24] With this in mind, Greer recommends that the U.S. Congress do the following: "Develop a special diplomatic unit to interface with these extraterrestrial civilizations, foster communication and peaceful relations."[25]

This nomination of a terrestrial diplomat to interface with extraterrestrial diplomats looks like it could have come right out of *The Day the Earth Stood Still*. During the era of the great contactees, in the 1950s, Gabriel Green nominated himself for this diplomatic appointment. Green claimed that one day a space visitor contacted him and stated that extraterrestrials had chosen him to lead America. Not being overly modest in the face of this unusual form of political draft, Green accepted the support of his otherworldly constituency. Using his organization, The Amalgamated Flying Saucer Clubs of America, as a base, he launched a campaign for the presidency in 1960 on a space and peace platform. He dropped out before the election, yielding to John F. Kennedy, but in running for the U.S. Senate seat from California in 1962 he won 171,000 votes.

The 1951 movie did not create the image of the flying saucer in American life. Flying saucers had been seen with considerable frequency beginning in 1947. But the movie certainly did serve to reinforce popular speculations regarding the political—and perhaps moral—implications of UFOs. It gave body to the image of the interstellar envoy. The original experience was most likely our perception of machine-made objects sailing uninvited through our national air space and outperforming our own aircraft. Then came the speculations: If these ships do not belong to us, and if they do not belong to the Soviet Union, then perhaps they belong to a third superpower somewhere in outer space.

If this is the case, it would be natural to ask why they are here. Perhaps they want us to negotiate with them. Perhaps the aliens will ally themselves with one superpower over against the other, just as the capitalist nations seek allies against the Communist bloc. Perhaps they want to establish peace between the superpowers with an organization like the League of Nations or the United Nations.

All such speculations reflect the conceptual categories of our political thinking on Earth. The more recent cases of Herbert Schirmer and Sergeant Moody appear to be extensions of this basic mindset. There might be much more to the UFO experience than just this conceptual framework through which we attempt to understand it. Nevertheless, our imaginations cannot integrate our new experiences without drawing on such established frameworks for thinking. This makes understandable the proposal for exopolitics made by Paola Leopizzi Harris: "It is logical that the creation of *Exobiology* [by Carl Sagan] goes hand-in-hand with the creation of *Exopolitics,* as we, on this planet, will need to study the implications but, even more, the protocols for contact!"[26]

INTERSTELLAR DIPLOMACY

Michael Michaud, a career foreign service officer working for the Department of State in Washington, D.C., has considered the possibility of negotiating with other worlds.[27] He says it is unavoidable that our basic interest would be to protect ourselves from any possible threat to Earth's security. That is first and foremost. Our second concern would be to assist in developing or to participate in a stable system of interstellar politics that provides an acceptable level of security for all. Only then could we have a third concern, for example, to learn from the aliens in order to advance our mutual knowledge of the universe and add to the tools of civilization. Michaud argues that this third concern, so often placed first on the list by scientific writers on the subject, would be meaningless or impossible if the first two concerns had not been satisfied. And, says Michaud, "There is no reason to believe that extraterrestrials would think or act differently."[28]

Given the probability that we would be dealing with a more advanced civilization, our posture should be one of calm confidence. We do not want to appear prematurely offensive or defensive. We must take great care in presenting the correct image. If we convey an aggressive image, we could trigger a war. If we convey an image of weakness, we could invite expansion in our direction. Because there is so little precedent, these early messages could be crucial.

An interstellar diplomat must start from the assumption that we are a potential threat to other races and they are a potential threat to us. Even if there did exist a great star empire or federation of planets that had overcome the problems of war for themselves—as was presented in *The Day the Earth Stood Still*—this would not eliminate their concern with external threats. Even if they were far in advance of Earth in both technology and political institutions, we still represent a potential danger. We have nuclear weapons and rockets to send to other worlds.

The chief argument raised by astronomers against the hypothesis that UFOs are spacecraft sent to Earth by extraterrestrial beings is the time-distance problem. Even if passenger vehicles could attain a speed close to that of light, it is still 4.3 light years to the closest star, Alpha Centauri, and about 20 light years to other likely candidates for planetary systems such as Zeta Tucanae and 82 Eridani. But Michaud conjectures that a concerned interstellar power might consider it well worth a 40-year round trip to Earth to look over a potential threat. And it is possible that alien lifetimes might be considerably longer than ours. In addition, we have our own speculations regarding the dilation of time produced by velocities near the speed of light and the possibilities of slowing down the human metabolic activities of the crew during flight. Perhaps extrasolar travel is not out of the question. Is it possible that we are now in the first stages of interplanetary negotiation?

TAKE ME TO YOUR LEADER

As a schoolboy I recall a genre of stories usually depicting an American astronaut having landed on an alien planet. Our hero meets up with a native of the planet and says, "Take me to your leader!" In one version, there is a male astronaut who is being escorted to the planet's leader. En route he spots a female inhabitant of the host planet. She is exquisitely beautiful but she is 15 feet tall. The astronaut turns to his guide and says, "Take me to your ladder, I'll see your leader later."

This raises the question: Is there likely to be a single leader at all? If the situation were reversed, and alien astronauts were to land on our planet and ask to be taken to Earth's leader, where would we take them? To the President of the United States? To the Secretary General of the United Nations? To Santa Claus? We do not have enough cooperation on Earth to have only one leader. Should we expect it of aliens?

If negotiations were to begin between ourselves and representatives of another world, we would soon ask just who they represent. There is the possibility that an alien planet would have as many cultures at different levels of development as Earth does. And they might not have any more political unity than we do. If the extraterrestrials did have competing states, it would be important to know if the individuals with whom we communicate represent a unified planetary body politic or only one state, alliance, faction, or other subgroup. We would need to know just how much authority their emissary had in the negotiations.

Suppose there are two almost equally advanced species in competition. Both might be sufficiently expansionist to have colonized many planets. We would want to learn which one is winning and which one is losing its grip. But we would not want to become involved unwittingly in an interstellar civil war. We may even have the opportunity to exploit the old divide-and-conquer technique familiar to terrestrial politics. Michaud suggests that after contacting one very powerful civilization, we might find it useful to look for a balance in the form of a rival superpower. Where would we fit in the balance of power? If we play our cards right, we could play one off against the other.

Model I: The Interstellar Diplomat

In order to gain political leverage, Michaud says, we should deny free access to the other planetary peoples to enter our solar system. With such tactics we might become "one corner of a galacto-political triangle." Hurray! We will have successfully exported stand-off politics.

3

Geopolitics and Exopolitics

Imagine your office in America has a coin sorter/counter. As long as only quarters, dimes, nickels, and pennies are thrown in the hopper, the machine sorts and counts automatically. Now, imagine that you have just returned from a multi-country trip to Asia. Your pocket is full of coins of various sizes from countries you've already forgotten. Suppose you throw these coins in the hopper. In moments you'll have a very confused machine. Some coins simply do not fit, so they cannot be counted.

Scholarship is like this. When the scholar invents categories for sorting the evidence, some evidence simply doesn't fit. It's anomalous. Now, I am offering four rather neat models for classifying the UFO phenomenon: the Interstellar Diplomat; the Research Scientist; the Celestial Savior; and the Hybridizer. I believe these models are illuminating and revealing. They help us dissect and comprehend the UFO phenomenon. However, these four models do not account for everything. Not by a long shot. Some sub-phenomena, such as crop circles, cattle mutilations, Area 51, and Men In Black, lie beyond the scope of what I will be able to help us comprehend. What lies within the scope of these four models, however, is vast, textured, nuanced, and potent. Government conspiracy is a sub-phenomenon within the larger UFO phenomenon, and

I place it within Model I: the Interstellar Diplomat, even if it does not fit perfectly.

One valve that pumps blood into the UFO heart is the preoccupation with a U.S. government conspiracy to withhold information from the general public. This concern over Washington's role is no peripheral matter. It belongs inextricably to the phenomenon itself. It is clearly political, but it does not fit precisely within the Interstellar Diplomat model. It spills beyond this category. It baffles me. Despite its ubiquity, I find it difficult to comprehend.

Public rage over government conspiracy is co-primal with the UFO phenomenon. The first book in the new genre of UFO treatments was Donald Keyhoe's *The Flying Saucers Are Real*. In Keyhoe's "Author's Note" prior to Chapter 1, the topic is the gathering of UFO data by the U.S. Air Force, which "denied the existence of flying saucers."[1] In one of the next of these early works, *Behind the Flying Saucers* published in March 1951, we find Frank Scully's "Author's Preface" dated Decoration Day 1950. Right on the very first page with text, before a single word regarding flying saucers is uttered, we find this blistering denunciation of the United States government:

> *Between the people and the government today lies a double standard of morality. Anything remotely scientific has become by government definition a matter of military security first; hence of secrecy, something which does not breed security but fear. If we see anything unusual, even in the skies, we the people must either freeze our lips, like a Russian peasant at the sight of a commissar, or give our names, addresses, business connections, and testimony to be screened and filtered by anonymous intelligence officers.... There is only one thing to do under such a setup. Expose their tactics.*[2]

Today, this clarion call to "expose" government tactics is called "disclosure" in UFO nomenclature.

Does this rage over government conspiracy combined with the revolutionary call for disclosure fit neatly into Model I, the Interstellar Diplomat? No. Parts of it overlap with Model II, the Research Scientist, and Model III, Celestial Savior. Even after this distribution, there may remain aspects of the conspiracy concern that do not fit in any of these. Yet, it belongs to the UFO phenomenon like a frame belongs to a picture.

Here's a fact: Ufologists have been at war with the U.S. government since the Roswell case of 1947. Why? What does this mean?

ROSWELL IN 1947

Let us situate this topic of governmental management of information. The date most ufologists attach to the onset of the current phase of the UFO phenomenon is June 24, 1947. On this day pilot Kenneth Arnold reported seeing nine disc-shaped objects traveling at twice the speed of sound near Mount Rainer in the state of Washington. His description gave birth to a new term in the English language: *flying saucer.*

During the first and second weeks of the next month, July 1947, excitement gripped Roswell, New Mexico, and its surrounding ranches. One rancher, William "Mac" Brazel, reported hearing an explosion during a storm on Friday night, July Fourth. Riding around his property the following day, Brazel came across what looked like wreckage scattered across part of his ranch, "a quarter mile long or so, and several hundred feet wide." He described the metal pieces: "You could wrinkle it and lay it back down and it immediately resumed its original shape. It was quite pliable, yet you couldn't crease or bend it like ordinary metal. It was almost like plastic."[3] On some of the debris, balsa-like sticks, Brazel found mysterious markings or figures and undecipherable writing. Brazel reported this to Sheriff George Wilcox, who in turn reported it to the military. At the Roswell Army Air Base, military personnel had been tracking mysterious objects on the radar for three days, so they welcomed this opportunity to locate what they might have been tracking.

Two others who arrived on the site, Jim Ragsdale and Trudy Truelove, claim to have found a strange craft in a crashed state. Ragsdale reported that there were "bodies or something lying there. They looked like bodies." It appears that this might actually have been a separate crash site near the Brazel site, perhaps looking like a single site.

The Roswell Fire Department showed up, as well as some New Mexico state police. A number of locals, including some archaeologists, had gathered at the crash site by the time the U.S. military convoy arrived. Immediately, Major Edwin Easley escorted all civilian personnel off the premises and he asked the MPs to take the archaeologists to the air base for questioning. The military cleaned up the area quickly, leaving virtually no trace of the debris.

Sergeant Melvin E. Brown was ordered to drive the truck with the five dead bodies of the alien flight crew. He was told not to look at what was in his truck, but he claims he took a peek. He described the aliens as "small [in size] with large heads and skin that is yellow or orange."

Mortician Glenn Dennis of the Ballard Funeral Home in Roswell received a telephone call from the base mortuary officer at Roswell Army Air Field. The officer asked for small caskets. He also asked for advice on how to preserve bodies that have been exposed to the elements. When Dennis showed up at the Air Field to make a delivery, he was told by an officer in an intimidating voice: "There was no crash here. You did not see anything. You don't...tell anybody you saw anything. If you do, you'll get into serious trouble."

After conducting his own investigation of the crash site on Monday, July 8, Major Jesse Marcel, of the 509th Bomb Group Intelligence Office, took some of the rubble home with him. He showed it to his wife and 11-year-old son, saying that the debris was from a "flying saucer."

The Roswell Army Air Base press release published that day included, among other things, the following line: The U.S. Army "was fortunate enough to gain possession of a disc through the cooperation of one of the local ranchers and the sheriff's office." The *Roswell Daily Record* included, "The intelligence office of the 509th Bombardment group at Roswell Army Air Field announced at noon today, that the field has come into possession of a flying saucer. According to information released by the department, over authority of Maj. J.A. Marcel...." This press release was immediately picked up by wire services and appeared in the *New York Times* and the *San Francisco Chronicle*.

Lt. Gen. Hoyt S. Vandenburg, Deputy Chief of the U.S. Army Air Force, read the papers. He immediately began to issue his own orders from the top down. At Vandenburg's request, the debris and the bodies were allegedly flown on a B-29 to Fort Worth, Texas, and then on to Wright-Patterson Air Force Base in Dayton, Ohio. Major Jesse Marcel flew with the material as far as Fort Worth, where he had his picture taken and published in the newspapers. In the photo, Marcel was holding what looked like wreckage from a balloon. Marcel claimed that the debris came from a weather balloon that had broken up. No space craft had been recovered. The excitement was all due to a mistake in identifying the fallen debris.

Brig. Gen. Roger M. Ramey, commanding officer of the 8th Air Force at Carswell Air Force Base in Fort Worth, followed orders he received from Vandenburg. He invited his picture to be taken by the press with material he described as "parts of a balloon." The particular balloon had attached a Rawin (pronounced *ray-win*) sonde, a foil-covered, balsa-framed item that could be tracked by radar. Years later, the U.S. Air Force identified the Roswell crash with a Mogul balloon, a high-altitude balloon used to monitor Soviet bomb experiments. The published pictures of Marcel and Ramey were accompanied by a message: The Roswell "saucer" was a misidentified balloon.

Roswell locals and ufologists strongly objected, accusing the military of bait and switch. What Marcel held up was not what Brazel said he had found. The subject of the captured space craft and recovery of five alien bodies dropped out of the conversation. For reasons not publically disclosed, the U.S. Army decided to make it appear as if nothing extraordinary had happened at Roswell.

If the previous account is accurate, we would conclude that, for unstated reasons, the U.S. military and perhaps other wings of government have been deliberately managing information. By denying honest testimony by citizen witnesses as well as military witnesses, a byproduct of governmental secrecy is the impugning of witnesses who report encounters with flying saucers. Is this sufficient for outrage? If not, then what happened next might be.

ROSWELL AND MJ-12

The UFO community has never forgiven Uncle Sam for this discourteous behavior; if anything, the sense of public outrage skyrocketed with the revelation of the MJ-12 documents.

The next chapter in the Roswell odyssey began on December 11, 1984, when a mysterious envelope was delivered to the Los Angeles home of movie producer Jaime Shandera. Shandera enlisted the help of William Moore, who in turn enlisted the help of Stanton Friedman, to analyze the contents of the envelope.

Inside the envelope was a roll of black-and-white film, which included photographs of secret U.S. government documents. The document gained the "MJ-12" moniker because one photographed item was titled, "Briefing Document: Operation Majestic 12, Prepared for President-elect Dwight D. Eisenhower (Eyes Only), 18 November 1952." If authentic, this briefing memo would have been written only a couple of months following the Robertson Panel discussed in Chapter 2. The author of this letter to Eisenhower was Adm. Roscoe H. Hillenkoetter (MJ-1), one of the early heads of the CIA. Among others in this select group we find Dr. Vannevar Bush, Harvard's Dr. Donald Menzel, and Gen. Hoyt S. Vandenberg.

The MJ-12 briefing memo reports the flying saucer sighting of Kenneth Arnold. Then it proceeds to take up the crash at Roswell:

On 07 July, 1947, a secret operation was begun to assure recovery of the wreckage of this object for scientific study...four human-like beings had apparently ejected from the craft at some point before it exploded. These had fallen to earth about two miles east of the wreckage site. All four were dead and badly decomposed due to action by predators and exposure to the elements.... Civilian and military witnesses in the area were debriefed, and news reporters were given the effective cover story that the object had been a misguided weather research balloon.[4]

There are some people, such as Ryan Wood and Paola Leopizzi Harris, who wish to implicate America's two leading physicists with MJ-12, Albert Einstein and Robert Oppenheimer. In June 1947, a month prior to Roswell, these two respected intellects were said to have drafted a six-page Top Secret paper titled, "Relationships With Inhabitants of Celestial Bodies." Among the many issues Einstein and Oppenheimer considered was colonization. What might happen if aliens from space should wish to colonize our planet? "If they are politically organized and possess a certain culture similar to our own, they may be recognized as an independent people.... A superior form of colonizing will have to be conceived, that could be a kind of tutelage, possibly through...the United Nations."[5] Certainly this form of exopolitics would require terrestrial and extraterrestrial diplomats.

ROSWELL 1997

With the disclosure of the scandalous MJ-12 documents and the mushrooming of public discussion, furor over the management of information by Uncle Sam was peaking on the eve of the 50th anniversary of the Roswell crash in 1997. A friend of mine, a ranking U.S. Marine working at the Pentagon, said, "Ted, the Air Force is about to publish its own answer to Roswell."

"Could you get me a copy?" I begged.

"I'll go to the printing office tomorrow."

When we met for dinner the following evening, I had my copy of *The Roswell Report: Case Closed.*[6] The text exudes a tone of ridicule aimed at those who believe something extraordinary happed in Roswell in

1947. Among other attempts to explain away the UFO element, the Air Force reported that in 1954 it had experimented with dropping humanoid dummies from balloons. Some of these anthropomorphic dummies landed in the region of New Mexico in question. The document suggests that the Roswell witnesses who claim to have seen alien bodies actually saw these experimental dummies. Recognizing that seven years stands between 1947 and 1954, the document suggests that the memory of witnesses may have been inaccurate; the Roswell witnesses got their dates mixed up.

Within weeks this Air Force document was widely read by ufologists. Nothing could be more insulting to the people of Roswell or to the UFO community. This crass attempt at disinformation on the part of U.S. government officials only poured gasoline on smoldering embers. Reactive anger against Uncle Sam flamed up.

One of the first things I did after arriving in Roswell in 1997 was buy a black t-shirt. On the front appears the face of a gray alien, almost but not fully smiling. On the back is written: "What do you think we look like...Dummies?" I still treasure the shirt, even though after many washings it hardly fits any more.

The festive 1997 Roswell anniversary was part carnival and part seminar. The all-stars of UFOdom graced the stage, including Erich von Däniken, John Mack, Whitley Strieber, Linda Moulton Howe, Stanton Friedman, Robert O. Dean, Kevin Randle, Donald Schmitt, and Budd Hopkins. Each took the podium purportedly to recite the historical events at Roswell. What I found stunning was how each of these speeches was dominated by angry denunciations of the U.S. government. If I understood the speakers correctly, the credibility of claiming that a crash had occurred at Roswell seemed to depend solely on the existence of information now being concealed by Washington. The answer to the big mystery regarding extraterrestrial visitation exists, the speakers contended, but it is being deliberately withheld by an authoritarian, stubborn, and paternalistic military intelligence network.

Friedman insisted that the controversial MJ-12 documents demonstrate clearly that beginning with President Truman in 1947, our government has been intentionally and systematically engaged in cover-up. Linda Moulton Howe chastised Washington for denying truth to the American people. Robert O. Dean, retired after 27 years in the U.S. Army with special NATO intelligence assignments, decried the totalitarian attitude of a government that had lost respect for its own citizenry. In his Roswell speech he cried for public resistance.

Kevin Randle argued, "Flying saucers are real. They are extraterrestrial, and the government, through its conspiracy of silence, has tried to keep us in the dark."[7] Randle, a former intelligence officer with the U.S. Air Force, says in his book, "There clearly was a directed program from inside the government whose job it was to obscure the truth. The room is littered with smoking guns. It is littered with cold pistols that provide us with additional information about UFOs."[8]

WHAT SHOULD WE BELIEVE?

How much of this can we reasonably believe? The Roswell crash account? The authenticity of the MJ-12 documents? The conspiracy on the part of the U.S. government?

Kal Korff is less than convinced that the MJ-12 documents are authentic. "At best, Friedman's research has uncovered only *circumstantial* evidence that indicates the MJ-12 documents *might* be authentic. However, it is important to remember that circumstantial evidence is *not* scientific evidence or even forensic evidence…. Friedman's investigation was hampered by the fact that there were and are *no original documents* with which to work."[9]

Korff says that insufficient evidence exists to support the notion that a flying saucer crashed at Roswell and, for that matter, anywhere else. "Unfortunately, as of this writing, there is no known, scientifically verifiable evidence that *any* UFO has ever crashed at any location on this planet. If indeed such an occurrence has ever taken place, then the hard evidence that proves it has so far remained elusive."[10] Korff goes further with an *ad hominem* criticism. "Let's not pull punches here: the Roswell UFO myth has been very good business for UFO groups, publishers, for Hollywood, the town of Roswell, the media, and UFOlogy."[11]

It is not my task here to judge the authenticity of MJ-12 nor the veracity of the Roswell crash reports. My task here is to demonstrate that public furor over the handling of UFO matters is equi-primordial with UFO sightings themselves. Complaints regarding a government conspiracy are built-in to the UFO phenomenon. If we are to understand UFOs, we need to include in our understanding the role played by Uncle Sam combined with public anger at Uncle Sam.

THE MYTH OF THE SKEPTICS

If Korff is cautiously skeptical, Joe Nickel and James McGaha are non-cautiously skeptical. They have read the Roswell history, and they see myth in that history. "We identify this [mythmaking] process—a UFO incident's occurring, being debunked, going underground, beginning the mythmaking process, and reemerging as a conspiracy tale with ongoing mythologizing and media hype."[12] Roswell fixes the more general UFO paradigm, they contend.

After the Air Force identified the sighting as a mistaken weather balloon in 1947, the story went underground. There it incubated and eventually spawned an antagonism against the government for its apparent conspiracy to withhold the truth about what happened. We can tell the myth-making story in four chapters. Chapter one: the *incident*, begins with a report by Mac Brazel that he saw a light and then later found wreckage. Chapter two: the *debunking*, amounted to a government identification of the wreckages as belonging to a Project Mogul weather balloon. Chapter three is: *submergence*. Upon hearing of the balloon explanation, the news dropped the subject. But ufologists continued to probe and speculate and gather data. They complained of a government cover-up, rendering the evidence they amassed ambiguous, yet still ripe for alien visitor interpretation. Chapter four is *mythologizing*. The underground story becomes "an elaborate myth. It involves many factors, including exaggeration, faulty memory, folklore, and deliberate hoaxing."[13] The fifth and final chapter is the *reemergence and media bandwagon effect*. Books were written, two UFO museums in Roswell were established, and a 50th anniversary festival was celebrated in July 1997, which drew tens of thousands of UFO aficionados.

What accounts for this pattern? Nickel and McGaha answer: Frustrated UFO investigators, because they cannot find the definitive case to embellish previous cases. "It appears that ufologists are always looking for a Holy Grail case to verify their belief in extraterrestrial visitation, and when that does not pan out (most UFO reports prove little more than misidentifications, ambiguous sightings, fake photos, and the like) they seek out the old cases and are rewarded with much more sensational testimony."[14] I find this to be a curious denunciation of ufologists. The skeptics circumstantially decry the myth-making propensity of so-called UFO believers—a propensity from which the skeptics themselves are apparently exempt.

Let me point out that the concept of myth applied here by Nickel and McGaha appears to be simplistic: a myth is a false story believed by someone other than me. No nuance here. What Nickel and McGaha seem to be oblivious to is the larger myth that frames their own inquiry, one that relies upon modern science to supersede atavistic mythological thinking. Knowledge saves, and skeptical scientific knowledge saves better than mythical knowledge.

My own employment of the concept of myth is more subtle and more comprehensive. I have been trying to show that the ETI myth within the wider modern worldview is structured according a pattern we have seen in the ancient world: the gnostic redeemer myth. According to this myth, knowledge saves, of course. The ETI variant of the gnostic myth functions within an evolutionary worldview replete with the doctrine of progress and reverence for knowledge in the form of intelligence, science, and technology. This is shared by both those who affirm the UFO myth and those skeptics who debunk it. It's the myth that underlies the myth, so to speak. The suppressed religious thirst for ultimate meaning in a comprehensive view of the universe gets quenched with the nectar of the gods—gods in the form of extraterrestrial aliens. Or it gets assuaged by the skeptic's worldview devoid of myths, gods, or religion.

THE CORSO CONTROVERSY

During the spring of 1997 leading up to the 50th anniversary hoop-la in Roswell, a publishing frenzy broke out. New books touting new takes on Roswell swarmed like locusts. One in particular occupied my attention: *The Day After Roswell*, by Col. Philip J. Corso, (Ret.). Corso's claims were dazzling, reinforcing the most extravagant asseverations and adding exaggerations beyond credulity.

Corso arrogated to himself secret knowledge ready to be divulged. He had served "in Army R&D" and as an "intelligence officer and adviser to General Trudeau" at the Pentagon.[15] Yes, indeed, there had been a crash at Roswell in 1947. Corso had personally seen the alien bodies. More importantly, the recovered star crafts had become the subject of reverse engineering. We earthlings—actually, the American military—had used its learnings to develop new technologies for both domestic and military usage. Space technology had jump-started terrestrial technology, thanks to Roswell.

When I arrived in Roswell for the festivities surrounding the 50th anniversary of the crash, I found parking lots filled with RVs and trailers, blue-collar families with children, charcoal smoke rising above Weber grills, and an all-around merry mood. The single topic most frequently discussed was not the Roswell crash itself, but rather the government cover-up. If I read between the lines, I was hearing two things: criticism of a government cover-up combined with a sense of admiration that Uncle Sam was able to pull it all off. During the reveling and excitement, Corso was courted like a hero. He was constantly mobbed by autograph-seekers and media reporters.

In his book, Corso lists recent technological advances that could not have occurred without the influence of tutelage from extraterrestrial intelligence. Some items on Corso's list: fiber optics, lasers, integrated circuits and microminiaturization of logic boards, irradiated food, particle beams, and electromagnetic propulsion systems.[16] If left to ourselves, current terrestrial technology might look like it did in the 1940s.

"The military found itself fighting a two-front war, a war against the Communists who were seeking to undermine our institutions while threatening our allies and, as unbelievable as it sounds, a war against extraterrestrials, who posed an even greater threat than the Communist forces," wrote Corso. "So, we used the extraterrestrials' own technology against them, feeding it out to our defense contractors and then adapting it for use in space-related defense programs." The technologies we learned from the dismantled space vehicles helped propel President Ronald Reagan's "Star Wars" program. "The Strategic Defense Initiative, Star Wars, to achieve the capability of knocking down enemy satellites, killing the electronic guidance systems of incoming enemy warheads, and disabling enemy spacecraft.... It was alien technology we used: lasers, accelerated particle-beam weapons, and aircraft equipped with stealth features."[17]

One item on Corso's list caught my attention, namely, the laser. The laser prototype had been taken from a crashed saucer at Roswell. In such cases, said Corso, contractors would be invited to re-design and patent such inventions; in the case of the laser, it would become the most lethal weapon in the Star Wars arsenal. What an achievement! Just think about it: The U.S. military captured a laser from a crashed flying saucer, reverse engineered it, perfected it, and then employed it in the 1980s to shoot down both Soviet missiles and extraterrestrial "spacecraft." Our clever military received saving knowledge from the heavens and is now using this knowledge to save the United States not only from its terrestrial enemies, but from extraterrestrial colonizers as well.[18] If only this were true. But, alas, it is not.

I happen to know one of the two persons who invented both the laser and the maser. *LASER* is an acronym for Light Amplification by Stimulated Emission of Radiation. *MASER* represents Microwave

Amplification by Stimulated Emission of Radiation. The two co-inventors of these two dramatic breakthroughs in technology received the Nobel Prize in 1965. One of the two, Charles Townes, an emeritus professor of physics at the University of California at Berkeley, nears 100 years of age as I write the following account.

When I asked Professor Townes whether he'd received the design for the laser from outer space, he was most puzzled. Why would I ask such a question? I supplied him with the relevant pages from Corso's book and asked if he would write me a response. I supply his letter on page 73. Among other things, Townes writes, "Philip Corso has almost no factual material correct so far as the maser and laser are concerned." Whereas Corso claims that the first maser was assembled at Bell Laboratories in 1956, Townes reports that it took place at Columbia University two years prior. Whereas Corso says that "all three branches of the military were working with researchers...to develop a working laser," Townes reports that "the military were quite uninterested until sometime after I had built the first maser." Referring to Corso's description, the word *nonsense* appears in Charlie's letter to me. Corso's facts are "easily refuted."

In his book *Starstruck* Albert Harrison writes, "Corso's account was riddled with mistakes and inconsistencies. The biggest problem for Corso's story is that we have a competing history of modern technology, one that is supported by a huge paper trail, personal reminiscences on the part of the inventors, and corroboration by independent eyewitnesses."[19] In other words, these technological advances on Corso's list all have their own inventors, their own paper trails, and their own stories that have nothing to do with influence from outer space.

One more aspect of Corso's claim tickles my funny bone. Note how Corso claims that the laser played a central role in President Reagan's Strategic Defense Initiative (SDI), commonly known as Star Wars, in the 1980s. This is correct, but more needs to be said about the technology involved. Recently, Townes told me a story: On one occasion, he caught a private moment with then President Reagan. Townes addressed the president: "Now, I have been following what is being said about

Geopolitics and Exopolitics

UNIVERSITY OF CALIFORNIA, BERKELEY

BERKELEY • DAVIS • IRVINE • LOS ANGELES • RIVERSIDE • SAN DIEGO • SAN FRANCISCO

SANTA BARBARA • SANTA CRUZ

DEPARTMENT OF PHYSICS
366 Le Conte Hall # 7300
TEL: 510/642-7166
FAX: 510/643-8497

BERKELEY, CALIFORNIA 94720-7300

July 24, 1997

Dr. Theodore Peters
Pacific Lutheran Theological Seminary
2770 Marin Avenue
Berkeley, CA 94708-1597

Dear Ted:

Philip Corso has almost no factual material correct so far as the maser and laser are concerned. On the bottom of p. 178 and the top of p. 179 he says "...extraordinarily high energy levels by the application of bursts of energy. The gas would release its excess energy as microwaves..." Bursts of energy were not used at all, but rather a simple flow of gas and application of a constant electric field. He then says "When the first maser was assembled at Bell Laboratories in 1956...". The first maser was assembled at Columbia University and first came into operation in early 1954. He then says "...theories about how this might be accomplished were circulating widely through the weapons-development community even before Bell Labs produced the first maser." This is not true at all. I was at Bell Labs and then at Columbia and there was no thought of such a device. Lower on the page he says "...all three branches of the military were working with researchers in university laboratories to develop a working laser." Actually, the military were quite uninterested until sometime after I had built the first maser. Later in the same paragraph he says "...in 1958...especially at Columbia University where, two years later, physicist Theodore Maiman constructed the first working laser." Maiman never worked at Columbia University. He did make the first working laser in 1960 but it was at the Hughes Laboratory in California.

Substantial parts of the rest of his material is nonsense, but perhaps the above illustrates the situation. It is clear that he simply enjoys saying what he would like to say without bothering to check on facts even where he can be easily refuted.

Thanks for sending me this chapter. I had not before seen this book and was interested to see the style of the author.

Very best regards.

Sincerely,

Charles H. Townes

CHT:mm

73

SDI. I happen to know a great deal about laser technology. Given what I know, Sir, it is impossible to develop the kind of space-based weapon you are planning."

"Yes, I know," said the president. "But, we want to scare the hell out of the Russians." The president did not say he wanted to scare the hell out of extraterrestrial colonizers. In addition, reverse technology or not, SDI was not technologically potent. What Corso did not know was that SDI was all a bluff.

DISCLOSURE

In the previous chapter, we met a medical doctor named Steven Greer from North Carolina, who has dedicated his free time to what he calls "disclosure." Greer wants to put an end to U.S. government secrecy, as well as to secrecy in other extra-governmental agencies and other terrestrial governments that have been sharing in the cover-up. He is collecting testimony and documents that will demonstrate "advanced spacecraft of extraterrestrial origin, called extraterrestrial vehicles (ETVs) by some intelligence agencies have been downed, retrieved and studied since at least the 1940s and possibly as early as the 1930s," and "that significant technological breakthroughs in energy generation and propulsion have resulted from the study of these objects."[20]

Why, we might ask, would Uncle Sam or any other official body be motivated to construct a network of secrecy and maintain it for three quarters of a century? Perhaps Washington is paternalistic, worried that the public might panic should news about alien visitations be released. Perhaps Uncle Sam wants to protect us from ourselves. No, says Greer, that's not why. "Contrary to the popular myth, since the 1960s concern over some type of public panic when faced with the fact that we are not alone in the universe has not been the major reason for secrecy."[21] What, then? Greer's answer: It's political and economic.

The knowledge related to UFOs/ET phenomena must have such great potential for changing the status quo that its continued suppression is deemed essential, at all costs.... The technological discoveries of the 1950s resulting from the reverse-engineering of extraterrestrial craft could have enabled us to completely transform the world economic, social, technological and environmental situation. That such advancements have been withheld from the public is related to the change-averse nature of the controlling hierarchy at the time—and to this day.[22]

The roadblock to disclosure is the "controlling hierarchy."

Greer is passionate about disclosure. His message is urgent. He asks us to pressure the U.S. Congress and other political leaders around the globe to hold hearings, to unlock the mysteries, to divulge the secrets, to expose the conspirators, to upset the hierarchy. Locked in the vaults of governmental secrecy are technological treasures that could enrich all of us on this planet. With our planet facing ecological disaster, the technology transfer from space to Earth could solve the problems we face, such as pollution, energy, food supply, climate change, and many others. Even more than technology, this knowledge descended from our skies could bring peace on Earth. Disclosure is the path to redemption.

Greer states that the "classified, above top-secret projects possess fully operational antigravity propulsion devices and new energy generation systems that, if declassified and put into peaceful uses, would empower a new human civilization without want, poverty, or environmental damage."[23] We are facing a "social and spiritual crisis," warns Greer. But, if we rise to the occasion, opportunity for planetary transformation awaits. "Can our spiritual and social resources rise to this challenge? Nothing less than the destiny of the human race hangs in the balance."[24]

So much more is at stake here than garden variety grumbling about governmental ineptness and inefficiency. Like the shamans in archaic tribal life, the secret agencies within our government have received truths from the heavens, revelations from what is beyond us. In this case, the heavenly truths brought down to Earth have descended via flying machines piloted by more technologically advanced UFO crews.

The knowledge of social and spiritual salvation is not sequestered in the heavens above; it now exists right here on Earth. Our difficulty is that Uncle Sam has appointed himself to play the roles of priest and guard; our Washington priesthood wants to protect and manage the slow dispensing of this redeeming knowledge. Greer urges us to break into the holy of holies, to rescue this saving knowledge on behalf of the entire human race. Those who successfully accomplish disclosure will become our gnostic redeemers. In sum, Model I, the Interstellar Diplomat, has bled over into both Model II, the Research Scientist, and Model III, the Celestial Savior.

JUST HOW ANTI-GOVERNMENT ARE THE UFOLOGISTS?

Shortly after the 1997 Roswell funfair, I offered a prophesy. This prophesy has not been fulfilled, which I'm glad about.

After the farm crisis due to catapulting interest rates in the late 1970s, renegade militia groups began to crop up in rural America. Feeling disenfranchised and very much at home with hunting rifles and other weapons, these groups began voicing some of the most anti-government rhetoric one could imagine. They readied themselves for an apocalyptic battle, the kind of battle the FBI and other law enforcement groups seemed ready to grant.

After witnessing the uncanny degree of hostility toward Washington among UFO believers in Roswell, I began to fear a potential alliance. I could imagine a coalition of militia military with ufology ideologues becoming a significant force for insurrection. In my own foreboding imagination, this seemed ominous and portentous. Such an accord never took place. These two forms of anti-government sentiment did not coalesce. Why?

Here is one candidate for explanation. After the attack on New York's World Trade Center on September 11, 2001, the mood of America changed. Suddenly, every American became a patriotic American. The common enemy, Al Qaeda, required national unity. The militias went quiet. Objections to government secrecy over UFOs kept within parameters, within the bounds of its focal concern without connoting a general distrust of Uncle Sam. In sum, both militias and ufologists became intimidated by patriotism.

However, there might be another explanation. This candidate for explanation is more subtle. Here is my hypothesis: The ufologist complaint against Uncle Sam is double-minded. On the surface, ufologists complain that agencies within the government are hiding information that should be shared with the wider public. This information allegedly has to do with the single-most important truth ever communicated to the human race. What the government knows and is hiding is scientific and technological knowledge that could save our planet from nuclear war and from environmental catastrophe. This hidden knowledge, once revealed, would deliver peace and prosperity on a global scale. Keeping such knowledge secret is a culpable crime, say the ufologists.

Beneath this surface complaint, however, lies an unspoken admiration and even pride in the awesome power available to the government. The orphic knowledge gained from heaven's descent to Earth turns secular Washington into a sacred place, an *axis mundi* that connects heaven and Earth. What is secret is actually esoteric. What is scientific knowledge is holy knowledge, redemptive knowledge. Oh yes, all of this is cast in secular and scientific language, but it emits sacred energy and enlists an inner response of awe and grace. In sum, what is going on in the soul of the ufologist has virtually nothing in common with those in the militias.

CONCLUSION

The complaint against the U.S. government for its conspiracy to manage UFO information fits within Model I, even though this complaint does not center on interstellar diplomacy. More complaints about a government conspiracy spill beyond Model I into Models II and III, into the Research Scientist and the Celestial Savior. We will look at these in more detail in the chapters to come.

4

Model II: The Research Scientist

If we are being visited by extraterrestrials, why? What is their purpose in coming? How are they going to behave while on our planet?

One way to project a possible answer is to imagine ourselves in their shoes. What would we do if we were to travel to another world? What did we do when we went to the Moon? American astronauts took soil samples and collected rocks to bring back to laboratories for analysis. They made countless atmospheric and other physical tests. Had they encountered small game, they surely would have considered capturing some to examine. Had they encountered humanoid creatures, they would have inquired after their physiological makeup.

Despite all that was said in the last chapter about the priorities of politics over science, we could not send diplomats to another world if our scientists did not invent the machines to send them. Space travel is unthinkable for us without the aid of the scientific community. Consequently, interplanetary expeditions are closely identified with the interests of science in our minds. We simply take it for granted that our space missions will be exploratory—their object is to gather scientific data.

This brings us to the second model for understanding the ufonauts: the Research Scientist. This subsystem of beliefs is familiar to all of us. We all have a mental picture of medical biologists or physical chemists dressed in their stained white lab coats, shifting mysterious liquids or powders from one test tube to another, and hastily scribbling notes of their observations onto a scratch pad. But before they can run their experiments, someone must bring in the materials to be analyzed. This becomes the task of the flying saucer scout ships, equipped with scientific gathering and measuring devices, which are presently surveying the planet Earth. The information they gather on Earth is sent back to their planet to be logged in scientific journals and written up in encyclopedias for school children to read.

Why are they here? They are here to learn about us and our world. When Hynek formulated the category "Close Encounters of the Third Kind," he seems to have had the scientific model in mind. He notes that there are similar descriptions coming from different places all over the world. We find the occupants of mysterious machines picking up samples of earth and rocks and carrying them aboard their craft, much as U.S. astronauts picked up Moon rocks. We find them exhibiting interest in human installations and vehicles. We "even find them making off with rabbits, dogs, and fertilizer!"[1]

SOIL SAMPLING AND ROCK COLLECTING

During the excitement of the 1967 UFO activity mentioned in Chapter 3, the Aerial Phenomenon Research Organization (APRO) received a report of UFOs engaged in full-fledged mining. Buzz Montague and his companion, both from Twin Falls, Idaho, went hunting and camped on a bluff overlooking a valley near the Spring Creek mines. He could not remember the precise date, but it was sometime in the middle 1960s. Looking through the 10-power scopes affixed to their rifles, they watched four shiny flying objects hovering over the dump. Each object had protruding from its top a hose-like device that was inserted into the piles of slag and moving around. When they had evidently vacuumed to their capacities, they flew up one at a time to a giant cigar-shaped mother ship hovering at roughly 1,000 feet. When the smaller craft reached the larger one, they fitted themselves into ready-made depressions, after which there was no indication that there had been a depression to begin with. After apparently transferring their load to the mother ship, the smaller objects would return to the slag heap. They made four such trips in approximately 45 minutes.[2]

Coral and Jim Lorenzen, now deceased but then directors of APRO, offer two theories to explain this incident. On the one hand, certainly, the space visitors may have been mining. On the other hand, the Earth they were probing had already been mined by humans, so the occupants of the craft might have been obtaining samples to determine the nature of *human* mining in that area.[3]

The Lorenzens also describe a fascinating case that took place at Vilvorde, seven miles northeast of Brussels, Belgium, in the middle of December 1973.[4] Having arisen from bed at 2 a.m., Monsieur "V.M." caught sight through his window of a creature in his garden. The creature was a small humanoid, about three and a half feet tall, and wearing a shiny, green one-piece suit; its head was encased in a transparent globular helmet.

The creature was carrying in its hands a device that closely resembled a vacuum cleaner or metal detector. It passed this device slowly to and fro over a pile of bricks that the witness had gathered together a few days previously. V.M. said that when he blinked his flashlight at it, the creature turned and seemed to give a responding hand signal. Then, with a waddling gait, the visitor walked off toward the back wall of the enclosed yard. Without hesitation it walked straight up the 10-foot wall with no change of pace and disappeared down the other side. Four minutes later, V.M. heard a noise similar to that of a cricket. Then a round object about 15 meters in diameter rose up, and he could see the humanoid outlined in the greenish light of a cupola on top of the craft. After pausing briefly at a height of about 60 feet, the machine shot out of sight into the star-studded sky above.

What we have here is perhaps an alien version of Neil Armstrong's picking up moon rocks and testing the surface for radioactivity. Because so many of the alien creatures are described as short and childlike, what we more likely have is a seventh-grade science class from an undiscovered planet orbiting Zeta Reticuli coming here to gather information for a semester research paper in geology. If the junior high schools of Zeta Reticuli can do it, so can the medical schools. Certainly an interplanetary research project would want to investigate the physiology of the living creatures on Earth and to that research project we turn next.

Also in 1973, November 4 to be exact, Rex Snow and his wife were awakened by a brushing sound against their Goffstown, New Hampshire, house. Mr. Snow looked and, to his amazement, saw two silver-suited beings, about four and a half to five feet tall, in his backyard. They seemed to be self-luminous, had oversized, pointed ears, and dark, egg-shaped eyeholes with large noses. One of the creatures held what looked like a flashlight while the other went about the yard picking up things from the ground and putting them in a silver bag.[5]

Then, in January 1975, just past 2 a.m., George O'Barski was driving through North Hudson Park, New Jersey, across the Hudson River from Manhattan. A 72-year-old teetotaler, O'Barski still managed his own liquor store in Chelsea, New York. He normally worked the evening shift, closing the store at midnight and finishing the bookkeeping and restocking about 2 a.m. Then he would drive home to New Jersey.

While taking his customary shortcut through Hudson Park, he noticed a scratching sound coming from the radio. He fiddled with the dial a bit, and then the radio went completely silent. Outside the car he heard a droning noise, like that of a refrigerator, increasing in volume. Suddenly he saw a brightly lit object fly by on the other side of a row of trees, traveling the same direction as his car. In seconds it had stopped and was hovering about 10 feet above the ground. The UFO, he said, was round, about 30 feet in diameter, and six to eight feet thick, with some sort of dome on the top. It was dark in color with regularly spaced vertical windows around the edge of the body. The windows gave off the light.

The craft came to rest above a grassy area in the park about 100 feet from O'Barski. He continued to drive by very slowly, coming to within

60 feet of the activity. He watched with a mixture of cautious dread and bewildered fascination.

A ladder apparatus made its appearance from a vertical opening. Immediately, at least nine, maybe more, uniformed figures descended the mechanical steps. Each was about three to four feet tall, clad in light coveralls that made them look "like little kids with snowsuits on." Their heads were covered by some sort of helmet, so the faces were not visible.

Each one carried a small, dark-colored bag and a little shovel or spoon-like instrument. He watched them dig in various locations near the waiting machine, putting soil into their bags. O'Barski explained the incident to investigator Ted Bloecher, New York State Director of MUFON, saying, "They came down the steps as though they had one mission in their entire life—to fill these little bags they had with these little spoons, or shovels, they had. The minute they got down, they started working."[6]

Finishing their soil-sample gathering in a few moments, the UFOlks reentered the ship. Its icebox-sounding engine started up again. The craft lifted off the ground and then shot up until it disappeared in the sky. O'Barski judged that the time elapsed from initial lift-off to its disappearance was about 20 seconds. In fact, the whole incident took less than four minutes. Then his car radio began to play normally. O'Barski drove straight home and went immediately to bed, pulling the covers over his head. "I've been held up in the store lots of times in 30 years by men with pistols and knives, and I've been plenty scared," he said, "but nothing like this, ever. I was petrified!"

The next morning O'Barski went back to the park and walked to the spot where the UFO had landed. There in a small area he found 15 little holes, triangular and about five or six inches deep. Ten months later another UFO investigator, Jerry Stoehrer, found the purported holes, still devoid of grass.

In November 1975, journalist Budd Hopkins along with Ted Bloecher and Jerry Stoehrer made an inquiry regarding the O'Barski case. They eventually came upon William Pawlowski, a former doorman at the Stonehenge apartments, which are located about 300 yards east of the alleged sighting. Pawlowski recalled seeing bright lights in the vicinity of the park about 2:30 or 3 a.m. on January 12, 1975.

Another former employee of Stonehenge apartments, Frank Gonzales, said he saw something round and very bright with windows in the park in front of Stonehenge at 2 or 3 a.m. on a Monday night in early January 1975. Bloecher figures that the Gonzales sighting may have taken place on January 6, whereas the O'Barski-Pawlowski sighting occurred on January 12. So it is Bloecher's judgment that the O'Barski claim is partially corroborated by at least one other witness, possibly more.

BETTY AND BARNEY HILL'S INTERRUPTED JOURNEY

One alleged case of a close encounter and personal contact with UFO occupants that received considerable media attention is that of Betty and Barney Hill. Barney worked for the U.S. Postal Service, and Betty, a social worker, made their home in Portsmouth, New Hampshire. The story of their late-night abduction into a spacecraft was first made public by John Fuller in two articles featured in *Look* magazine in 1966, "Aboard a Flying Saucer," and subsequently in a book, *The Interrupted Journey.*[7]

The adventure began on the night of September 19, 1961, when Betty and Barney Hill were returning from a short vacation. They were driving from the Canadian border down US 3 to their home in Portsmouth. The couple noticed a brightly lit object off to the right, flying parallel to their car. After Betty watched it through binoculars, Barney stopped the car a couple of times to get out and take a look. It was clearly a machine-made craft of enormous dimensions with a double row of windows. A red light appeared on the left side of the object followed by a similar one on the right. The machine hovered at treetop level, apparently waiting.

Barney stopped the car, got out, and walked across the field to within 50 feet of the craft. "Barney!" yelled his wife. "Barney, come back! Do you hear me?"

Out in the field Barney was watching the ship that had just tipped toward him. Through the windows he could see the silhouettes of at least a half dozen humanoid figures staring directly at him. All but one turned from the window and began scurrying about. The fins bearing the two red lights spread themselves out further and the machine began to land. An extension began to lower from the underside.

Barney's eyes were fixed on the eyes of the one crewmember still staring at him. He had never seen eyes like that before. Suddenly fearing capture, Barney turned and ran to the car, started the engine, and raced down the road. Although unable to see the flying saucer through the car windows, they heard a strange, electronic beeping sound. They each began to feel an odd tingling sensation and became drowsy.

When their heads cleared they noticed a road sign: Concord 17 miles. That meant there was a distance of 35 miles about which they could remember nothing. Both their wristwatches had stopped, so when they arrived home and looked at the kitchen clock, they realized something else: There were two hours about which they could remember nothing.

During the weeks following, Betty had repeated nightmares that seemed to prolong the fear generated by her UFO experience. She dreamed she encountered a roadblock on a lonely New Hampshire highway. A group of strangers approached the car. She lost consciousness and awoke to find herself and Barney aboard a strange craft. She and Barney were assured that no harm would come to them and that later they would not be able to remember what happened. At this point the nightmares would end.

Later, Barney began to exhibit signs of general distress. In the summer of 1962, physically exhausted and discomforted by an ulcer, he sought medical and then psychiatric help. Eventually, both he and Betty found themselves in the office of Boston psychiatrist Benjamin Simon, who began hypnotherapy on January 4, 1964.

Through hypnosis, Dr. Simon sought to open up the Hills' shared amnesia and tried to recapture the traumatic experience that brought on the emotional disturbances they were feeling. Under independent hypnosis, both Betty and Barney reported similar stories describing their abduction. That night, the car had come to a roadblock and the Hills were forcibly taken aboard the waiting craft.

Barney described the creatures as having grayish, almost metallic-looking skin, and dressed in dark clothing. They had large craniums, which diminished in size progressively toward the chin. The eyes seemed to continue around to the sides of the heads, so it appeared that they could see several degrees beyond the lateral extent of our vision. The nose was flat with only two slits for nostrils. (Betty, in contrast, said they had large noses like Jimmy Durante's.) The mouth had no lips and consisted of a horizontal line, with a short, perpendicular line on each end. Later, after an analysis by Marjorie Fish, it was determined that these creatures were natives of the double star system Zeta Reticuli One and Two.

Betty's testimony about the abduction activities was more detailed than Barney's, though there were a few incongruities between the two reports. She explained that one creature spoke English—"He had sort of a foreign accent"—and he told her to go on up into the flying ship. They spoke with Barney via mental telepathy. She was guided in by two crewmembers.

Betty was escorted down a corridor and put in a room. As she turned she saw Barney being taken past the doorway and into a different room. When she complained, saying that she did not want to leave the side of her husband, she was given a matter-of-fact answer: "No, we only have equipment enough in one room to do one person at a time. And if we took you both in the same room, it would take too long."

The image she describes seems to be of a hospital or laboratory; Betty even referred to one of the Zeta Reticulians as a doctor. The doctor then took a machine that looked like a microscope with a big lens and examined her skin. Aides took an instrument resembling a letter opener and scraped off small particles of skin from her arm. They placed the skin particles on a small piece of cellophane or plastic and put it in the top drawer.

Then, with a lighted instrument, the doctor examined Betty's eyes, ears, nose, and throat. The doctor also cut off pieces of her hair and fingernails (evidently aware that these could be removed without causing pain) and put them in the drawer.

After asking her to remove her dress (no sexual advances were made) they rolled her from back to stomach and back again on a table, testing her reflexes with a needle-like instrument as her body rested in each position. While she was on her back the doctor put a six-inch-long needle into her abdomen via the navel, saying it was just a simple test for pregnancy. When Betty complained of pain, another assistant rubbed a three-fingered hand over her eyes and the pain went away. Following the physical exam, the doctor courteously helped Betty zip her dress.

In the meantime, the examiners in the other room had discovered Barney wore dentures. Being surprised that his teeth were removable, they checked Betty's teeth only to find they were permanent. In reviewing this account, Hynek imagined the scholarly paper this doctor would give at the next science convention on the home planet. The doctor will announce that this expedition to Earth disclosed that African-American males have teeth that can be removed but Caucasian females have teeth that do not come out.[8]

Author Budd Hopkins later added an item not reported by Fuller. "Barney Hill recalled that a sperm sample had been taken from him by his captors (This important detail was omitted from Fuller's book on the Hill case, *The Interrupted Journey*; it was probably considered too sensational to include in what was already an 'unbelievable' account)."[9] This sperm collection would be the kind of thing one might expect from an extraterrestrial scientist performing research on *Homo sapiens*. As we will see in a later chapter, sperm collection might also be part of a hybrid breeding experiment.

In their parting conversations, the space doctor apologized for having frightened the couple, and assured them that they would be unable to remember the details of their experience. After Betty and Barney were returned to their car, the craft began to glow, rose gently, then shot away into the heavens.

UFOs: God's Chariots?

FOLIE À DEUX

The Hill account was elicited through hypnosis. This led to the introduction of a new term in the field of UFO research, *folie à deux* (a folly or delusion shared by two persons). The *folie à deux* disorder was first identified in 19th-century French psychiatry by Charles Lasèque and Jean-Pierre Falret. It is also known as Lasèque-Falret Syndrome.

Hypnosis is a pathway to the truth as it is felt and understood by the patient. The truth is what the patient believes to be the truth. What the patient believes to be the truth may or may not be consistant with the extra-personal, objective truth. Hypnosis cannot discriminate precisely between illusion and objective experience. "Human memory is notoriously undependable," writes Gwen Farrell. "During the recovery process, a memory may be affected by events currently happening in the individual's life or other untapped memories existing in the subconscious mind." After seven months of psychotherapy with Betty and Barney, Dr. Simon concluded, "Nothing is finally settled. Nothing is absolutely proved regarding the alleged abduction."[10] Despite this rather ambiguous conclusion, Dr. Simon's method of hypnotic regression to retrieve forgotten memories became a stock-in-trade for UFO investigators.

Dr. Simon offered four hypotheses that might account for the descriptions given by Betty and Barney Hill: (1) the Hills are psychotic and suffer from joint psychosis, *folie à deux*; (2) this is an intentional hoax; (3) the story is fundamentally true; and (4) the dream hypothesis. Simon considers the most tenable hypothesis to be number 4. Recall that Betty experienced terrifying nightmares in the weeks following the trip in question. She described these dreams to her friends in the presence of her husband. Dr. Simon believes that during the three years before hypnotherapy the information in Betty's dreams was transferred to Barney so that he presented similar information in the hypnotic interviews. Regardless of Simon's own judgment regarding the Hills, the phrase *folie à deux* took on a life of its own.

It is interesting to note with what enthusiasm Dr. Leo Sprinkle is willing to endorse hypothesis number 3. He writes, "Despite the weight of authoritative views which raise doubts about the authenticity of the stories, this investigator tends to accept the view that the events probably occurred."[11]

Harvard's John Mack would agree with Leo Sprinkle. "Despite Dr. Simon's belief that the Hills had experienced some sort of shared dream or fantasy, a kind of folie à deux, they persisted in their conviction that these events really happened, and that they had not communicated the corroborating details to each other during the investigation of their symptoms."[12]

During the alleged abduction, Betty was shown a map of the stars indicating the home of her abductors, Zeta Reticuli Two.[13] She was not told explicitly what she had seen on this map, so when she reproduced the explanation later it was discovered that Zeta Reticuli was the viewpoint.[14] This has greatly impressed astronomers who examined the map.

On his TV show one afternoon in November 1966, Mike Douglas asked noted astronomer, I.M. Levitt, about the story told by the Hills. Tending to discount it, Levitt said the reported physical examination was not exotic or advanced enough to have been carried out by technicians from a more advanced civilization. He contended that in the future, Earth's scientists will be able to place a human on a table, and with the use of electronic instruments and computers, give a physical examination, diagnosing any problems without laying a hand on the patient. Skin scraping and reflex tapping represent crude and potentially outdated methods of medical diagnosis.

Coral and Jim Lorenzen countered Levitt's debunking of the Hill experience. They pointed out that the physical examination to which the Hills were subjected did not appear to be concerned with diagnosis of illness. It was, rather, a scientific analysis of the physical makeup of Earth's inhabitants. The diagnostic machine projected by Dr. Levitt would have to be designed with knowledge of the creature being examined. It is just because they lacked this knowledge that an expedition was sent to research life on our planet.[15]

The ufonauts who abducted Barney and Betty Hill appeared to be extraterrestrial scientists sent to Earth for the purposes of conducting research. Perhaps they would eventually write scientific papers for pub-lication on their home planet orbiting Zeta Two Reticuli.

THE PASCAGOULA FISHERMEN: MORE EXAMINATIONS, BETTER EQUIPMENT

Like Betty Hill, Charles Hickson and Sandy Larson were allegedly given physical examinations by alien scientists from outer space.

Charles Hickson is one of the now-famous Pascagoula, Mississippi, fishermen along with Calvin Parker. Their dramatic abduction took place at the climax of the "Flap of '73."[16] Between January and October 1973, UFOs were sighted in Maryland, South Carolina, Missouri, Oregon, Pennsylvania, Ohio, Illinois, California, and Georgia. Particu-larly in late summer and early fall there was a high concentration of re-ports regarding hovering objects with brightly colored lights in central and southern Georgia, Alabama, Tennessee, and Florida. Then Georgia governor Jimmy Carter, along with 20 other people, saw a UFO in the form of three contiguous balls of flashing red and green light one night in Thomaston, Georgia, following Carter's speech to the local Lions Club. In September, NBC-TV broadcast a rerun of its popular documentary movie, "In Search of Ancient Astronauts," based on Erich von Däniken's *Chariots of the Gods?* The first showing had been in January of that year. In October, a news release from Tass in Moscow reported that Soviet scientists had picked up strange radio signals from space and considered the possibility that they came from another civilization. The atmosphere was charged with UFO excitement.

On the evening of Thursday, October 11, 1973, Hickson and Parker went fishing by the ramshackle grain elevator near Schaupeter shipyard on the Pascagoula River. At age 42, Charles Hickson had been a shipfit-ter for the Ingalls shipyard, but was currently working as foreman on a crew for the F.B. Walkers shipyard. Calvin Parker, age 19, was a longtime friend of the Hickson family: Charlie's oldest son, Ed, nearly the same age, had been Calvin's buddy until Ed went into the Marine Corps in 1972. Two weeks prior to the UFO incident, Calvin Parker had left his father's farm in nearby Tucker's Crossing to live with Hickson and work as a welder at the shipyard.

Right after catching two flathead catfish, they allegedly witnessed a brightly lit, oval or round flying vehicle that made a buzzing noise, and which hovered two or three feet above the grass. Three 5-foot-tall beings—later referred to by Hickson as "robots"—floated out of the hovering machine and over to the aghast fishermen. Their light gray, elephant-like skin (or covering) was wrinkled. They had pointed ears and only a slit for a mouth. Instead of hands they had pincers or claws at the ends of their arms.

The three creatures clasped the shuddering shipworkers in their claws (at which point Parker fainted), and floated them aboard. Hickson reports that the light was very bright in the craft—so bright that his eyes may have been damaged. Inside he was given a physical examination or inspection.[17] Perhaps the Reticulian physiologists were continuing their research on the anatomy of earthlings begun during their study of Betty and Barney Hill.

During a conversation between Charles Hickson and myself in my office at Loyola University in New Orleans in 1976, the following exchange took place:

Peters: *Just what happened to you inside the craft?*

Hickson: *Well, they held me suspended in the air. I never touched the floor. Then something like an eye came right out of the wall toward me and stopped at my face.*

Peters: *Do you mean a living eye?*

Hickson: *No. It must have been something mechanical. Maybe it was like an X-ray machine. I'm not sure.*

Peters: *How large was it?*

Hickson: *It was about this big. (Hickson held out his hands indicating it was about the size of a football.) It was larger in the front* *and tapered back, sort of like a bicycle headlight. And the front was made of something different from the edges and back. It was not attached to anything I could see. It was just hanging there.*

Peters: *Do you mean it had no connecting wires or cables?*

Hickson: *No, none that I could see.*

Peters: *What happened next?*

Hickson: *Well, it came right up to me and stopped. It slowly went down the front of my body as if it were taking pictures or something. I believe, but I'm not sure, it went under me and up my back and over the top of my head. Anyway, soon I saw it come down and stop again in front of my face. Then it went back toward the wall and disappeared.*

Peters: *What do you think they were doing to you?*

Hickson: *It was some sort of examination.*

Note that the diagnostic eye or X-ray machine never actually touched Hickson's body. It appears that in the 12 years since the abduction of Betty Hill the equipment of the Reticulian examiners has been modernized. This no doubt should please Dr. Levitt.

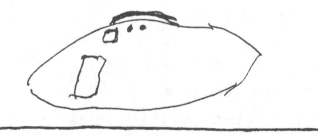

Freehand sketch of the craft that allegedly abducted Charles Hickson and Calvin Parker, October 11, 1973, as drawn by Mr. Hickson for Ted Peters, October 19, 1976.

Model II: The Research Scientist

After an estimated 20 or 30 minutes Hickson and Parker were freed. They set off to telephone the U.S. Air Force at Keesler Field in Biloxi, at which time they were told the Air Force is no longer interested in UFOs. They allegedly tried to tell the local newspaper, the Mississippi *Press-Register*, but it was closed. Eventually, at about 10:30 p.m. they got ahold of Sheriff Fred Diamond, who listened to their story. Within 48 hours the media had alerted the world. Hickson made TV appearances on the shows of Dick Cavett and Mike Douglas. Their attorney and publicity agent, Joe Colingo, reportedly hoped to earn a million dollars from book and movie rights, but apparently the proceeds have been surprisingly modest. On this last point, Hickson told me he discharged Colingo because "Colingo just wanted to make a buck."

Dr. James Harder, a professor of engineering at Berkeley and an amateur hypnotist and investigator for APRO, arrived two days after the incident to interview the fishermen. He questioned them under hypnosis and concluded, "There was definitely something here that was not terrestrial." Hynek arrived the same day and conducted the interviews in conjunction with Dr. Harder. Hynek's conclusion was positive but more reserved: "There is no question in my mind that these men have had a very terrifying experience."

Self-appointed UFO debunker Philip Klass implies that the whole incident could be a hoax. He bases his argument primarily on the procedures surrounding the administering of the lie-detector test. Hickson did not take the test until October 30, and then only at the behest of Joe Colingo, who was being pressured to verify the story before Hickson was to appear on the Dick Cavett Show. Colingo arranged for the test to be given in his own office by an uncertified polygraphist whom he had imported from New Orleans. Parker was absent at the time of the polygraph due to a "nervous breakdown." This aroused Klass's suspicions that something less than the truth was verified.[18]

On one occasion I traveled to the site of the abduction in Pascagoula with a newsteam from WWL-TV New Orleans. Hickson met us there.

He stressed that he was convinced there is life "on other worlds up there." He indicated that he has been contacted subsequently by extraterrestrial beings and that he hopes someday he and his family may leave this Earth with their help; the Hicksons plan to go with their space escorts to a new and better world beyond the sky. When I pressed him to tell me just how they had gotten in touch with him, he said it was through mental telepathy.

Telepathically, these space beings have communicated with Hickson about the future of the world, which is awesome in scope. They have assured him personally, however, that they have only good intentions and that he need not be afraid any longer. They have also planted something in him—something undetectable via medical examination—which permits them to monitor his every activity. These elements are characteristic of the Celestial Savior model for interpreting extraterrestrials that we will describe in greater detail later in the book.

With regard to the lie-detector controversy already mentioned, Hickson told me off camera that Klass wrote "damned lies" in his reporting of the encounter. Just to clear the record, Hickson told us he was undergoing hypnotherapy and taking both polygraph and voice-stress lie-detector tests from professionals of unchallengeable credentials. When we returned to New Orleans, newscaster Bill Elder took the videotape of his interview with Hickson to a detective agency for a lie-detection examination on a Truth Analysis Psychological Stress Evaluator. Hickson passed with a 94 percent score. He passed every question relating to the facts regarding the case. The only area of doubt had to do with his speculations regarding the future departure of his family from Earth courtesy of the UFO travel service.

One humorous footnote: After hearing about his son's UFO abduction on the news, the father of Calvin Parker rushed to Pascagoula to find his son. Arriving at the hospital where the two men were being examined, he exclaimed: "I tol' that boy never to ride in cars with strangers. Now he goes 'n' gets himself picked up in a flying saucer!"

Model II: The Research Scientist

SANDY LARSON'S KIDNAPPER SCIENTIST

A closer approximation of the Betty Hill episode occurred almost two years following Pascagoula. A cocktail waitress named Sandy Larson of Fargo, North Dakota, was driving with her daughter and daughter's boyfriend from her home to Bismarck to take a real estate sales examination. They had set out early in the morning of August 26, 1975, around 3:30 a.m. As they were traveling on Interstate 94 about 39 miles west of Fargo they heard "a big noise." Then eight or 10 round, orange, glowing objects came down out of the sky. They recall pulling up next to a camper truck. The driver of the vehicle also acknowledged he had seen them too.

One mile down the road the frightened threesome arrived at Tower City and entered a restaurant to call the police and report what had happened. When Mrs. Larson looked at the clock on the restaurant wall, she was astonished to see that it read 5:23. Where had the time gone? They had driven 40 miles at 70 miles per hour and it took them more than an hour and a half. An hour of their lives was missing.

By 8 a.m. they arrived in Bismarck, and Mrs. Larson experienced an unusually heavy menstrual flow, though it was not the normal time for it to occur. Several weeks after the trip she began experiencing terrifying nightmares. Eventually, she sought to retrieve the missing hour through hypnotic regression with the help of University of Wyoming psychologist Dr. Leo Sprinkle and two UFO investigators, Jerome Clark and J. Allen Hynek.

Under hypnosis she described being abducted by a UFO occupant whose head was wrapped completely in elastic-like bandages and whose body resembled brown vinyl. She described the creature as "mummy-like." The mummy's eyes glared at her, and, she told Jerome Clark, "It seemed like their eyes can control my brain." (Later, she revealed there were two creatures.)

She said she was taken aboard the craft, stripped naked, and given "a complete medical exam." Some sort of knife or needle-like instrument was pushed up her nose, and several times during the examination her nose was swabbed with something. She claims that prior to this examination she had suffered from a chronic sinus condition. After the experience, it completely disappeared. The space examination may have caused an extra menstrual period but it also cured her sinus condition. An even trade?

Earlier, because of her sinus condition, Mrs. Larson had visited a terrestrial doctor for help. The doctor performed a painful operation in which he cleaned out her sinus passages with a sharp, knife-like instrument. The doctor told her she would require an additional operation, and she was very frightened at the prospect of enduring the pain a second time. Because the UFO doctor cured her sinuses, she did not have to return to her terrestrial doctor for the second operation.

Mrs. Larson also said her sexual organs were inspected aboard the UFO. In addition a bright light was placed on her face and around her head. She said that during the examination, the examiner frequently pushed some buttons on a panel board. Perhaps these were buttons to a computer because according to Dr. Levitt, a computer would be a much better place to store diagnostic information, similar to the top drawer that was used in the Betty Hill case.

United Press International (UPI) quoted Mrs. Larson as saying, "Even our heads were opened and all parts of our brains looked at...we were dissected like frogs." However, Dr. Sprinkle phrases it somewhat differently: "She said it was as if she were a frog being dissected. Now this is the kind of statement we have gotten from other people who claim to have been abducted. It's a sort of feeling of indifference. They don't seem to mean any harm. They're like scientists coldly doing their work."[19]

Mrs. Larson's 15-year-old daughter, Jackie, also underwent hypnosis, but she did not report being taken aboard the UFO. She seems to have lost track of the experience. Her daughter's boyfriend, reported by Mrs. Larson to have been taken aboard the UFO with her, refused to participate in the investigation for personal reasons.

The August 26th episode was not the last Mrs. Larson would see of her alien abductors. On the evening of December 2, 1975, she saw a strange shooting star in the sky. That night, she went to bed around 2:30 a.m., but was suddenly awakened sometime between 3 a.m. and 4 a.m. There in her bedroom stood the two mummy-like ufonauts she had met the summer before.

They placed her between them, and she said she felt "magnetized" by them. Then all three floated through the wall. She said this happened in her physical body. It was not an out-of-body experience.

She was taken to a bright orange UFO, just like the ones she had seen in August. Aboard the UFO she felt dizzy and nauseated. Although she closed her eyes out of fear, she said she felt she was in the presence of a great light.

The aliens landed and took her into a square, windowless building that was located in the middle of a desert-like landscape. In the building she was met by another ufonaut with a bright light surrounding its head. The alien began to communicate with Mrs. Larson via mental telepathy, asking her how human minds worked. The alien researcher seemed to be working with the notion that all humans on Earth are bound together in a sort of high mind, and that individual personalities are only secondary.

The being would not state the purpose for coming to our planet, but promised that it would be revealed in the future. The researcher was neither friendly nor unfriendly, but gave off an aura of authority. Mrs. Larson told journalist Jerome Clark she thought of the alien as a "scientist."

The scientist warned Mrs. Larson not to tell anyone of her experience because no one would believe her. Then the two mummies returned and escorted her back home and tucked her into bed. She awoke again at 6:30 a.m.

On April 18, 1976, she was again taken from sleep, floated into a hovering UFO, and placed on the examination table with wires attached to her head. She was later returned to her bedroom.[20]

In discussing the Sandy Larson case, *Detroit News* staff writer Lowell Cauffiel explores the possibility of a connection with the October 1975 showing of the NBC-TV program *The UFO Incident*.[21] This program was a dramatized portrayal of the noted Betty and Barney Hill abduction in 1961. Cauffiel suggests that other abductions might have been influenced by the program. He mentions in particular the Travis Walton case of November 5, 1975. Walton, a tree-cutter for the forest service in Arizona, was allegedly abducted by a UFO and held captive for five days. During this time he was also given a scientific physical examination. While he was missing, other cutting crew members confirmed via polygraph that they had engaged in no foul play and that a UFO had been sighted.

The Walton incident occurred shortly after the TV broadcast about the Hill case. Sandy Larson's did not. Does this eliminate speculation about a possible connection? It may be helpful to note that the *National Enquirer* published a two-page article on the forthcoming TV special, complete with photos of the actors and a synopsis of the plot, in their August 19, 1975 issue. Mrs. Larson claims her abduction took place on August 26.

Hynek, in his hallmark style, said: "She (Mrs. Larson) seemed to live through a frightening experience (that is, through the catharsis in hypnosis). I believe she thinks she was taken aboard a UFO. I don't think she is lying, in other words."[22]

Whether these reports are lies, hoaxes, dreams, or objective accounts, the interpretive structure is what interests us here. What the witnesses report they are seeing are extraterrestrial scientists on a field trip to Planet Earth, which coincides with Model II: the Research Scientist and forms our interpretation of otherwise strange events.

TERRESTRIAL SCIENCE STUDYING EXTRATERRESTRIAL SCIENCE

We find the research scientist on both ends of the telescope. What we see in UFOs are research scientists coming to Earth to gather data. At the same time, we ask our own scientists to gather data about UFOs. "From a science point of view, I can't ignore the data (on UFOs). The phenomenon is just so beautiful, so powerful, so curious that it demands some scientific involvement," says NASA's Richard Haines. "Science can get interested in the phenomenon if it has some good, firm data to work with."[23] Our terrestrial interpretation of unexplained flying objects is aided by comparing what is unidentified with what we are familiar with, and we are familiar with what scientist look like. The aliens look like our scientists. It follows that we should ask our scientists to study the alien scientists.

However, there is more to science than merely gathering and assessing data: Science improves our lives. How will this science benefit humanity? Executive Director of MUFON Jan Harzan answers this question by asking: "Will man become more accepting of his fellow human beings once he realizes that he is not alone in the universe? Will human understanding ultimately reach a level where wars cease and mankind begins to look at all humanity as his brother, to be taken care of and served rather than destroyed? One can only hope, and it is with this hope that MUFON proudly bears the mission statement: 'The Scientific Study of UFOs for the Benefit of Humanity.'"[24]

THE EXTRATERRESTRIAL BREEDING EXPERIMENT

What has been subtle in the previously mentioned cases becomes more obvious in the work of UFO investigator Budd Hopkins. Hopkins' theory states that the ufonauts are in fact extraterrestrial scientists who are engaged in an ongoing breeding experiment with earthlings. Hopkins has collated data from dozens of reports, especially abduction cases such as those described previously. He notes a common pattern that includes three often repeated elements: (1) people who have had abduction experiences remember almost nothing about them until their memory is revived through hypnosis; (2) many abductees have had more than one experience, the first one generally occurring in childhood around the age of six or seven; and (3) some even report visible, physical scars indicating that an incision had been made. This suggests the analogy of alien medical researchers, perhaps taking cell samples. Or even more dramatically, it suggests alien zoologists studying an endangered species of animals: us. If Hopkins' theory holds, then UFO abductees are human subjects who have been "tagged."[25]

His paradigm case is that of Kathie Davis, a mother of two living in Copley Woods, Indiana, who wrote to Hopkins after reading his 1981 book, *Missing Time.* She reported an extraordinary UFO experience, which Hopkins investigated through the use of hypnotic regression. This yielded not one but numerous UFO contacts, which indicated that Kathie had been continually monitored by alien scientists.

Born in Indianapolis in 1959, Kathie and her older sister Laura were first contacted by spacelings during the winter of 1966. Living in Detroit at the time, they were playing outside in the snow when a loud noise and flash of light led her into a friend's house. The friend, a little boy, morphed into a small, large-headed, gray-skinned entity. Today, Laura remembers nothing of the incident. What Kathie remembers comes from hypnosis. In July 1975, 16-year-old Kathie sighted four spiraling lights while visiting Rough River State Park in Kentucky. She also talked with a normal-looking man, who closely resembled her, and two companions.

In early 1977 Kathie became pregnant out of wedlock but experienced a miscarriage. In December 1977 and again in March 1978, Kathie was abducted, taken aboard a UFO, and was subjected to a gynecological operation. Hopkins believes she was artificially inseminated in December, and the alien breeders removed the fetus in March.

Kathie married in 1978. In 1979, while pregnant with her first son, Robbie, she was abducted again. While lying on the UFO operating table, thin probes of some sort were pressed into her nostrils. Robbie was born in July of that year. Her second son, Tommy, was born in September 1980. Kathie divorced in 1981 and moved with her two children back into her parents' home.

On June 30, 1983, a UFO landed near her parents' home, and Kathie was abducted once again. This time a probe was inserted into her ear, and she subsequently started to suffer the effects of what appears to be radiation poisoning. At this point she wrote to Budd Hopkins and the investigation began.

On October 3, 1983, Kathie encountered a gray-skinned figure while shopping at a local store. Later that night she was abducted from her bedroom and taken to a UFO. After a physical examination she was shown a small child, whom she believed was her own daughter. The child, 5 years old but small for her age, had patchy hair, very large eyes, and an unusually shaped cranium. Hopkins concluded that what Kathie saw was a hybrid, the child of a marriage of heaven and Earth.

To substantiate his breeding theory, Hopkins cited numerous other cases, although not all abductees were women; sometimes men were taken, and so were samples of their sperm. Included in his list are four men who were abducted and raped. He even adds a component to the Betty and Barney Hill case. Hopkins says that a sperm sample was taken from Barney by his captors, a fact not reported in Fuller's account in *The Interrupted Journey?*[26] All these cases, says Hopkins, follow a pattern: (1) initial contact of a child by aliens in which a small incision is made in the child's body; (2) abductions during puberty or young adulthood, sometimes taking sperm samples from the male abductees; (3) artificial insemination of mature women followed by removal of the fetus on a separate occasion; (4) possible genetic tampering; (5) resulting in a psychological impact on the human subject consisting primarily of fear and anxiety.[27] Hopkins stops short of speculating on the ultimate purpose of this apparent medical plan to create a race of alien-human hybrids.

The Hopkins theory is a clear instance of the model of the Research Scientist; according to Hopkins, abductions do not fit the Celestial Savior model. Yet, what Hopkins reports spills beyond Model II alone. This has led me to propose Model IV: the Hybridizer. Let's look at Hopkins' argument a bit more closely.

First, Hopkins treats the aliens as strictly objective. Scientists must be objective; this means they cannot allow their personal feelings to distort or prejudice their work. So the alien medical technicians go about their work devoid of human feeling. In order to drive this point home, Hopkins spends pages speculating on the meaning of Kathie Davis's April 1986 abduction, when the aliens sought instruction on the care of an infant. The ufonauts needed to learn how human touch and human emotion played a role in the healthy development of the child. Despite the technological superiority of the UFO scientists, they apparently know nothing about human compassion. Therefore, Hopkins can add, "one simply cannot reconcile the idea of kindly, helpful, all-powerful Space Brothers" with these gray-skinned scientific types.

Second, he employs such a narrow understanding of religion that very little can fit into it. Something is religious, he says, when it literally distinguishes between good and evil. Then he ascribes the religious dimension of the UFO phenomenon to sci-fi movies in a list that includes *War of the Worlds, The Body Snatchers, The Day the Earth Stood Still,* and *Close Encounters of the Third Kind.* What makes all these movies religious, says Hopkins, is that they assume a black-white division between good and evil, between gods and devils. Such movies assume that we can distinguish sharply between right and wrong. The authentic aliens who abduct and breed earthlings, in contrast, do not have a message that we can fit into this pattern. Rather, says Hopkins, the alien visitors are simply ethical, that is, they mean us no harm.

The Hopkins argument is hopelessly naive. First, he fails to distinguish between sci-fi and the UFO phenomenon in the movie theater. These two ought not be confused with one another. The distinguishing key is this: the sci-fi movies, especially in the 1950s, used an embellished model of international war to create a suspense-filled drama showing earthlings battling an invasion from the outside. Hopkins is correct in discerning the battle theme in *War of the Worlds* or *Body Snatchers*—today we might add movies such as *Independence Day* or *District 9* and television series such as *Falling Skies*—although it is primarily a battle between aliens and us, not between gods and devils. In the movie *Avatar* the invading enemy is us, not them, yet the warfare theme prevails.

What Hopkins misses is this: the sci-fi genre fails to comprehend what is at stake in the UFO experience. Only two movies, *The Day the Earth Stood Still* (1951) and *Close Encounters of the Third Kind* (1977) genuinely reflect the UFO phenomenon. In these two films there is no fundamental conflict between Earth and the star people. In addition, these movies are religious in an oblique way. They are religious because they portray the star people as rooted in a cosmic apprehension of ultimate reality, and because the heavenly visitors come to Earth to teach us a saving truth. We will elaborate on this covert religious dimension in later chapters. For Hopkins to assume that he can define religion on the basis of making a black-white distinction between good and evil is simplistic, even wrong. To let Hollywood determine one's theology is also suspect. Hopkins is most misleading because he confuses the interstellar battle theme with its opposite, the peace-on-Earth theme.

What is going on here, I think, is that Hopkins is working quite self-consciously with the interpretive model of the Research Scientist, and in doing so he is trying to distance himself from the Celestial Savior model. The abductees "are neither devoured nor saved," he says.[28] The ufonauts' gray skin and officious manner of going about their business connotes a transcendence of human emotion, just what is needed for serious scientists to go about their laboratory breeding experiment.[29]

CONCLUSION

It is easy to imagine that aliens in outer space have the same basic scientific impulses for research that we have. It is easy to imagine that we are their guinea pigs. No doubt the extrasolar counterpart to our National Science Foundation is offering research grants to scientists at a university on a planet orbiting Zeta Reticuli Two. One grant may have gone to their department of exogeology to study the rocks of Earth. Another grant may have gone to some exophysiologists to study our anatomies, and a third to some bright exopsychiatrist to study our minds. Unfortunately, the empirical study of Sandy Larson was biased because the alien psychiatrist had already read about the "oversoul" in the writings of the American transcendentalists and ancient Hindus. Because so much of our life is understood in terms of ever ongoing scientific research, it is easy to ascribe similar purposes to alien visitors.

I am not saying yay or nay to the extraterrestrial hypothesis. What I wish to point out is that regardless of the objective nature of the stimulus given to us by UFOs, there is at work a strong tendency to perceive and interpret them in terms of the belief systems of our culture. Our culture is shot through and through with a scientific mentality and a kind of reverence for research. This element in our belief system cannot help but dispose us to interpret our experience with UFOs in a science-oriented direction. What UFOs are in their own "objective" reality may be a good deal more—or a good deal less—than what we interpret them to be.

5

Will the True Scientist Please Stand Up?

There are two questions that orient most discussions of UFOs: (1) do UFOs present an anomalous phenomenon of sufficient importance to warrant serious scientific study? (2) is the extraterrestrial hypothesis (ETH) true, that is, are UFOs interplanetary vehicles sent to earth by extraterrestrial intelligences?

There are three sides involved in the UFO controversy, and they can be defined by their answers to these two questions. The organized UFO study groups such as MUFON or those attending the annual International UFO Congress in Arizona, along with only a few professional academics, will most likely answer yes to both questions. Both the Condon Report and the established scientific community that dominates our universities will answer no to both questions. A minority of reputable professional scientists, such as the late J. Allen Hynek and Jacques Vallée, who are perceptive enough to recognize the distinction between the two issues, may answer yes to the first while either answering no to the second or withholding judgment on it until conclusive evidence is available. This last position is the one assumed here.

However, as most people see it, the controversy has only two sides. The argument is between the first two positions mentioned above: either pro UFO-ETH or con UFO-ETH, the so-called *believers* and *unbelievers*. Astronomers such as Sagan, Hynek, and others seem to be in agreement that statistically it is plausible to argue that there is intelligent life somewhere else in the universe. Since the mid-1990s astronomers have been locating and identifying exoplanets orbiting stars within the Milky Way. The best candidates for hosting life are those in the habitable zone (HZ). The HZ is sometimes called the "Goldilocks Zone": not too hot and not too cold, but just right for liquid water. If the Milky Way contains between 100 billion and 400 billion stars, and if each star is accompanied by one planet in the HZ, well…do the math.

Although astronomers are happy with the ETH *per se,* they argue that it has no relationship to UFOs. Sagan contended that, given the very vast number of possible destinations in the universe, it's statistically unlikely that a spaceship would come to us. Franklin Roach writes, "I think it likely that there are many extraterrestrial civilizations in our galaxy, but I think the evidence of UFO sightings does *not* support the hypothesis of visitations by these extraterrestrials."[1]

On the other side, MUFON and former ufology groups such as APRO and NICAP accept the statistical arguments in favor of intelligent life elsewhere, but then go on to argue that many UFOs seen in Earth's skies are driven by such beings. Terrestrial engineers could not manufacture machines that do what UFOs do.

The debate between proponents and opponents of UFO-ETH is widespread and often bitter. The argument spawned an excellent historical study by David Michael Jacobs, *The UFO Controversy in America.*[2] We are ready for another updated study of this sort.

What is interesting to note is that each position in the debate accuses the others of being unscientific. Establishment science, which rejects ETH in reference to UFOs, accuses the pro UFO-ETH side of being amateurish and incapable of performing objective, thorough, and rational research. Those supporting UFO-ETH complain that the orthodox scientists have such an initial bias against UFOs that they do not take UFO investigation with sufficient seriousness to yield objective conclusions. What

Will the True Scientist Please Stand Up?

I find interesting is the unquestioned allegiance to the ideal of good science held by both sides. There is no real struggle here between scientific and nonscientific thought, despite the personal attacks or mudslinging that occasionally blacken the debate. It is a struggle between good science and inferior science. Both sides seek to be better scientists than their opponents. Both sides appeal to the same basic system of beliefs and values. Both sides claim to be seeking an empirical and rational truth.

Why is there this devotion to science? In the history of civilization there have been other paths to truth suggested: mystical meditation, magic, ecstatic prophecy, casting lots, examining the entrails of slain chickens, reading holy writ, and so on. Why are these paths excluded and only that of empirical science accepted?

The answer lies in the fact that the worldview or belief system of natural science envelops us at every turn. Our intellectual tradition, our universities and public schools, even our common-sense reasoning, all have the stamp of scientific method. The famous biologist Jacob Bronowski emphasizes this point: "Dream or nightmare, we have to live our experience as it is, and we have to live it awake. We live in a world which is penetrated through and through by science, and which is both whole and real."[3]

It appears to me that the contours of the UFO debate present another expression of the mind-set or system of beliefs that makes Western culture what it is. The worldview of the modern West simply presumes that the concept of nature is all-inclusive and that everything we experience can be explained according to the rational principles of natural science. There is no room left anymore for miracles, supernatural forces, demons, spirits, or even personal meaning. Anything mysterious we happen to encounter is simply "not yet explained." We are confident it will be explained as soon as sufficient research is performed. And the explanation will simply add more data to a system of naturalistic thinking, the axiomatic principles of which are fixed and unchanging.

The use of the term *natural phenomenon* in the UFO controversy clouds recognition of this underlying agreement. When authorities such as Menzel or the Condon Committee refer to a UFO sighting as a misinterpreted "natural phenomenon," they mean an earthly or otherwise familiar phenomenon. They are referring to misidentified airplanes, clouds, balloons, birds, meteors (which are technically extra-earthly before they land on Earth), kites, planets, stars, atmospheric reflections, visual after-images, hallucinations, or hoaxes. The saucer sighter is said to have Mis-Identified a Flying Thing (MIFT). In using the term *natural* phenomenon to refer to all such things, what is implied by its opposite? A supernatural phenomenon? An unnatural phenomenon?

When an advocate concludes that a particular UFO cannot be classified as a natural phenomenon, he or she does not necessarily mean it is supernatural. It is still natural! What is intended is that the UFO is at least anomalous with reference to our familiar experience and may even be extra-earthly. It may better be classified as having its origin in outer space along with meteors, comets, stars, and other planets. UFO believers assume that the heavenly bodies are natural phenomena.

Extraterrestrial Intelligences are also natural phenomena in the broadest sense, then, because they are part of this great, big, wide natural universe. ETI do not disobey the laws of nature. It is just that because they are more technologically advanced than we are, they employ those natural laws in more sophisticated ways. Nature is the same on Earth, Mars, the supposed planets of Tau Ceti, Zeta Reticuli, Alpha Centauri, or anywhere in the heavens.

Both sides of the controversy operate with this basic assumption. Both share an image of what makes good science good, and both seek to embody that image in their own work. Professionals and amateurs alike understand themselves as natural scientists. Perhaps this is the reverse side of understanding the ufonauts as scientists engaged in similar pursuits.

Look Who Is Calling the Kettle Black

On January 9, 1969, after two years of intensive study and an expenditure of half a million dollars of taxpayers' money, Dr. Edward U. Condon of the University of Colorado released his *Final Report of the Scientific*

Study of Unidentified Flying Objects. A panel representing the prestigious National Academy of Sciences released an accompanying report, saying, "We are unanimous in the opinion that this has been a very creditable effort to apply objectively the relevant techniques of science to the solution of the UFO problem.... On the basis of present knowledge the least likely explanation of UFOs is the hypothesis of extraterrestrial visitations by intelligent beings."[4] Establishment science had spoken!

The question that guided the Condon inquiry was not that of the ETH but rather that of the scientific value of UFO study. The question and answer appear on page one of the report.

The emphasis of this study had been on attempting to learn from UFO reports anything that could be considered as adding to scientific knowledge. Condon's general conclusion was that "nothing has come from the study of UFOs in the past 21 years that has added to scientific knowledge. Careful consideration of the record as it is available to us leads us to conclude that further extensive study of UFOs probably cannot be justified in the expectation that science will be advanced thereby."[5]

Hynek criticized the Condon Report for, among other things, confusing the question of the scientific value of UFO study with the question of the ETH. Note in the earlier quotation that the National Academy of Sciences confuses them as well. In Hynek's opinion, study of the UFO phenomenon might very well yield valuable scientific information regardless of theories about the ETH. Hynek said that "Condon's recommendation to cease granting further scientific attention to UFOs does not serve the best interests of science."[6]

To argue that the Condon Report sought to shut off all further scientific investigation into UFOs may not be precise. It recommended specifically that there be no ongoing program involving public expenditure in this enterprise. This meant that some of the research proposals lobbied for in congress by NICAP and others should be voted down. It meant that the Department of Defense should study UFOs only to the extent that UFOs are a defense matter. It meant that Project Blue Book should be discontinued. Condon did say there may be some fruitful areas of study relating to UFOs in the fields of psychology or sociology. He also qualified his original recommendation by saying, "We believe that any scientist with adequate training and credentials who does come up with a clearly defined, specific proposal for study should be supported.... Therefore, we think that all of the agencies of the federal government, and the private foundations as well, ought to be willing to consider UFO research proposals along with the others submitted to them on an open-minded, unprejudiced basis."[7]

Even in Condon's positive recommendation for research support, however, note that only the scientist who has "adequate training and credentials" deserves support. This betrays one of Condon's criteria for distinguishing truth: He believes credentials are needed, and credentialed scientists disregard UFOs whereas only amateurs are likely to take them seriously. The ranking of the in-group over the out-group on the basis of professional credentials is a frequent tactic taken by the established scientists. Believing true science to be their own private possession, they invoke a chauvinistic class bias in favor of their own special intellectual elite.

Condon referred to organizations such as NICAP, founded in 1956, and APRO, founded in 1952, as "amateur organizations."[8] Then he said, "From 1947 to 1966 no attention was paid to the UFO problem by well qualified scientists."[9] In the introduction to the report, the work of these groups is dismissed by Walter Sullivan simply because "their memberships consisted largely of people sympathetic to the view that UFOs may be controlled by an alien civilization."[10] In other words, sympathy with the ETH disqualifies one for scientific research.

In Boston on December 26 and 27, 1969, the American Association for the Advancement of Science held a symposium on unidentified flying objects. The planning was done under the able leadership of Thornton Page, an astronomer at Wesleyan University and research associate at the NASA Spacecraft Center in Houston, along with Carl Sagan, then professor of astronomy and director of the Laboratory for Planetary Studies at Cornell University. In an attempt to block the planning of the symposium, Dr. Condon circulated letters from himself and two others presenting objections. He wrote, "The UFO buffs are a slippery lot, and do a great deal by 'insinuendo,' so that it is usually useless to try to find out what they are really contending." He went on to attack the integrity of ufologists by saying that if AAAS gave a platform to the "UFO charlatans," it would aid them in their "deceptive and fraudulent operations."[11] Condon failed to hold up a barrier and the symposium was held as planned. No "amateur" UFO buffs were invited, however.

One of the participants in that symposium was Dr. Donald H. Menzel. Menzel, Paine Professor of Astronomy and Astrophysics at one of the most prestigious of established academic institutions, Harvard University, seemed to thrive on calling his opponents amateurs. A veteran UFO debunker for 25 years, Menzel said NICAP and APRO were cults, and, "usually lacking proper scientific background for the studies, they made many mistakes and confused the issues." And supporting Condon he writes, "Do not take these amateur groups lightly. They can do considerable harm to science with their vociferous demands for costly government studies. I hope the silent majority will speak up against this situation. I think the Condon Report will hold the barrier."[12]

Another so-called scientific reason for rejecting the ETH is that those who espouse it evidently believe it too enthusiastically. Condon, Menzel, and others refer to them as UFO "enthusiasts" or "true believers," which seems to be sufficient grounds for dismissing the content of what they believe. Many newspapers praising the Condon Report accompanied their remarks with the observation that "true believers," regardless of the quality of evidence presented, would not change their view. True believers were occasionally lumped together with members of the British Flat Earth Society who, despite photographs and astronauts' eyewitness accounts, "refuse to believe the earth is round."[13]

In the Condon Report, Sullivan wrote that "a great many people want to believe the extraterrestrial hypothesis.... The feeling has been attributed to a hope that some sort of superior beings are watching over our world prepared to intervene if things get too bad."[14] The *New York Times* received a letter from Dr. Donald E. Ehlers, president of the Boothe Memorial Astronomical Society, praising the Condon Report by saying the Committee showed courage because it "discounted a growing religion."

William K. Hartmann, a professor at the University of Arizona and a coauthor of the Condon Report, dismisses the credibility of true believers as religious fantasy. He argues that true believers are unscientific because they will not accept relevant evidence when it contradicts their beliefs. "It doesn't matter whether the fantasy is true or not; in the dogmas of astrology and witchcraft, the lack of empirical evidence seems to have little effect.... The evangelical spirit whispers, 'Believe it because you want something to defend.'"[15]

Now what seems to be advocated here is the following position: If UFOs can be identified with religion, then they certainly require opposition from science. Science and religion never mix! Or do they? Later, I will argue that they have mixed in perhaps an unnoticed way. For the moment, it seems acceptable to all concerned—even to NICAP and APRO on occasion—that if we can point to our opponents and find an element of religion in what they believe, then, ipso facto, we can dismiss that position as unscientific.

Who's calling the kettle black? This superconfidence in an elite group of scientists who supposedly know the truth borders on the fanatic. If a credentialed scientist begins to have sympathy with the ETH explanation for UFOs, the biggest single hurdle will be the risk of ostracism by professional colleagues. Secular orthodoxy is exclusive.

Hynek was one sympathizer with the proposition that UFOs are scientifically important, and he suffered no small amount of ridicule from his colleagues. Of course, he had built a 20-year reputation as a UFO debunker before it became widely known that his views had changed. Prior to retiring, Hynek was the chairman of the Department of Astronomy and director of the Lindheimer Astronomical Research Center at Northwestern University. Even so, Menzel blistered Hynek for doing inferior science by allowing too much subjectivity to enter into his work.[16]

Another scientist who was unable to escape the destructive forces of professional ridicule was James E. McDonald. McDonald was the senior atmospheric physicist at the University of Arizona's Department of Atmospheric Sciences and author of *Unidentified Flying Objects: Greatest Scientific Problem of Our Times* (an address to the American Society of Newspaper Editors). A UFO skeptic earlier in his career, McDonald "converted" after doing research on Air Force files during the 1960s. It became his judgment that "the extraterrestrial hypothesis [is] the only presently plausible explanation for the now-available facts."[17]

Menzel criticized McDonald because he was "highly subjective" in gathering facts to support the ETH. "This is not science," Menzel said.[18] Condon went beyond this level of criticism and called McDonald a "kook." Paleontologist George Gaylord Simpson referred to McDonald's support of ETH as a "monument to gullibility."

But the worst episode of ridicule occurred in the halls of state before the House Committee on Appropriations. McDonald was called to testify representing the National Academy of Sciences during the debate over the supersonic transport (SST) plane in 1971. Having studied the problem thoroughly, McDonald said the SST would reduce the protective ozone layer of the atmosphere. He expressed concern that this might cause an additional 10,000 cases of skin cancer per year in the United States.

Congressman Silvio Conte of Massachusetts interjected that McDonald was an expert on UFOs and that he believed the 1965 power failures in New York were caused by flying saucers. McDonald corrected Representative Conte, saying that this was not his conclusion. Rather, he simply said that there was sufficient correlation between UFO sightings in the areas of power failures to warrant further investigation. During this exchange some members of congress openly laughed at McDonald. The evidence regarding the effect of the SST on the ozone layer was set aside while Conte launched an attack on the witness's credibility.

Conte insisted on linking the skin cancer hypothesis with UFOs. McDonald, of course, protested that no relationship between the two existed. Despite the fact that others present defended McDonald's credentials by calling him a "very distinguished atmospheric physicist," Conte said that "A man who comes here and tells me that the SST flying in the stratosphere is going to cause thousands of skin cancers has to back up his theory that there are little men flying around the sky. I think this is very important."

In June of that year, at the age of 51, McDonald committed suicide. The extent of the impact of this ridicule on McDonald is unknown, but it is difficult to believe it was not a factor.[19]

UFO-ETH

Despite the elitist bias on the part of establishment science that permits it to ridicule its opponents as "amateurs" or religious "kooks," the UFO-ETH advocates do not respond in kind. They avoid *ad hominem* retaliation, at least for the most part. One might expect them to employ sour grapes rationalization and say, "To hell with the scientific big-shots! We don't need them anyway!" But this does not occur for two reasons. First, the UFO buffs are just as enamored with the methods and ideals of science as the established professionals are. Their approach is to do better science than the big-shots. Secondly, APRO, MUFON, NICAP, and CUFOS (Center for UFO Studies) have had a long list of academic scientists who serve as advisers and consultants in their research. Consulting panels include PhDs from reputable universities in biology, medicine, physics, engineering, astronomy, psychology, philosophy, and theology. In other words, they are not all amateurs, not by any means.

I recall watching a TV interview in 1974 with nuclear physicist Stanton Friedman. The interviewer asked him if there was any evidence that UFOs were intelligently controlled craft from an extraterrestrial civilization. Answering affirmatively, Friedman said: "A vast amount of scientific studies, of photographs, of landing trace cases, where after a UFO was seen landing and taking off, one finds the equivalent of burned circles, burned rings, the soil changed in color and texture, or vegetation destroyed--a whole host of excellent radar-visual cases with multiple witnesses and multiple radar sets, in short, better than the evidence against most crooks is the evidence for UFOs."

What is implied in this kind of argument is a strong reverence for scientific method. Belief in UFOs depends upon evidence! Friedman is not defending UFO-ETH on the authority of holy writ, or because of extrasensory messages delivered to him by supernatural spirits, or because it is politically prudent. He intends his conclusion to stand or fall with scientific argumentation alone.

The French mathematician and astronomer and NASA consultant on the Mars Map project, Jacques Vallée, published four books advocating that the scientific community take UFOs seriously. Though not quite a staunch advocate of UFO-ETH, he does believe that serious research into the matter will be fruitful to science. And, like Friedman, he wants to be guided only by the evidence. He writes: "Our problem, therefore, is clear: We must analyze the evidence already gathered, in such a way that we neither presuppose nor pre-exclude any possible conclusion. And this is not at all what previous investigators seem to have done."[20]

Everyone seems to agree that impartial examination of the facts by qualified researchers is required for good science. Then why doesn't everyone agree that UFOs are sent here from an extraterrestrial civilization? Ufologists answer that the established scientific community has so committed itself to an anti-ETH position that it operates with a bias in its research. It is not impartial. It is unable to evaluate the evidence honestly because the conclusion has been determined in advance. A truly open-minded investigation cannot be carried out when the conclusion is assumed from the outset. In short, the ufologists accuse the established scientists of falling short of performing genuine scientific research.

The great English biologist Sir Julian Huxley was somewhat unmasked in the UFO debate for being less than fully open and ready to consider UFO-ETH. After a banquet speech in which he had impugned UFO believers, he was buttonholed by a UFO buff named Gordon Creighton. In a 1996 issue of *Flying Saucer Review*, Creighton asked Professor Huxley if he had ever read any of the scientific writings on UFOs or studied the evidence.

Huxley: *No. What evidence, which writings?*

Creighton: *Books and articles by Vallée and Hynek, for example.*

Huxley: *Who are they?*

Creighton: *Astronomers.*

Huxley: *But why should I read astronomers? I'm a biologist.*[21]

Menzel, too, opened himself to the charge of jumping to premature conclusions in "UFOs" when he declared, "I confidently predict that no amount of investigation will bring evidence in support of the extraterrestrial hypothesis."[22] Ufologists sense in this attitude a reluctance to examine evidence in an objective manner.

WILL THE TRUE SCIENTIST PLEASE STAND UP?

This question of bias is best illustrated in the furor that developed over the Condon Committee's report, especially where Donald Keyhoe and the NICAP were concerned. The Condon Committee had solicited the aid of the NICAP because its files apparently contained the most extensive and thorough data on UFO sightings. The quality of the NICAP's records was higher than that of the Air Force's.[23] NICAP welcomed the opportunity and eventually shuttled 1,000 of its more than 9,300 case reports to the Colorado researchers. Keyhoe said NICAP would offer its full cooperation as long as he was convinced the study committed itself to an unbiased and objective evaluation of the facts. In one of his letters to Condon, Keyhoe wrote: "We do not ask any guarantee of a positive conclusion. We do ask a guarantee of an impartial investigation and evaluation of evidence from qualified, honest observers."[24]

Publicly the Condon committee had pledged itself to just that ideal—impartial investigation by qualified observers. In the project contract Condon signed with the U.S. Air Force, he wrote: "The work will be conducted under conditions of the strictest objectivity by investigators who, as carefully as can be determined, have no predilections or preconceived positions on the UFO question."[25]

However, four days following the signing of the contract, Condon was quoted in the *New York Times* as saying, "It is highly improbable they exist. The view that UFOs are hallucinatory will be a subject of our investigation, to discover what it is that makes people imagine they see things."[26]

Keyhoe was infuriated. Was he betrayed? He telephoned Condon and Condon denied the statements. "It's the press that's at fault. I've been badly misquoted," he told Keyhoe.

Only three months later, on January 25, 1967, Condon delivered a speech before the Corning New York section of the American Chemical Society. He told the audience the government should get out of the UFO business, and the press quoted him as saying, "My attitude right now is that there's nothing to it, but I'm not supposed to have a conclusion until we finish." In other after-dinner speeches Condon drew upon some of the more ridiculous contactee stories for anecdotes, making light of the whole UFO affair.[27]

But the bombshell was the release of a memorandum by project coordinator Robert Low.

Our study should be conducted almost exclusively by non-believers, who, although they couldn't possibly prove a negative result, could and probably would add an impressive body of evidence that there is no reality to the observations. The trick would be, I think, to describe the project so that, to the public, it would appear a totally objective study, but to the scientific community would present the image of a group of non-believers trying their best to be objective but having an almost zero expectation of finding a saucer. One way to do this would be to stress investigation, not of the physical phenomena, but rather the people who do the observing, the psychology and sociology of persons and groups who report seeing UFOs.[28]

NICAP members thought this was proof that not only did Condon and his staff not take UFOs seriously, but that they were clearly biased. An impartial investigation seemed impossible. Keyhoe threatened to pull out but, on a couple of occasions, was cajoled into remaining. NICAP finally did withdraw support before the project was completed.

In the published report, Condon said, "NICAP had made several efforts to influence the course of our study. When it became clear that these would fail, NICAP attacked the Colorado project as 'biased' and therefore without merit."[29] NICAP's response, understandably, was that it did in fact try to influence the investigation; it tried to influence it in the direction of greater objectivity and thoroughness.

This battle has made the Condon Report notorious and gave rise to a slogan propounded by UFO researchers: *True science stands for the investigation of the unexplained, not the explanation of the uninvestigated.*

"Although the Condon Report hurt UFO research, it had absolutely no influence on the UFO phenomenon itself, which continued to be reported, unaffected by societal events," is the assessment of David Jacobs.[30] Who would receive these reports?

With the termination of the Condon committee, there arose a new determination by amateur UFO researchers. The Mutual UFO Network, born in 1969, is currently a vibrant, healthy, international organization of ufologists with a fine monthly journal. On the MUFON agenda is the investigation, cataloguing, and analysis of UFO reports. Because of the Condon Report, the U.S. Air Force no longer gathers such information (at least officially). MUFON sells blue and white t-shirts; on the back of one is written: "Doing the Air Force's Job Since 1969."

Thomas Bullard prophesies: "Science may die by its own hand, if overconfidence forecloses inquiry and leads to a preference for pontification over learning."[31]

MISEDUCATION?

The point of this chapter has already been made, but I would like now to append a couple of comments about UFOs and education. The question is: Should UFOs be discussed in our schools? Professor Condon represents establishment science and desires to keep all competitors from gaining an open hearing, which is made clear when he criticizes the "miseducation" taking place in our schools. When one sees a term such as "miseducation," watch out. It hints that we might have a battle going on here, a battle between orthodoxy and heterodoxy. In this case, it is the battle between orthodox science and heterodox ufology.

Condon's final report include the following passage:

A related problem to which we wish to direct public attention is the miseducation in our schools which arises from the fact that many children are being allowed, if not actively encouraged, to devote their science study time to the reading of UFO books and magazine articles.... We feel that children are educationally harmed by absorbing unsound and erroneous material as if it were scientifically well founded. Such study is harmful not merely because of the erroneous nature of the material itself, but also because such study retards the development of a critical faculty with regard to scientific evidence which to some degree ought to be part of the education of every American."[32]

In sum, if the public schools teach American orthodoxy, then keep unorthodox doctrines such as belief in UFOs away from our children. The Condon Report continues:

Therefore, we strongly recommend that teachers refrain from giving students credit for school work based on their reading of the presently available UFO books and magazine articles. Teachers who find their students strongly motivated in this direction should attempt to channel their interests in the direction of serious study of astronomy and meteorology, and in the direction of critical analysis of arguments for fantastic propositions that are being supported by appeals to fallacious reasoning or false data.[33]

Orthodox science will maintain its control by censoring what children read and what teachers may grant academic credit for.

Later in the report, Condon referred to a 1966 Gallup poll that reported 48 percent of American adults believe flying saucers are "something real" and five million claim to have personally seen a UFO: "The poll showed that increased amount of formal education is associated with an increased tendency to believe in the reality of flying saucers. Perhaps this result says something about how the school system trains students in critical thinking."[34]

Condon's commitment to this identification of ufology with astrology, spiritualism, psychokinesis, and other pseudosciences was passionately presented in his speech "UFOs I Have Loved and Lost" before the American Philosophical Society in Philadelphia in April 1969: "In my view publishers who publish or teachers who teach any of the pseudo-sciences as established truth should, on being found guilty, be publicly horsewhipped, and forever banned from further activity in these usually honorable professions."[35]

Ufology in Higher Education

We can only applaud Condon's concern regarding students in our schools and how they should be guided to develop a "critical faculty with regard to scientific evidence." However, should our students not be given academic credit for reading books or magazine articles about UFOs just because they are written by proponents of UFO-ETH? I for one do not draw that conclusion. I believe such reading material may help develop students' "critical faculty" and find profitable use in the classroom.

The first observation to make is that young people (people of all ages, for that matter) are quite fascinated with the subject of UFOs, especially UFO-ETH. The phenomenal book sales on the subject rank almost as high as sex novels and whodunits. Erich von Däniken claims to have sold millions copies of his various books on UFOs. My dentist told me his 10-year-old daughter was reading his book *Chariots of the Gods.*

Will the True Scientist Please Stand Up?

I have had the opportunity to speak and lead discussions on UFOs with all kinds of audiences: college assemblies, teenage workshops, ladies' circles and garden clubs, men's service clubs, and even a sixth-grade classroom. There is a wide-spread fascination with the subject. Once while I was visiting a sixth-grade class, the discussion had gone on for an hour when the bell rang; instead of leaving for lunch the class voted to stay and continue the discussion. And it seems to me that the curiosity and the kind of questions people ask are practically the same for both young and old, well-educated and poorly educated, male and female, black and white, and so on.

This is important to note at a time when S.A.T. scores have been dropping and when our public school systems seem to be losing students' interests. For various reasons, students are poorly motivated to attain even the three Rs, let alone a critical faculty. So many young people live in a world of TV, iPhones, and ear buds that it is extremely difficult to interest them in reading anything. Consequently, their reading ability falls. If a teacher discovers that his or her students have sufficient interest in a subject to read about it, then it would behoove that teacher to take advantage of it. Apparently Professor Condon would tell such a young person to put away *Chariots of the Gods* and pick up a dry, boring astronomy, meteorology, or physics textbook. Many a schoolteacher knows that this tactic will teach the majority of fledgling students to be nonreaders.

Is there perhaps a more creative approach that Condon has overlooked? I believe there is. It seems to me that the teacher could capitalize on student interest in UFOs by pursuing the subject and in the process raise critical questions. When questions are raised about the distance a UFO must travel from one star to another, lead the student to the astronomy textbook. When attempting to find whether a sighting was a real flying saucer or a mirage caused by a temperature inversion in the atmosphere, lead the student to a meteorology textbook. When asking how it is possible for flying saucers to make right-angle turns while traveling at high speed (do they have their own portable gravity control devices?)

lead the student to the physics textbook. If the ufologists Condon so despises are in fact wrong, then they will have had their day in court and found guilty, fair and square. But more important, the students will have followed a critical argument step-by-step and witnessed science at work on a topic relevant to their own interests.

The teacher in this situation, of course, will have to do some planning. The students should not be left entirely alone, but then this is true for all areas of supervised study. The teacher must embody and demonstrate the critical faculty we wish to have passed on to the student. Condon is right when he says that a teacher who teaches "the pseudosciences as established truth"—that is, teaches without employing a critical faculty—ought to "be publicly horsewhipped."[36] Actually, I don't advocate corporal punishment for school teachers.

While teaching philosophy and religion at Newberry College in central South Carolina during the 1970s, I developed and taught an interim course on UFOs and incorporated some of the ideas outlined previously. I was stimulated to do so because I developed a furious rage against the scholarship of Erich von Däniken similar to what Condon has shown against the NICAP, APRO, and other ufologists. Having taught courses on religion in archaic society and on hermeneutics (theory of biblical and literary interpretation), I felt I could see how and where von Däniken was misinterpreting the evidence in a crude way. But his books were on the bestseller lists, and students were carrying them around and asking for my reaction to his views. My occasional pompous tirades against von Däniken's scholarship were not enough. Something more creative had to be done.

I announced the course on UFOs and more than 65 students (just short of 10 percent of the small campus student body) asked to take it. I accepted 18 and made it a discussion seminar. On the first day of class I asked: "How many students think von Däniken's thesis about extraterrestrials visiting earth is reasonably well substantiated by the evidence?" Fourteen answered "yes" and four said "probably." I asked the same question on the final day of class. Seventeen said "no" and one said he was not sure yet.

During the course, students were asked to go to the library to see if other scientists and scholars would confirm or disconfirm von Däniken's theories. When, for example, they read how von Däniken said space travelers built the pyramids in Egypt, the students studied about Egypt. When they read in von Däniken that ancient astronauts carved the statues on Easter Island, set up a rust-proof pillar at Delhi, and built roads for the Mayans and for other Indians on the plain of Nazca, the students studied archaeology. When they read that, according to von Däniken, the Ark of the Covenant was a radio transmitter and that Ezekiel saw a UFO instead of God, the students consulted the Bible and scholarly interpreters of Scripture. The students discovered by themselves, and with only a modicum of structured guidance by the instructor, that von Däniken's data could be better explained by other theories. In the course evaluation at the semester's end, the majority of students said that the single best feature of the course was that it aided them in developing a critical faculty.

But the change of mind did not go in only one direction. I recall one somewhat humorous episode of a skeptic who became converted into a UFO believer. It was not a student in this case; it was a professor of education, Dr. Margaret Buckley. One of Dr. Buckley's hobbies is archaeology. I asked her if she would lecture to my class on the construction of the pyramids. She gladly did so and explained that von Däniken's ancient astronaut theory is superfluous because the details describing their construction by terrestrials using slave labor were in some cases hieroglyphically written inside the pyramid.

But Dr. Buckley did not stop there. She took the opportunity to launch into a professorial diatribe against pseudoscience. She said anyone who claimed to believe in UFOs had to be a "freak" or a "kook" or "mentally unbalanced." Surely such people could not take UFOs seriously and still claim to be well-educated! I took this humorous shot to have been aimed at me as well.

The following January I offered the interim course a second time and invited Dr. Buckley to speak again. However, during the intervening year Dr. Buckley had had her own UFO experience. Early in the evening of January 14, 1974, she and a friend were traveling down Interstate 26 west of Columbia, South Carolina. Flying parallel to the horizon at great speed she saw a ball-shaped object, bluish-white in color, with a yellow to red tail, perhaps of fire. She was certain in her own mind that it was not an airplane because of its speed; nor was it a meteor because of its long, horizontal flight path. She and others stopped their cars along the highway to watch. It eventually crossed the highway and then disappeared over the horizon. Dr. Buckley came to my class the second time to testify on behalf of UFOs.

After leaving Newberry College, but before coming to Berkeley to teach at the Graduate Theological Union, I took a position teaching in the Religious Studies department at Loyola University in New Orleans. There I proposed to offer the course again. This time I titled it "UFOs: Science? Psychosis? or Salvation?" Perhaps afraid of the image this would create, an administrator temporarily changed it to the innocuous title of "Science and Religion." Eight weeks later the Common Curriculum Committee met and rejected the course entirely. (Later I was asked by members of the Committee to resubmit my course proposal and was given genuine encouragement.) At the time, I was called into the dean's office to receive the bad news. The Common Curriculum Director, Dr. Richard E. Johnson, told me the course had been rejected. But before I left, he said, "By the way," and then launched into a personal story. It was a story about the time he saw two UFOs.

6

Celestial Chariots and Terrestrial Pseudoscience

In the summer of 1975 I received a grant from the National Endowment for the Humanities to participate in a high-gear seminar on the philosophy of science at the University of Notre Dame. A dozen PhDs from universities around the country were gathered under the leadership of the now-deceased Professor Ernan McMullin.

On one occasion Erich von Däniken was brought up. It was greeted with sneers and jeers around the seminar table. I asked why. "Because he's a crackpot religious nut," someone said, and everyone nodded in agreement. I asked how many in the room had actually read any of von Däniken's writings and could pinpoint his errors. Only a couple had even bothered to look at his books. "I wouldn't touch it with a 10-foot pole" was the attitude expressed.

It struck me that this reaction was a strictly emotional and chauvinistic defense of establishment science. Would it not be more true to the ideals of the science and scholarship they were defending to bring a scientific critique to von Däniken's theories, in support of their own position? I too find von Däniken's theories preposterous, but it would be hypocrisy to decry von Däniken's view without offering a fair evaluation. In this chapter, we will look briefly at von Däniken's theory and then evaluate the evidence he uses to support it.[1]

THE HERMENEUTICAL QUESTION

Erich von Däniken believes that ancient texts currently out of date should be reinterpreted in modern terms. One thing that is out of date is faith in God. If we translate ancient faith in God into modern terms, von Däniken says we should rely upon reason to affirm the ancient astronaut theory. What our ancestors thought were gods were, in fact, astronauts visiting Earth from outer space.

To illustrate von Däniken's method, let's look at his interpretation of the dramatic apocalyptic work we know as Enoch. The books of Enoch are filled with heavenly visions of divine glory. But, says von Däniken, we must reinterpret what is said to eliminate references to the divine and substitute extraterrestrial beings.

> ...the 'throne of Great Glory'—Enoch told how the majestic leader arose and 'came to me and spoke to me with his voice'.... It's not really a scene that you can ascribe to God. Two extraterrestrials... collected Enoch, disinfected him, dressed him in a spacesuit, and brought him to the command bridge of the mother ship, and God welcomed him 'with his voice'.... It's about time that the old texts were presented in a modern, comprehensible form to make it possible to plumb their meanings. May doubt shatter the old authorities, and reason triumph over faith.[2]

This is von Däniken's hermeneutical method: Reinterpret ancient texts, monuments, petroglyphs, artifacts, and such so that they fit the ancient astronaut scheme of explanation. This method includes a rejection of traditional religious understandings and their replacement with a modern materialist worldview that respects if not reveres science. What this method leads to is an entirely new worldview, a metanarrative that includes both Earth's history and cosmic history. It is to that metanarrative we now turn.

UFOs—God's Chariots?

We earthlings were created in the image of god-like beings from space. Erich von Däniken speculates about the origin of intelligence in our evolution, and in the process he develops the following wild but enticing vision: Back in some unknown and remote past, perhaps in some distant galaxy, a gigantic battle raged between two races of intelligent creatures. In their retreat the losers boarded spaceships and flew to destinations unknown to the pursuing victors. Seeking to hide from the enemy, who might decide to track them down and wipe them out completely, the losers sought to colonize a planet that would be inhabitable yet not so similar to their own as to be an obvious target for their enemy's search. They chose Earth.[3]

The Earth was satisfactory but not ideal. For many years the interstellar colonialists continued to wear gas masks on the new planet while waiting for their biological systems to adapt to our terrestrial atmosphere. As evidence for this stage in the drama, von Däniken points to primitive cave drawings of humanoid figures that appear to be wearing helmets and heavy clothing. He repeatedly compares these drawings to photos of modern astronauts in space garb that protects them from the atmosphere (or lack of it) on the Moon.

Earth's new visitors dug tunnels. Fearing that their pursuers might survey the Earth with technical devices, the losers made elaborate tunnel systems for hiding. Von Däniken claims to substantiate this hypothesis, particularly in *Gold of the Gods,* where he describes a visit he made to such a tunnel or cave in Ecuador. In the cave containing a "gigantic hall" with an entrance "as big as the hangar of a Jumbo Jet," von Däniken claims to have found a table and chairs made of plastic or steel, a veritable zoo of carved animal statuary, what could be interpreted as a model airplane, and some as yet untranslated engravings on metal "which might contain a synopsis of the history of humanity."[4]

UFOs: God's Chariots?

As a diversionary measure, these troglodytes placed electronic transmitters emitting coded reports on what was then the planet orbiting the sun between Mars and Jupiter. Falling for the ruse, the victors annihilated this planet with a gigantic explosion. The remains of the destroyed planet still float in space between Mars and Jupiter in the form of thousands of small lumps of stone, known as the planetoid belt. Believing the losers to be destroyed, the victors withdrew to their home planet and ceased to be a menace.

With peace achieved, the cave dwellers emerged from their subterranean refuge to find on the surface of the Earth a quaint but promising stage in the evolution of life. Resolving to create the human race *in their image,* they had sexual intercourse with already existing monkeys. It was hoped that the resultant offspring would have the physical countenance of the ape but the intelligence of their superhuman creators. The record of this celestial-terrestrial marriage is to be found in the mysterious text of Genesis 6:1-4, where "the sons of God came in to the daughters of men, and they bore them children." And in the promise to Abraham in Genesis 12, they promised that these offspring would have descendants as numerous as the stars in heaven.

But as time passed the creators were not uniformly happy with their creatures. Evolution was moving too slowly. The former losers having become absolute rulers (that is, gods) often became impatient and declared divine war upon humans. Von Däniken believes the cities of Sodom and Gomorrah (Genesis 19) were destroyed not merely by "fire and brimstone" but by thermonuclear explosions.[5] Evidently the gods used airplanes to harass humans, because archaeologists have found so many caves and underground fortifications, which appear to von Däniken as refuges from air attack. The myths of primitive religions all include stories of gods in the sky, even the Bible.

Von Däniken claims the vision in Ezekiel 1 refers to a flying machine made by the astronauts-become-gods. Ezekiel describes what he saw: A fiery whirlwind in the midst of which appeared four living creatures each with four faces and two wings; beside each was a construction that looked like a "wheel within a wheel"; the wings of the creatures did not move, yet they and the wheels "rose from the earth" together; "and there came a voice from above the firmament over their heads." Von Däniken likens the object in the vision to the multipurpose amphibious helicopters used by the American military. All the wheels rise at the same time when it leaves the ground. The voice speaking to Ezekiel is that of an astro-divinity giving the prophet information and instructions as to what the Hebrew people should do. Note that Ezekiel is receiving a revelation, to be sure; it is just that the revelation comes from a humanoid creature rather than the almighty and spiritual God posited by Judaism and Christianity.[6] One reader of von Däniken's theory, Joseph Blumrich, was so impressed by this interpretation that he applied his knowledge as an engineer to demonstrate just how he believes Ezekiel's vision does report a spaceship. He published his argument in a book titled *The Spaceships of Ezekiel.*

Von Däniken goes on to say that these gods continued to fly about our planet in their Vimanas,[7] occasionally constructing a pyramid in Egypt or Mexico,[8] erecting statues on Easter Island,[9] turning a stone stairway upside down at Sacsahuaman,[10] standing up a lonesome, rust-proof pillar at Delhi,[11] and in general leaving all sorts of mysteries for later generations to unravel. Then they disappeared.[12]

God Is IT

Von Däniken is no atheist. He says that the picture of God held by Jews and Christians is really a case of mistaken identity. When the Bible speaks of revelations of the divine it is really speaking about contact with space visitors. But still we may ask: How did the space visitors originate? Where did it all begin? Why is there something and not nothing? That primordial origin of all things is what von Däniken labels "IT": that is, God in the fullest sense of the word. But the Bible is a primitive book that still mistakenly refers to visiting astronauts as God, says von Däniken.

In referring to the creation of human beings, von Däniken is quick to point out the use of the plural pronoun in Genesis 1:26: "Then God said,

'Let us make man in our image, after our likeness.'" If there were only one God, von Däniken asks, then wouldn't he refer to himself in the singular? The conclusion left with the reader is that the "us" and "our" refer to the race of extraterrestrials who are creating a race of earthlings.[13] Traditional conservative Christian reflection on this passage understands the plural pronoun to be a reference to the three persons of the Trinity. More recent neo-orthodox Christian thinking, following the great German Old Testament scholar Gerhard von Rad, understands the plural to be a reference to God in the company of his heavenly host, for example, angels, cherubim, and so on. This is important for the theology of the Bible. The Bible says no one has ever seen God in all his majesty. No one can see God as he actually is. If human beings were in the exact image of God, then God's mystery would be totally uncovered. The use of "our image" means that to be human is to share in the goodness of heaven, but the human image is sufficiently independent of God so as never to be idolatrously mistaken for God himself.

After the creation of human life through God's word in Genesis 1, von Däniken then refers to this creation again by the marriage of daughters of Earth with sons of God (members of God's court), in Genesis 6. But is this a fair interpretation of even the most literal reading of the Bible? Between chapters 1 and 5 we have Adam and Eve (fully human) living in the garden of Eden and then expelled, the birth of Cain and Abel, and then the appearance of Adam's descendants right down to Noah's three sons, Shem, Ham, and Japheth. If it was the Bible's intent to describe the creation of humans as the result of sexual intercourse between celestial beings and terrestrial monkeys, then this incident would have appeared at the beginning of the process. According to von Däniken's logic Adam and Eve would have been monkeys, not humans. And if they were created in the image of the gods (Genesis 1:26), then the astronauts were monkeys. The inconsistencies of von Däniken's argument boggle the mind of any rational thinker. But we must push on.

The ultimate sin of humanity, which precipitated its Fall, says von Däniken, was having sexual intercourse with animals. Interbreeding with animals impeded the direction of evolution hoped for by the space travelers. Because *Homo sapiens* had been the product of a marriage between extraterrestrials and apes, the first few generations of this new breed could be sexually attracted toward either side of the family: human or beast. A sexual human-animal cult "was practiced with gusto and enjoyment by the people of antiquity,"[14] and evidence for it is found in the literature of many ancient cultures. Von Däniken reminds us of the god Pan (the devil called upon in modern Satanic rituals) who is depicted as a humanoid with goat's feet and a goat's head. The Centaurs, who violated the wives of the Lapithae, were said to have "human torsos and horses' bodies."[15] He even is able to quote Leviticus 18:23: "You shall not lie with any beast and defile yourself with it, neither shall any woman give herself to a beast to lie with it: it is perversion."

Human-animal interbreeding represents a Fall from divine grace because it arrests the evolutionary development of humanity toward a higher species. Von Däniken believes the bestial nature of humans, expressed in their inclination to have sex with animals, is the original sin that we inherit and from which we seek to escape. The Fall, furthermore, precipitated divine judgment and punishment by the gods. Moses announced that the punishment for sharing sexual relations with an animal would be death (Leviticus 20:15). Perhaps the destruction of Sodom and Gomorrah was the result of such acts.

It is the supposed cruelty of these space-divinities that leads von Däniken to conclude that they are certainly inferior to the omniscient God of love postulated by the Jewish and Christian religions. "The same God who had created man decided to destroy His work. And He did it often. Why?...I doubt whether an infinitely good god has feelings of revenge."[16]

This question has been asked often before, and in the philosophy of religion it is called the *theodicy problem*. Originally coined by the philosopher Gottfried Wilhelm Leibniz, the term *theodicy* comes from the Greek words *theos* (God) and *dike* (justice), and it literally means "justification of God." Sometimes the question is asked this way: If God is supposed to be both all-powerful and also all-loving, then why does he permit evil in the world? Is he all-powerful, and therefore the author of evil? Or is he all-loving, and therefore unable to overcome the power of evil? Traditionally, Christians have pointed to the cross and the resurrection of Christ to answer this question, saying that as Jesus suffered, God also suffers from evil. Yet the resurrection of Jesus promises God's ultimate triumph and the obliteration of sin and death everafter. Von Däniken offers a different answer. He says that the true God ought not to be confused with the lesser divinities from space, whom earthlings mistakenly have labeled as gods. He says, "The great God of the universe has absolutely nothing in common with the 'gods' who haunt legends, myths, and religions, and who effected the mutation from animal to man."[17] But if the "great God" had nothing to do with what we earthlings view as a pretty important event—our own creation—then why is God so "great" in our eyes?

In the concluding chapter of *The Gold of the Gods* von Däniken renames God "IT." Here he chastises the bickering and infighting within and between the memberships of the various religions of the world. Certainly the great god IT could not be the object of their worship because they are constantly squabbling. On the other hand, von Däniken finds that he cannot side with the atheists either. To say there is no god at all leaves at least one very big question unanswered: Where did everything come from in the first place? After entertaining various scientific theories about the origin of the universe, he recognizes the respected dominance of George Gamow's big-bang theory. According to the big-bang theory, 18 or more billion years ago everything that now exists was concentrated in a single ball of proto-hydrogen gas. This ball of gas exploded and sent gas hurling in every direction. This gas eventually began to solidify into suns and planets. The present continuing expansion of the universe is the result of all things still reeling from this single primordial explosion.

Von Däniken likes this scientific theory better than the creation accounts in Genesis. But he still asks: Where did the primal stuff for the beginning explosion come from? He concludes that IT was a neutrum that existed before the big bang. "IT caused all the worlds in the universe to originate from the explosion. IT, incorporeal primordial force, the decisive primordial command, became matter and IT knew the result of the great explosion. IT wanted to reach the stage of lived experience."[18] He recommends that we say good-bye to the familiar and well-loved "fairy stories" of the Bible to contemplate the indefinable IT.

The neuter neutrum got lonely and decided to create a world with which IT could relate, according to von Däniken's story without fairies. When we think of an "it" we think of a thing. An "it" that is a neutrum would be a thing that stands alone, unrelated to other things. It would be impersonal and uninvolved. But this neutrum became personally involved.

Thus, IT for von Däniken is really not an it at all. It is a person. In ordinary parlance we believe an "it" is a thing. A *person,* in contrast to a thing, has feelings, desires, and intentions. Von Däniken, then, has mis-named his God IT, because IT is in fact personal. It likewise has desires and intentions; it acts to create the universe with the aim of developing life. Therefore, IT is really a person, and not so very different from the Judeo-Christian God whom he has already rejected.

Von Däniken believes he has shown scientifically that Jews, Christians, and other religious believers are all fouled up on their image of the gods. He does not, however, surrender the idea that there is one ultimate and divine ground of all being. Perhaps an analysis of the quality of von Dän-iken's scientific investigation will help us decide how much of what he says is believable.

DOES VON DÄNIKEN HAVE PROOF?

Von Däniken has two methods for proving his theory correct. His first method is to try to make us believe that other scientists who dis-agree with him are ignorant blockheads. The second method is for von Däniken to examine the sites of ancient relics and to reinterpret the pas-sages of ancient scriptures in order to gather evidence supporting his theory. Let us begin with the first method.

Von Däniken claims to be doing scientific scholarship, but in the judgment of other scholars he is seen to be doing pseudoscience. As suggested earlier, von Däniken (as well as other ufologists) participates in a wider, more general system of beliefs, which can be loosely identified as scientific or naturalistic. In this sense von Däniken is a *genuine* scientist but a poor scientist.[19] If we work with a more stringent definition of "scientist"—meaning only those who do good scholarly research—then von Däniken will appear as a *pseudo-*, or false, scientist.

Our word *science* comes from *scientia*, which means "knowledge." More specifically it has come to refer to the process of gaining knowledge through the examination of evidence combined with thorough and objective argumentation. The "Mathematical Games" columnist for *Scientific American*, Martin Gardner, describes the characteristics that distinguish the pseudoscientist or crank from the orthodox scientist. First, pseudoscientists work in almost total isolation from their colleagues, that is, they have no fruitful dialogue with fellow researchers. Of course, modern cranks insist that their isolation is not desired on their part; it is due, they claim, to the prejudice of the established scientific community against new ideas. Pseudoscientists never tire of reminding their readers about the numerous examples of novel scientific views that did not initially receive an unbiased hearing, but which later proved to be true.

The second characteristic of pseudoscientists, which greatly strengthens their isolation, is a tendency toward paranoia. Gardner lists five ways in which these paranoid tendencies manifest themselves in pseudoscientists: (1) they consider themselves geniuses; (2) they regard their colleagues as ignorant blockheads; (3) they believe themselves unjustly persecuted and discriminated against; (4) they focus their attacks upon the greatest scientists and the most-established theories; and (5) they often write in a complex jargon, in many cases making use of terms and phrases they themselves coined (neologisms). Do any of these characteristics fit Erich von Däniken? With the exception of the last one I suggest that they do.

Von Däniken's writing style is irregular and it skips from topic to topic. Although the reader is sure something is being proved it is not always obvious what that is exactly. A close look, however, seems to reveal five reasons why von Däniken believes the established scientific community either has not considered his position or, if they have, why they have rejected it unjustly. First, the present stage of scientific investigation is out of date because practicing scientists do not ask questions about the past based on our most recent knowledge about space travel, that is, they presuppose that people in ancient times could not fly. Consequently, they cannot accurately assess such evidence when they find it.[20] The only conclusions that are available to research are those that are discovered in response to the questions asked. If one does not ask the right questions, then the right answers never appear. Von Däniken claims that if the science of archaeology does not pose questions regarding its data based upon what we now know about space travel, then the possibility of an explanatory theory that includes space travel is beyond the purview of the theorist. In principle, there is nothing wrong with what von Däniken is saying here; it is simply sound interpretation theory.

Second, von Däniken argues that present-day scientists are stubborn and refuse to admit the need to change their methods and theories.[21] He accuses scientists of insisting that "new discoveries" fit "into accepted patterns."[22] More specifically, modern scientific methods presuppose that our present civilization is the most advanced civilization in the Earth's history; consequently, they are blind and prejudiced against any evidence proving that civilizations higher than our own have existed here before us.[23] Present archaeological theory, for example, explains artifacts only in terms of "primitive" religion and refuses to entertain other possibilities.[24] "Archaeology," he writes, is "tied up in a straitjacket of preconceived views. Eyes have grown blind, ideas become dead. Science says that it cannot accept imaginative solutions because they have no empirical or demonstrable foundation."[25] (Von Däniken recognizes that science prefers "empirical or demonstrable" evidence to that of pure imagination.) With this kind of prejudice, von Däniken argues, the orthodox scientific community has shut itself off from the truth before it begins investigating the evidence. Here we have a symptom of the pseudoscientist: the established scientists are presented as prejudiced blockheads who cannot see past their noses.

The third reason is an extension of the second. Von Däniken claims that modern science will not consider any theoretical explanations that tend to disprove the accuracy of the Jewish and Christian Bibles. He says, "even the scholars of the nineteenth and twentieth centuries...were still caught in the mental fetters of thousand-year-old errors, because the way back would inevitably have called in question parts of the biblical story."[26] He is saying that modern science and religion have combined forces to defend the integrity of the Bible. This contention reveals von Däniken's complete lack of awareness of Western intellectual history and his insensitivity to the touchy relationship between science and religion today.

At the Center for Theology and the Natural Sciences at the Graduate Theological Union in Berkeley, California, my colleague Bob Russell and I have studied the relationship between science and religion since 1981. We have witnessed battles between evolutionary biologists and their attackers among creationists and intelligent design advocates. We have witnessed battles between stem-cell biologists and their attackers among Roman Catholic bioethicists. We have witnessed physicists and theologians tendering consonant accounts of the origin of the universe, and we have witnessed evolutionary theorists and theologians tendering consonant accounts of human nature.[27] One thing we have never witnessed is an alliance between establishment scientists and religious scholars to defend the integrity of the Bible. It is as amazing as it is ludicrous that von Däniken perceives a scientific-religious alliance conspiring in defense of the accuracy of the Bible! Perhaps here is an example of the grandiose dimension of paranoia: What greater establishment could a theorist seek to triumph over than a unified Judeo-Christian scientific conspiracy?

Alleged prejudices in scientific practice are the fourth reason establishment science rejects his thesis, according to von Däniken. There is, he says, a conspiracy to withhold the truth. "What are people really afraid of?" he writes. "Are they worried that the truth, protected and concealed for so many thousands of years, will finally come to light?"[28]

This conspiracy shows a slight inclination toward persecuting von Däniken as well. Identifying himself with Thomas Edison and Leonardo da Vinci, he refers to himself as one of those "visionaries who were violently attacked or, what is often harder to stomach, laughed at condescendingly by their contemporaries."[29] The projection of a conspiracy in opposition to the pseudoscientist is one of the most serious symptoms of paranoia. In all fairness to von Däniken, I must add that *although* the projection of a conspiracy is certainly present in his work, it is not as salient a theme as are the others.

The fifth argument von Däniken raises in behalf of his own claim is that the orthodox scientific community has been wrong in the past; therefore, it just may be wrong now too.[30] After all, he says, the law that the sun orbited the Earth was held for thousands of years, and less than a hundred years ago it was held that objects heavier than air would never be able to fly. Even Einstein was not a believer at first. Just because von Däniken stands alone in the face of gigantic opposition from the scientific establishment does not mean he is wrong. The scientific establishment has been wrong before. Does it not follow that they are wrong again? Here is an obvious theme pseudoscientists play over and over to their own advantage.

IF NOT PROOF, DOES VON DÄNIKEN HAVE EVIDENCE?

At this point we may suspect that von Däniken is a pseudoscientist, but an examination of his argument based on literary and archaeological evidence will indict him for sure. The formula that he repeats over and over again is comprised of four steps:

1. Report an interesting archaeological discovery or passage from ancient literature.
2. Describe it as semi-explained or even baffling.

3. Raise a leading question regarding its origin, sometimes suggesting intervention from outer space.

4. Move on to another subject.

For example, von Däniken examines Easter Island and reports his amazement at the hundreds of gigantic statues, some of which are 33 and 66 feet high and weigh as much as 50 tons.[31] Originally these colossi wore hats, and the stone hats weighed more than 10 tons apiece. The stone for the hats was found at a different site from that used for the bodies, and the hats had to be hoisted high in the air. The usual explanation is that the stone giants and their hats were moved to their present sites on wooden rollers and put in place by the conventional "heave-ho" methods. Von Däniken rejects this. He is amazed that we should think primitive people capable of this kind of engineering. He speculates that even 2,000 men, working day and night (for how long?), would not be enough to carve these colossal figures out of the steel-hard volcanic stone with rudimentary tools. In addition, the island is so small it could scarcely have provided food for more than 2,000 inhabitants. So von Däniken dangles questions before the reader: Then who did the work? And how did they manage it? Von Däniken then turns to another topic.

Because we do not know for sure just who did the work, we are supposed to conclude that highly skilled technicians from space were responsible. Because von Däniken cannot believe the Easter Islanders were responsible, and because we cannot prove that visiting astronauts did not do it, then this becomes proof that extraterrestrials were in fact responsible. In logic this kind of argument is called the fallacy *argumentum ad ignorantiam,* or the argument from ignorance. The fallacy has this basic form: because I cannot prove something false, then it follows that it must be true. Von Däniken depends upon this fallacious form of reasoning throughout his writings. In *The Gold of the Gods,* for example, he writes, "Of course, I cannot 'prove' my theory, but no one has produced arguments to convince me of the contrary. So I am going to follow it through to the bitter end."[32]

With regard to Easter Island itself, perhaps a few additional facts will reveal the quality of von Däniken's scientific investigation. It seems that for the purposes of this discussion the Norwegian explorer Thor Heyerdahl has resolved these mysteries in his book *Aku-Aku, the Secret of Easter Island* .[33] Heyerdahl explains how he convinced some of the natives of Easter Island to demonstrate the procedure for carving and erecting the statues. The demonstration showed that with simple stone implements it would take six men about a year to carve a 15-foot statue. And at Heyerdahl's invitation, 180 men pulled a statue weighing between 25 and 30 tons across the island with ropes using the conventional "heave-ho" method. They further demonstrated how the colossi were stood upright by pushing stones under a log lever, and how ramps were constructed to put the hats on top.

Another piece of evidence von Däniken uses in support of his theory is the ancient pillar at Delhi.[34] This column is made of iron and, despite exposure to the weather for more than 4,000 years, it shows not even a trace of rust. So von Daniken asks if it could have been produced by some celestial engineer whose scientific capacities were well in advance of our own. Clifford Wilson says von Däniken should have looked at the Delhi pillar more carefully, because there is in fact rust on it.[35] Furthermore, to find examples of advanced technology in our distant past could also mean that earthlings had advanced technology in our distant past; it does not necessarily warrant a postulate about visitors from space.

Another technique frequently employed by von Däniken is pyramidology, or the baffling numbers game. For example, he asks, "Is it really a coincidence that the height of the pyramid of Cheops [in Egypt] multiplied by a thousand million 98,000,000 miles corresponds approximately to the distance between the Earth and the sun?...Is it a coincidence that the area of the base of the pyramid divided by twice its height gives the celebrated figure pi = 3.14159?"[36] In *Fads and Fallacies in the Name of Science,* Gardner analyzes this pseudoscientific use of the baffling numbers technique. He says that if you set about measuring a complicated structure like the pyramid, you will quickly have on hand a great abundance of lengths to play with. And if you have sufficient patience to juggle them about in various ways, you are certain to come out with many figures that coincide with important historical dates or figures used in the sciences.

Supposing that the number five has a particularly numinous quality, Gardner opens a world almanac to the entry on the Washington Monument. Its height is 555 feet and 5 inches. The base is 55 square feet, and the windows are set at 500 feet from the base. If the base is multiplied by 60 (or five times the number of months in a year) it equals 3,300, which is the exact weight of the capstone in pounds. Also, the word *Washington* has exactly 10 letters (two times five). And if the weight of the capstone is multiplied by the base, the result is 181,500—a fairly close approximation of the speed of light in miles per second. If the base is measured with a "Monument boot," which is slightly smaller than the standard foot, its side comes to 56 1/2 feet. This figure multiplied by 33,000 yields a figure even closer to the speed of light. It should take an average mathematician about 55 minutes to discover the "truths," working only with the meager figures provided by the Almanac.[37]

One other argument raised by von Däniken will be of interest to Bible readers. He writes, "Without actually consulting Exodus I seem to remember that the Ark was often surrounded by flashing sparks," so "undoubtedly the Ark was electrically charged!"[38] Having dramatically and *conclusively* proved by this investigation that the Ark was electrically charged, he goes on to argue that God was really a space being with whom Moses communicated via an electrical transmitter whenever he needed help or advice. But, we might ask, why didn't von Däniken bother to consult Exodus? Does he expect us to accept his interpretation of a Bible he admits he has not read it? In contrast to von Däniken, I *have* consulted Exodus and could not locate the flashing sparks.

Up to this point I have not suggested that von Däniken is engaged in deliberate fraud. This possibility needs to be entertained, however. As mentioned earlier, in his book *The Gold of the Gods* von Däniken claims to have visited certain caves in Ecuador where he found ancient furniture made of plastic, a menagerie of golden animal statuary, and a library of imprinted metal folios containing chronicles of an ancient civilization. He names the guide who led him to the subterranean treasures as Juan Moricz. The editors of *Der Spiegel* interviewed Moricz, however, and he stated that von Däniken "never set foot in the caves" about which he wrote. According to Moricz, the account of the cave excursion recorded in *The Gold of the Gods is* a blatant embellishment of a story Moricz had told von Däniken. In an interview for the August 1974 issue of *Playboy* magazine, Timothy Ferris asked von Däniken: "Which of you is telling the truth?" Von Däniken answered that they both were telling "half the truth." He went on to say, "In German we say a writer, if he is not writing pure science, is allowed to use some *dramaturgisch Effekte* [sic]—some theatrical effects. And that's what I have done."

The thoroughness and quality of von Däniken's scholarship just cannot permit him to be ranked with the legions of scientific researchers who laboriously scrutinize trains of experiments before advancing a guarded hypothesis about what is probably the case. I am not flatly saying von Däniken's overall thesis is wrong; my intention is rather to say that if we make scholarly integrity part of what defines *genuine* science, then Erich von Däniken must be placed on the *pseudo*science side of the ledger.

CONCLUSION

Von Däniken seems to be advocating a reinterpretation of the foundations of religion in terms of the modern Western naturalistic and scientific mind-set. According to Gregory Reece, "Von Däniken transforms the gods into humans and finds the answer to the mysteries of ancient civilizations in the literal stars rather than in the metaphorical heavens."[39] Because our modern system of beliefs accepts the naturalistic paradigm (loosely put) presupposed in scientific research, the ancient biblical reports of miracles or spirits appear as anomalous phenomena. They can no longer be explained in terms of the modern paradigm.

UFOs: God's Chariots?

Von Däniken assumes unquestioningly the validity of the naturalistic-scientific way of thinking, so he proceeds to hammer and chisel away at ancient scriptural testimony, to reshape it, and to make it fit the modern paradigm. His ancient alien theology naturalizes all supranatural claims. Von Däniken and his disciples are providing us with a secular theology, a non-religious theology, a theology without belief in God.

7

Ancient Alien Theology

I attended a lecture delivered by Erich von Däniken to an audience of about 4,500 at the University of South Carolina on March 9th, 1976. It was a slide presentation that supposedly gave evidence for his "scientific" theory in which the planet Earth had been visited by extraterrestrial intelligences in the ancient past. He spoke for nearly two hours and then entertained questions for another two hours. The audience was not as indefatigable as he, so by the time he stepped down from the podium to give autographs, only a third of his listeners remained.

What interested me was that nearly three-fourths of the questions raised by the audience were religious in nature. One woman wanted to know if Jesus was from outer space. A fundamentalist-type preacher stood up, Bible in hand, and proclaimed that on judgment day von Däniken would find himself in hell. Von Däniken was attempting to promulgate a scientific theory, but the audience was hearing a new theology. The audience was not interested in science per se. It was concerned about religious beliefs.

One question from the audience could be important in this regard. A man asked what started von Däniken on his search for ancient astronauts. Von Däniken's answer was quick and precise: "Religious doubts." He explained that he had been raised a Roman Catholic but in his later years at a Swiss gymnasium (high school) he found he could no longer accept the Christian faith as it had been told to him. He had read the philosophies of Friedrich Nietzsche and Arthur Schopenhauer, which severely challenged his traditional beliefs; so he set out to find a scientific explanation for Christian doctrines. Ancient astronauts became the answer to his quest.

Have von Däniken's doubts contributed to the development of a new secularized theology? An ancient astronaut theology? Do we find a double mind at work in our culture? On the one hand, we want to believe our ancient traditions, such as the biblical account of our origin. On the other hand, we want to dismiss ancient sacred literature because it's pre-modern, pre-scientific. Can we have both? Yes. All we need to do is adopt the ancient astronaut theory about the origin of the human race and the origin of our belief in the heavenly gods.

At a more subtle level, the ancient astronaut theory leads us to worship science, not the extraterrestrial angels bringing us science. Science—whether terrestrial or extraterrestrial—is responsible for making us who we are. And if there is any hope of redemption, it will come from scientists either on our planet or another planet.

ANCIENT ALIENS AND THE ORIGIN OF OUR GODS

In 2010, the History Channel hosted a widely watched series called *Ancient Aliens*.[1] Now, virtually everyone is familiar with the speculation that Earth has been visited by a more highly advanced extraterrestrial civilization. In addition, this ancient alien visit explains why things are the way they are today. According to the ancient astronaut theorists, extraterrestrials came to Earth with their advanced science and found our ancestors, either primates or early hominids. Extraterrestrial engineering augmented that of our primitive ancestors, which accounts for the Egyptian pyramids, the architecture of the Incas and Aztecs, and the placement of statues on Easter Island, Stonehenge, and numerous other ancient wonders. In addition, alien scientists genetically modified the terrestrials, thereby giving a jump start to the evolution of *Homo sapiens.* We human beings now benefit from alien DNA in our genome.

Accounts of this alleged dramatic event can be found in the petro-glyphs and scriptures of ancient peoples such as those in Sumer, Egypt, and Israel. If, when reading the Bible, we replace references to God or the gods with references to aliens in spacecraft, we will see that it all fits together. Gods and ET are the same, or, alternatively, between us and the inexpressible god is a layer of extraterrestrials, according to the ancient astronaut theorists.

Ancient astronaut theorist Scott Alan Roberts, founder and publisher of *Intrepid Magazine,* reinterprets the Adam and Eve story in Genesis to show how the evolution of the human race was jump-started by an alien. Earth's evolution was moving too slowly, so an ancient astronaut inserted some extraterrestrial DNA. According to Roberts, the serpent in the Garden of Eden was actually a reptilian alien. Eve engaged in sexual intercourse with both the serpent and with Adam, and gave birth to two boys, Cain and Abel. Abel was Adam's progeny. Cain was the hybrid. Cain killed Abel. This meant Cain's genes would survive and provide a DNA boost to the rest of humanity, expanding the genetic distance between primates and humans. "So let's engage in a little gap-filling exercise of our own; the so-called missing link may very well have been DNA provided by visitors from another world."[2]

Established scientists, let alone theologians, would think this is rubbish. Nevertheless, a growing popular view of science includes belief that archaeological and textual evidence support the ancient alien hypothesis. The observation so important to us here in *UFOs: God's Chariots?* is this: Every position in the ancient alien controversy identifies itself as scientific. Science is driven to slake our ontological thirst, to determine our essence by finding our origin.

Philip Coppens summarizes what is at stake in the ancient alien theology: "It is clear that civilization was indeed guided by gods, by a non-human extraterrestrial intelligence. Though today we would consider this to be the bailiwick of religion, it is not; it is about directly experiencing another reality and contacting this intelligence."[3] Again, even though it may appear that science is replacing religion here, it is more accurate to say that science is a re-expression of religion in secular guise. Science has become the modern religion.

Second only to von Däniken in popularity among adepts of the ancient alien theology is the late Zecharia Sitchin (1920–2010). His book, *The Twelfth Planet,* established him as the intellectual leader among reinterpreters of archaeological evidence on behalf of the ancient astronaut hypothesis. Sitchin argued that many of our ancient Hebrew words in the Bible have been mistranslated as referring to the divine; they actually refer to spaceships. Sumerian texts testify that a 12th planet exists in our solar system, and, further, aliens from this planet visiting Earth provided the DNA material that gave the initiative for human evolution. Mysteries surrounding our interpretation of the biblical Nephilim in Genesis 6:4—where the "sons of God" inseminated the "daughters of men"—is now resolved. Sitchin's final book title tells the story in a nutshell: *There Were Giants Upon the Earth: Gods, Demigods, and Human Ancestry: The Evidence of Alien DNA.* Similar to von Däniken, Sitchen's story of origin recasts what were previously religious accounts of origin in the language of the modern scientific worldview. However, his science comes from the stars, not from the local university laboratory.[4]

Today's functional or practical religion is science. Some of us dump traditional religion and substitute science. Others try to translate religion into scientific terms. The latter is the task of the emerging ancient alien theology.

GOD WITHOUT MIRACLES

R.L. Dione, a school teacher from Old Saybrook, Connecticut, has published a couple of tidy tomes titled *God Drives a Flying Saucer* and *Is God Supernatural?*, which might serve as an early version of ancient alien theology.[5] Like von Däniken, he seeks to reinterpret the past from the standpoint of space-age presuppositions. In Dione's case, the past is the Bible, and the presupposition is that flying saucers or UFOs are piloted by humanoid creatures from outer space.

After attempting to prove that flying saucers are real and need to be taken seriously, Dione affirms that UFOs visited Earth during biblical times as well as in modern times. He claims that the occupants of flying saucers are responsible for the Scriptures, prophecies, and miracles that are so important to the Christian religion. God, he argues, is not *supernatural* but rather *supertechnological,* and is capable of producing all acts hitherto attributed to miraculous powers by technical-mechanical means. God is really a humanoid creature living on another planet who made himself immortal through technology and has created the human race on Earth in order to watch our evolution for his own entertainment.[6]

Dione seems compelled to translate everything in our religious tradition that hints of the supernatural into naturalistic terms. His own credo is a stern faith in natural science, and he maintains that miracles, Christian or otherwise, break no laws of nature. We will realize that miracles can never occur as soon as science has understood all the laws of nature. God is a technician, not a magician.[7]

On the inside cover page of Dione's *Is God Supernatural? The 4,000 Year Misunderstanding* the daring purpose of the book is announced:

> *This is a book on religion (in complete accord with the Scriptures) which never once resorts to mystical, magical or supernatural explanations of anything; and which attacks, with complete candor, the most battling concepts of religious doctrine, stripping them once and for all of their aura of mystery.*

Although it appears that Jesus healed the crippled and the blind, what really happened, according to Dione, was that extraterrestrials had previously hypnotized certain people (so that their infirmities were psychosomatic) and programmed them to respond to Jesus at a posthypnotic suggestion. The Bible records visits of supernatural beings known as angels, but they were really messengers from outer space who were trying to influence the course of human affairs according to God's interplanetary directives. With regard to the Virgin Mary—who was undoubtedly a virgin at Jesus' birth—the angel Gabriel was a biological specialist who artificially inseminated the Mother of God with a hypodermic needle. The semen, of course, came from the supertechnological deity somewhere in the outer reaches of space.

The apparition of Our Lady of Fatima in 1917 can be explained, says Dione, as a UFO hovering above the ground, shedding a mist that gave it a luminous glow, and then communicating telepathic messages calling the people of Portugal to repentance and faith.

Dione works laboriously to reinterpret what are usually referred to as miracles in the Bible so that they come out natural rather than supernatural. God and UFOs both belong within the pale of the natural world we understand through reason. He even says the Bible supports him in this because the Bible did not employ the concept of the supernatural. "So ingrained are we with the false assumption that God is supernatural that many will be shocked to learn that God's scribes never used the meaningless word."[8]

Dione is correct, of course; the Bible did not have a concept of the supernatural. But what Dione neglects to observe is that the Bible had no corresponding concept of the "natural" either. The concept of nature—meaning that the universe operates according to a set of impersonal laws, without divine intervention—is a modern concept. It has its roots in the Greek philosophers and medieval theologians who emphasized the role of divine reason in the world. The modern concept of nature is still more recent, developing only after the Renaissance, when the role of God in ordinary affairs was deleted completely by the Western intellectual mind. Unless you have a concept of the natural that excludes God, then it makes no sense to speak of God as supernatural.

The Bible, in contrast to the modern world, saw God involved in everything. The clouds would not rain nor the sun shine unless directed by the will of God. If we could picture God as an ancient, such as Saint Augustine did, God would be saying to the sun just before dawn, "Okay, get up and do it again today!" Miracles were seen as the hand of God at work in someone's personal life in a special way. They were wondrous and amazing. However, traditionally, miracles were not supranatural in the modern, beyond-nature sense. Yet, Dione thinks that if he can naturalize miracles, then he can rout traditional supranaturalist religion.

Such naturalistic thinking leaves us with only two choices. We may simply embrace the naturalistic mind-set and jettison the concept of God altogether. This is what atheists do. Or, we may try to recast the image of God so that he becomes part and parcel of the natural world. One way to do this might be to speak of God as a humanoid from an extraterrestrial civilization that is superior to our own, but still subject to the same basic laws of nature. Von Däniken and Dione seem to be following this route.

THE BIBLE AND FLYING SAUCERS

A more cautious and more sophisticated defense of a von Däniken Dione–type theology is offered by the Reverend Barry Downing in his book *The Bible and Flying Saucers.* Downing is a Presbyterian minister and holds a PhD from the University of Edinburgh. He is a consultant on religion for the mutual UFO Network (MUFON).

It is Downing's contention that the ufonauts deliberately created Judaism and Christianity. The intermediaries whose work stimulated the biblical religion were called "angels." The angels were messengers from another world. They came to Earth in flying saucers to deliver messages sent from Dione's supertechnological deity somewhere in the heavens.

Downing, along with other biblical scholars, recognizes that the beginning of the Hebrew religion occurs with Moses and the Exodus from Egypt, not at creation. The book of Genesis tells us about the world's creation and God's promise to Abraham. Between Abraham and Moses the people lived on that promise. A full-fledged religious tradition, however, did not emerge until after the Ten Commandments were given to Moses at Mt. Sinai en route to the promised land.

It was a UFO in the form of a cloud-by-day and a pillar-of-fire-by-night that led the Hebrew people out of the chains of slavery in Egypt

(Exodus 13:21). Some flying saucers seen today are described as cigar-shaped. Standing on end, one could appear as a cloud pillar during daylight hours, and glowing at night, it could certainly appear as fire.

But because a UFO as a mechanical device can be understood only by us in a modern technological society, it is no wonder these ancient people lacked the vocabulary to give it its proper label. "There is no reason to expect Biblical people to call a flying saucer a flying saucer even if they saw one," writes Downing. "'Cloud' is the Bible's 'short' form for some sort of space vehicle which seems to look and operate very much like modern flying saucers."[9]

The ancient astronaut theory offers a great deal toward reinterpreting what happened at the Red Sea in such a way as to remove every shred of the miraculous. According to the orthodox version of the story, the Hebrew slaves left Egypt and were fleeing Pharaoh's cavalry and chariots, who were in hot pursuit behind them. Their escape appeared blocked when they arrived at the banks of the Red Sea. But Moses, following the Lord's directives, stretched out his rod. Miraculously the sea parted, and the Israelites passed through on dry land. Pharaoh's army was less fortunate. The chariots got stuck in the mud, trapping the soldiers as the waters inundated the army. Yes, God intervened, Downing admits, but it was not a miracle. It was a UFO.

Downing says a UFO parted the waters with the beam from an anti-gravity (anti-G) device. Many ufologists hypothesize that if flying saucers are in fact mechanical spacecraft, then they must have some sort of autonomous gravity system that permits them to perform amazing flight patterns within Earth's atmosphere, apparently free from the influence of Earth's gravity. The anti-gravity hypothesis is a favorite speculation among UFO buffs. Downing argues, "If a UFO were to hover over the body of water which the Israelites were to cross, and if it were to apply a sufficiently strong anti-G beam to the area, which the Israelites desired to cross, the water would quite probably be forced back."[10]

Dione agrees with Downing that UFOs are responsible for both the cloud and the Red Sea parting, but he says that static electricity was employed rather than an anti-G beam. Dione argues that static electricity draws water, so the UFO guiding the Israelites simply drew water vapor around itself, giving it a cloudy, luminous appearance. The same principle accounts for the parting of the sea waters. Dione says two gigantic, cylindrical UFOs submerged themselves in the bottom of the Red Sea, parallel to, and 10 to 15 yards apart from each other. Their charges drew water to them, forming two mounds of water and, in return, leaving a vacated pathway between the two.

Both Dione and Downing agree that Moses was in communication with the pilot of the UFO. Downing describes how Moses went alone to the top of Mt. Sinai to converse with the being in the "cloud." He came back down with God's law. Downing says that before Sinai the Israelites had almost no religious tradition except for the promise given to Abraham by angels. But after Sinai they had the fundamentals of a religion, which has now been practiced for more than 3,000 years.

> *If the Mosaic tradition accurately describes events that happened in history, and if flying saucers exist, then I think we can be fairly certain that beings in a UFO quite similar to—if not identical to—a flying saucer were the immediate cause behind the Old Testament religion. This proves neither that God was working in the Old Testament nor that the lie was not working in the Old Testament. We have shown that many of the fantastic things reported in the Old Testament apparently happened in much the way as the Bible has reported them. The Old Testament may have a fairly high degree of scientific accuracy.[11]*

With regard to the New Testament, as one might predict, Downing emphasizes how often Jesus said he was "not of this world." In John 6:42 Jesus supposedly said, "I am come down from heaven." In John 8:23 Jesus tells his disciples, "You are from below, I am from above; you are of this world, I am not of this world." Downing says that Jesus came to our world from another planet in order to perform a mission. When it had been accomplished he returned to that world above in a "cloud," that is, in a UFO.

Jesus' birth was sufficiently irregular to suggest the influence of UFOs. An angel, Gabriel, is said to have visited Mary prior to the birth (Luke

1:26). Recall that Dione said Gabriel was a biological specialist who artificially inseminated Mary with semen from a stud in outer space. This accounts for both the virgin birth and Jesus' claim that his father was in heaven. He chose to enter our world through birth rather than to land publicly in a spaceship so that fewer people would suspect that Jesus was different. Downing pictures Jesus' career in terms of a spy working undercover. "I cannot help thinking here that Jesus is portrayed in the Bible in much the same way as our modern-day 'spy' stories. Jesus came from a foreign world into our world and started to gather together a small band of people who would owe their allegiance to his world (heaven). Jesus is really an 'undercover agent.'"[12]

Jesus' resurrection from the dead and ascension into heaven similarly required UFO aid. There was an earthquake associated with the crucifixion and resurrection of Jesus. Downing speculates that this was caused by the arrival of the angels in their UFO. The ship's anti-G beam may have caused a disturbance similar to that which occurred at the Red Sea. Somehow the angels raised Jesus from the dead and, work done, were calmly sitting there to be seen by Mary Magdalene and the other women who arrived at the tomb Easter morning. Later, Jesus ascended into the heavens via—you guessed it—the cloud-shaped UFO.

Of course when the Bible talks of resurrection from the dead it does not refer only to the resurrection of Jesus. All the faithful will be raised from their graves on judgment day, on the day when we will see "the Son of man coming in a cloud with power and great glory." Downing is not precisely clear on exactly how resurrection from death will be accomplished, but then neither is the Bible. Downing emphasizes that our resurrection is scheduled to occur at the second coming of Christ. He quotes part of the popular passage describing the so-called Rapture (1 Thessalonians 4:17), and says that those who have been raised from the dead will be forcefully taken "in the clouds to meet the Lord in the air."[13] Presumably, flying saucers will be employed to catch us "in the air."

Downing's revisionist biblical history can incorporate the abduction phenomenon. "Abduction images are also part of the biblical story. After all, Elijah was taken up into the sky—abducted—never to return, and likewise Jesus was taken up in a 'cloud,' never to return."[14] The spiritual and the secular find a most curious betrothal in the UFO phenomenon. It is a relationship fraught with tension, however. Downing apologizes: "I realize this point of view is inconvenient for both religious tradition-alists and for scientists who do not want religion mixed with their UFO research."[15]

When it comes to the relationship between science and religion, Downing deliberately treats the religious concept of the divine as a sub-ject for scientific inquiry. "The God hypothesis ought to be seen as a legitimate scientific hypothesis.... There is no logical reason why God might not be the ultimate cause of UFO events."[16] On the one hand, he has reinterpreted biblical reports about God in terms of UFOs. Now, he reinterprets contemporary reports of UFOs in terms of God.

Reverend Downing is clearly the most sophisticated UFO theologian we will examine in this book. He likes to distinguish his own theory from those advocated by von Däniken and Dione. The Presbyterian cler-gyman says he agrees with von Däniken that the biblical religion was started by beings from another world, but he disagrees with the thesis that these beings were misidentifications of the one God of the universe. For von Däniken, our religion is more or less an accident, whereas for Downing it is the deliberate work of God. Downing also disagrees with Dione's assertion that God is merely a finite supertechnological human-oid. He accepts as true the statement of John 1:18, "No one has ever seen God."[17]

Similar to von Däniken and Dione, however, Downing wants to make the religion of the Bible palatable to modern naturalistic and sci-entific tastes. He accepts all the rules appropriate to scientific procedure. He wishes to make observations with an open, unbiased mind and allow only evidence to guide the observer into constructing the most probable explanation. He feels he cannot read the Bible having already decided in advance that flying saucers had nothing to do with its contents. He argues that one must at least be open to the possibility of a UFO influence on

Jewish and Christian religion in order to conduct an objective examination of the data.

The religious problem, of course, is that our modern naturalistic system of beliefs makes the Bible appear to be an outdated book of atavistic mythology. "Science will no longer let us believe in angels, or in miracles, or in the Ascension of Christ."[18] Downing says it is intellectually dishonest for Christians to continue to support the orthodox Christian interpretation of the biblical materials as reports of supernatural events.

But rather than write off religion and forget it, Downing seeks to defend its veracity. He does so by reinterpreting the Bible in terms of UFOs. The result, he hopes, will be a new naturalistic theology that is acceptable to the modern scientific mind-set. Unless Christian doctrines can be recast into concepts compatible with modern thought, religious faith will be dismissed. UFOs may be our last hope. "If flying saucers do not exist, then much theology will probably continue its present course which leads down the road to the death of God."[19]

I concur with Downing that today's theologians must interpret the ancient Bible in light of our contemporary worldview, especially our scientific way of understanding the natural world. Yet, in my judgment, the attempt to explain the textured and symbolic language of ancient scripture in terms of nuts 'n' bolts craft visiting us from the stars fails to meet the standards of the best science. Downing risks the kind of reduction implied in a remark by author and actor William Bramley: "The bottom line is that Christianity in all its guises and incarnations is just a UFO cult."[20]

FALLACIOUS REASONING?

The ancient astronaut theory has its critics. Anthropologist Kenneth Feder, for example, criticizes the ancient astronaut believers for undervaluing the intelligence of our ancestors in creating their respective civilizations. To attribute ancient architectural achievements to space architects, for example, fails to recognize how smart our human race was at that time. "To assume that the achievements of ancient humanity were made by visitors from outer space is to grossly underestimate the intelligence and capabilities of our ancestors and to ignore the enormously fascinating actual archaeological record."[21]

On the one hand, I would agree with Feder that ancient astronaut theorists underestimate the intelligence of our terrestrial ancestors. On the other hand, I offer a different criticism of ancient astronaut believers. My criticism begins with the observation that human civilization—especially at the city-state stage, where architecture and technology can be examined by us—is uneven around the world. For example, we find pyramids in Egypt and pyramids in Mesoamerica, however, we find the wheel in Egypt and no wheel in Central America. It is utterly unfathomable to think that a common source would deliver the wheel to one continent and not to the other. In addition, one might ask: If the aliens were so smart, why did they not bless our human ancestors with electricity?

Much more plausible than the extraterrestrial hypothesis is the assumption that each civilization developed or failed to develop at its own pace with its own history of discovery and organization. In many cases, evidence exists that tells us the history of each civilization, and these histories seem quite adequate without appeal to any extraterrestrial influences.

Some critics of ancient astronaut theorists like to sneer. Included among the sneerers is skeptic Michael Shermer, a writer for *Scientific American* magazine. He accuses ancient alienists of committing the fallacy of *argumentum ad ignorantiam,* the argument from ignorance. Logicians agree that it is fallacious to argue that because we are ignorant of alternative explanations, our own explanation is automatically correct. Because of ignorance regarding who built the Egyptian pyramids, ancient astronaut theorists conclude that they must have been built by aliens from space. However, argues Shermer, we are not ignorant. We know how the pyramids were built. The tools for their construction have been discovered at the quarries, and descriptions of the construction appear inside the pyramids. This knowledge applies to the Nazca lines of Peru, the Easter Island statues, and all other such evidence appealed to by ancient astronaut theorists. I concur with Shermer that such existing evidence suffices, making appeal the to extraterrestrial visitation superfluous.

We have seen Erich von Däniken commit this fallacy. However, it is not obvious to me that *argumentum ad ignoratniam* is the fallacy most frequently committed by ancient astronaut theorists. They are aware of the evidence Shermer musters; they simply don't believe what passes as accepted scientific explanations for ancient artifacts. They substitute appeal to visitors from space to replace standard views common to the scientific establishment. UFO science is science, simply renegade or maverick science.

In my own judgment, ancient astronaut theorists commit a different fallacy: They violate the principle of parsimony. Or, to say it another way, they don't shave with Occam's razor. This logical razor is named after medieval theologian William of Occam. According to this principle embraced by scientists and philosophers alike, reasonable people presume the following: When we are confronted with two competing explanations, we should prefer the simpler one. Explanatory factors should not be unnecessarily multiplied. Applied here it looks like this: We have pyramids, and we have knowledge regarding the dates of their construction. We know that ancient Egyptians existed and we know they claim to have built the pyramids. We do not know for certain that aliens from space exist, so to appeal to space aliens unnecessarily multiplies unconfirmed factors. To explain the construction of the pyramids as the actions of the Egyptians is the simpler explanation and, hence, the preferred choice. This principle of parsimony applies to numerous other cases appealed to by ancient astronaut theorists.

If we look more closely at Shermer's application of the wrong fallacy, we might uncover another motive on Shermer's part, namely, to criticize the Intelligent Design school in the debate over evolution. "Ancient aliens arguments from ignorance resemble intelligent design 'God of the gaps' arguments: wherever a gap in scientific knowledge exists, there is evidence of divine design. In this way, ancient aliens serve as small 'g' gods of the archaeological gaps, with the same shortcoming as the gods of the evolutionary gaps—the holes are already filled or soon will be, and then whence goes your theory?"[22] To summarize, Shermer argues that Intelligent Design (ID) critics of Darwinian evolution commit the god-of-the-gaps fallacy, therefore, so do the ancient astronaut theorists.

We note a few things here. First, Shermer argues from analogy: Because ID advocates fill in their ignorance with appeals to the god-of-the-gaps, so do the ancient astronaut theorists. Second, ID advocates claim the gaps should be filled in with intelligent design, implying that God is the designer, whereas ancient astronaut theorists replace ancient myths about gods with claims about visitors from outer space.

Might Shermer himself be committing the fallacy of *argumentum ad hominem* (circumstantial)? It looks like it, and here is why: Shermer argues that because ID advocates commit the fallacy of *argumentum ad ignorantiam*—and because we can dismiss ID for filling in nonexistent scientific gaps with belief in God as the designer—it follows that ancient astronaut theorists may be dismissed for the same reason. Or to say it another way, because we in the scientific community do not like ID advocates, we will not like ancient astronaut theorists either. On the street corner, this fallacy is called "name-calling." Should Shermer wish to avoid fallacious reasoning, he could simply supply confirmable evidence to refute the claims made of each school—Intelligent Design and ancient astronaut theory—to provide positive evidence that supports his superior theory.

What is important in this discussion is that both establishment scientists and ancient astronaut theorists, right along with UFO aficionados in general, all belong to a culture that reveres science. All parties celebrate science. All of us want to think scientifically. Even if establishment scientists want to exclude UFO believers from sharing their barbecues, honest observation would show that a single scientized mindset is shared by all conversants.

CAN RELIGION BECOME FULLY SCIENTIZED?

What is startling about the claims of von Däniken and other would-be ancient alien theologians is that they actually humanize and trivialize

God. They make natural what we believe to be supernatural. They make physical what we accept as spiritual. They say that what we once thought to be extraordinary is really ordinary.

In their view, the Ark of the Covenant was awesome not because of its spiritual power but because of its electrical power. Moses did not pray to a God who had created the entire universe and whose infinite being was present everywhere in it—von Däniken says Moses prayed instead to a single individual space visitor in a high-altitude flying saucer by means of a walkie-talkie radio. Electricity and radios we understand; spiritual power and prayer we do not. How great it is to have a Bible that is now believable because we have found the key for translating its mysteries into concepts we can understand!

Science and religion can now become friends, according to this particular UFO theology. In the past, scientists have accused religious people of simply making up the idea of a God in order to provide an emotionally soothing explanation for things we could not otherwise explain. The idea of a God who created our world and the belief that the angels are watching and caring for us was said to be the fabrication of an insecure unconscious. We were told that mystery leads people to superstition and religion, but now that science is explaining away many mysteries, we no longer have any need for superstition and religion. Science used to look down on religion as primitive and out of date. Now, however, followers of UFO theology can triumphantly claim that the idea of God is not a product of our unconscious wishes and imaginations; our idea of God was revealed to us by space beings. In fact, it was through a marriage of these superscientific visitors with prehuman beasts on Earth that we have the intelligence common to our species today. This is recorded in the Bible, in Genesis 6, albeit in a form difficult to interpret correctly. We are children, not of a supernatural God, but of space travelers who continue to watch over us with electronic surveillance from their flying saucers—something like the FBI and CIA. Religion was given to us; we did not make it up. And, further, religion has found a way to explain itself without resorting to miracles or anything else supernatural.

But if we adopt such an ancient alien theology, will all the distinctively religious questions be resolved? I suggest that UFO theology has kicked up a lot of dust, but when that dust settles we will see that it has simply pushed some religious questions about transcendent reality back another step.

Paul Tillich, the renowned Protestant theologian, said that when the 5-year-old child asks, "Where did the sky come from?" he or she is asking a religious question. It is religious because it questions the source of all reality, the ground of all being. This basic question about the ultimate ground of all things is finally—whether the asker knows it or not—the question of God. In the past more sophisticated people than our 5-year-old child have asked about the first cause or source of all things. For example, they asked if things in our world today are in motion, and if things that move must be caused to move by other moving things, then somewhere some time ago was there an unmoved mover? Someone or something originally set things in motion. Aristotle and St. Thomas said it was God.

If Tillich is correct—that questions about the ultimate ground of all reality are religious questions—then many such questions remain after the UFO theologians are done. For example, if the ancient astronauts created human intelligence on earth, who originally gave intelligence to them? If these ancient extraterrestrial visitors gave us our religion (as Downing claims), where did they get it? Where did the sky with all its stars and planets come from in the first place? The question of the first cause or source of all things may have been extended in time and space, but it still remains.

The God of the Bible ought not to be confused with either his angels or his alleged astronauts. This God is the origin and destiny of the entire cosmos, the alpha and the omega of all things. Hence, even if extraterrestrial humanoids do in fact exist, they are saddled with the same basic religious concerns that we have. They will necessarily be finite creatures brought into being at the will of the one infinite creator.

FROM SCIENCE TO SYMBOL...ALMOST

Pertinent to our discussion is the creative theoretical work of Jacques Vallee. What Vallee brings to the subject of UFOs is sensitivity, nuance, texture, and the courage to move beyond the limits of conventional thinking. He recognizes that the current scientific model for understanding UFOs has its limits, and he is willing to indulge in speculation regarding the role being played by symbol, myth, and religion. Vallee offers a thought experiment: Instead of the extraterrestrial hypothesis why not consider an extra-dimensional hypothesis? Instead of ETI, might our visitors represent extra-dimensional intelligence (EDI)?

For this creative thinking he must be congratulated. However, as he proceeds in his analysis, Vallée's actual method differs very little from that of von Däniken and the other UFO theologians. He inadvertently superimposes the modern scientific mindset upon religious phenomena, a mindset that he not-so-secretly plans on defending to the bitter end. This prevents a full-fledged breakthrough.

Vallée sees himself as moving away from the extraterrestrial hypothesis and toward a parallel universe or paranormal hypothesis. He wants to move from the physical to the psychical dimension of UFOs. Extra-dimensionality replaces extra-terrestriality. Otherwise, his method remains unchanged.

> ...I believe that the UFO phenomenon represents evidence for other dimensions beyond spacetime; the UFOs may not come from ordinary space, but from a multiverse which is all around us.... [UFO] manifestations cannot be spacecraft in the ordinary nuts-and-bolts sense. The UFOs are physical manifestations that simply cannot be understood apart from their psychic and symbolic reality. What we see here is not an alien invasion. It is a spiritual system that acts on humans and uses humans.[23]

What Vallee believes he is doing is changing the location for UFO origin. Rather than from outer space, he suggests UFOs come from a space-time dimension that parallels yet co-inhabits with the one we experience here on earth. According to Vallée, UFOs constitute "windows," so to speak, whereby communication is shared between parallel dimensions. What I believe Vallée is actually doing is incorporating religious testimony into a scientized metaphysics.

Vallée's method compares contemporary UFO experiences with premodern reports of fairies and elves. He finds remarkable similarities among them: light symbolism, communication, abductions, and so on. In addition to fairy stories, Vallée occasionally includes religious phenomena, such as Ezekiel's apparition of the wheel within a wheel (Ezekiel 1); the appearance of the Virgin Mary to Juan Diego at Guadalupe in 1531 and to Bernadette Soubiroux at Lourdes in 1858; Joseph Smith's vision of the angel Moroni in 1823; and the miracle at Fatima in 1917. After examining all the various wrinkles in these reports, Vallee irons them out neatly so they all have the same flat appearance: They are UFO cases.

The mechanism of the apparitions, in legendary, historical, and modern times, is standard and follows the model of religious miracles. Several cases, which bear the official stamp of the Catholic Church (such as those in Fatima and Guadalupe), are—if one applies the definitions strictly—nothing more than UFO phenomena where the entity has delivered a message having to do with religious beliefs rather than with space or engineering.[24]

In the academic world this is known as *reductionism*, the premature reduction of something complex and outside one's sphere of understanding into something simple and manageable. Vallée is encouraged to look for possible connections between UFOs and past religious miracles, but to conclude so quickly that reports of past miracles can be reduced without remainder to UFO sightings is a bit premature, to say the least. Yet this is the method that typifies what I am calling UFO theology.

What Vallée has accomplished by this, in his own mind, is to challenge the bulk of contemporary UFO researchers who are anxious to find an explanation for UFOs that fits the paradigm of materialist science. Most UFO researchers want to find a nuts-and-bolts spacecraft that transports intelligent entities from one solar system to another, much as our rocket ships transport our astronauts. Vallée argues that many UFO reports simply do not fit this model. Many reports include psychic phenomena, telepathic communication, religious messages, and prophecies of future events. To handle such things we need to turn to the realm of myth, symbol, and even religion.

Yet, even with this insight, Vallée cannot seem to make the break from standard science. He wants to examine the religious qualities of the UFO phenomenon, but he wants to do so strictly from within the safety zone of science. He asks us to engage in open-minded expansion of rational thought, that is, he wants science to grow but to remain science in the process.

> *Although the UFO phenomenon is highly complex and stretches the boundaries of the scientific method, I am not prepared to abandon the rational approach to knowledge for conclusions based on faith, intuition, or the alleged messages received by "channels" and contactees.... We have a rare opportunity to improve scientific techniques and to glimpse beyond the limits of ordinary reality.*[25]

Vallée's loyalty to the scientific conceptual set is tenacious, almost fanatical. Genuine religion comes to him as a threat. For Vallée to get caught up in "faith" or "intuition" represents getting lost in an eddy of intellectual chaos. He protects himself from such chaos by never leaving the security of his fenced-in existence. He appears to be brave when he challenges other scientific types to come out of their respective backyards to entertain the possibility of a connection with religion, but then he retreats immediately to his own. I picture him as a restless prisoner who finds the door to his cell unlocked. He opens it, but rather than walk through it to freedom, he remains inside and rattles the bars.

Vallee's scientific parochialism, along with a borderline paranoia, becomes obvious when we ask: Just who or what is behind the UFO phenomenon? Recall that for Dione and Downing it was God, albeit their God was a trimmed-down and scientized version of the ancient belief in same.[26] But there is no mention of God at all in the Vallée theory. Instead, those responsible for the UFO phenomenon are super-technologists who are bent upon manipulating the human race through influencing our culture and our thought patterns. Vallée seems to assume they are non-benevolent realities who are seeking to control human behavior by provoking our curiosity and then confusing us with mixed messages. They lie. They deceive. They are, in fact, masters of deception.[27] Most importantly, Vallée simply cannot give up working with the idea that somehow, despite all the psychic and paranormal dimensions to the phenomenon that he recognizes, behind it all, lies some sort of advanced technology.

> I am not regarding the phenomenon of the UFOs as the unknowable, uncontrollable game of a higher order of beings.... Everything works as if the phenomenon were the product of a technology that followed well-defined rules and patterns, though fantastic by ordinary human standards.[28]

Although Vallée differs from the other UFO theologians in that he does not want to use the term *God* or *gods* to describe those responsible for UFOs, what he has in common with them is the theory that they are a scientized and technologized race who perform apparent miracles for the purpose of communication.

REINTRODUCING THE RELIGIOUS DIMENSION

Vallee believes the issue is whether or not UFOs come to us from outer space. He answers no. Most people associate UFOs with ETI. Vallée believes he is revolutionizing UFO research by turning our attention away from the extraterrestrial hypothesis toward a co-terrestrial or parater-restrial dimension.[29] It is my judgment, however, that this is at best a side issue. It does not even account for what is most valuable in Vallée's work. Vallée's greatest contribution, I think, is his demonstration of the inadequacy of the model of the research scientist and the opening of UFO investigation toward the religious qualities of the phenomenon. Even though Vallée does not walk through the door he has opened, we will in this book.

Vallée is less reductionist than debunkers or skeptics. It is the position of the late Carl Sagan, for example, that interest in UFOs derives from "unfulfilled religious needs. Flying saucers serve, for some, to replace the gods that science has deposed."[30] What Sagan does not take seriously, of course, is that religious needs might be important. Nor does he consider the possibility that something might be wrong with modern science if it fails to meet these needs. Sagan's remark may be more an indictment of modern science than of the gods that science has deposed.

The reductionist thesis is advanced as well by philosopher Paul Kurtz, a prominent figure in the Committee for the Scientific Investigation of Claims of the Paranormal in Buffalo, New York, which publishes the *Skeptical Inquirer*. In a lengthy philosophical book, *Transcendental Temptation*, Kurtz advances what he calls "scientific humanism." In the process he blasts away mercilessly at Christianity, Judaism, Islam, and anything that even remotely smells religious. Included in his attack is a diatribe against UFOs. The problem with UFOs and their accompanying extraterrestrial hypothesis, he says, is that they smack of religion.

We have no decisive proof, no hard corroboration evidence, that UFOs are extraterrestrial...UFOlogy is the mythology of the space age. Rather than angels dancing on the heads of pins, we now have spacecraft and extraterrestrials. It is the product of the creative imagination. It serves a poetic and existential function. It seeks to give man deeper roots and bearings in the universe. It is an expression of our hunger for mystery, our demand for something more, our hope for transcendental meaning. The gods of Mt. Olympus have been transformed into space voyagers, transporting us by our dreams to other realms.[31]

Kurtz is much more reductionist than Vallée. Kurtz assumes that UFOs can be reduced to mere human fantasy, to the product of our dreams. He is not willing to treat UFOs as a phenomenon, as a complex that includes what is perceived as well as the perceiver. Kurtz assumes he can get away with this as long as he assumes that everything religious is by definition the sole product of human subjectivity. Yet, there is much truth in what Kurtz says, despite his unnecessarily hostile attitude. Yes, indeed, we humans seek "deeper roots and bearings in the universe." Yes, indeed, UFOs seem to bear many of the qualities once possessed by the Olympian gods—qualities that we moderns are denied enjoying because modern science has prohibited it.

In sum, we have seen in this chapter how theoreticians try to make direct religious judgments regarding the nature of UFOs. Some have a very positive appreciation for UFOs. Others are skeptical and dismiss them completely. In all cases, unfortunately, the people we have studied (with the possible exception of Barry Downing) seem to be quite ignorant regarding the breadth and subtlety of the nature of religion and human spirituality. They operate completely out of a scientific conceptual set, making them unable to understand sympathetically just what is going on. They fail to recognize the translucent quality of religious symbols that remind us of the abiding presence of transcendent reality. They fail to understand that when the human spirit prompts questions regarding ultimate reality, they must come to expression in symbolic form, and, furthermore, that this prompting is the stimulus of ultimate reality working within the human spirit.

Conclusion

After the first edition of *UFOs: God's Chariots?* was published, I received numerous invitations to appear on radio and television talk shows. On one occasion, von Däniken and I debated one another on a Detroit radio station. On another occasion, I was interviewed by Pat Robertson on his television broadcast, *The 700 Club*. One caller asked me, "Dr. Peters, was Elijah actually picked up and taken to heaven by a flying saucer rather than by a fiery chariot?" I heard myself saying something I had not predicted I would say. I cited 2 Kings 2:11: "A chariot of fire and horses of fire separated the two of them, and Elijah ascended in a whirlwind into heaven." Then I added, "If the Bible says it was a chariot of fire, then I wonder: Could it have been a chariot of fire?"

8

Model III: The Celestial Savior

From what has been said thus far, we can see that the model of our extraterrestrial visitors as scientific researchers gives way at certain points to a more religious interpretation, and it occasionally gives way to the ritual abuse model (the fourth model). In this chapter we will deal with the third model, the Celestial Savior model.

Although most discussions of the UFO-ETH are cast in scientific terms, many descriptions of UFO experiences carry considerable religious or spiritual overtones. If God's heaven has been traditionally thought of as "up there," and if "up there" now refers to stars and planets, and if beings from planets in Earth's heavens are now visiting us, does this mean the ufonauts are divine? Or, if the teachings of our space visitors have mystical dimensions or transformatory power, might they connote the ancient concept of the gnostic redeemer? Is the ancient myth of "saving knowledge descending from the heavenly realm of light" alive and well in today's UFO phenomenon? This is the question we will explore in this chapter. Let's start with the scientific dimension and watch how it morphs into the religious dimension.

From Science to Salvation

Let's begin this section with two UFO experiences and then move to analysis. The first experience is the Jim Moroney case. It begins with the model of the Research Scientist and then drifts over into our next model, the Celestial Savior.

This account was not from Moroney's active memory, but rather his forgotten memory accessed through hypnotic regression. Moroney says that at 2 a.m. on the morning of August 9, 1987, he pulled his truck into Deacon's Corner Truck Stop outside of Winnipeg, Manitoba, in Canada to take a nap. However, he was interrupted by a presence accompanied by a paralyzing fear, a foreboding. He could not move his mouth. He could not scream. He unlocked the truck door to exit and found himself being dragged into the interior of something hovering just above his truck cab. "Inside a circular, amphitheatre-type of room with tiered steps," he saw "six stoic, identical-looking beings, all dressed in a kind of uniform. They had the typical large heads that many contactees have described, and stood about 4-and-a-half feet tall. They stared intently at me with large, blue eyes."

As the story unfolds, Moroney interprets a "blast of light" in terms of a "decontamination chamber." He reports that he was given a physical examination by these apparently extraterrestrial scientists wearing "what looked like white lab coats." They could speak to him in "perfect English." After the ordeal was over and he found himself relaxed, he said there was a tremendous sense of relief and sudden "salvation."[1]

Just a quick and dirty analysis will unmask the structure of a secularized religious experience: the blast of light signifies enlightenment of the gnostic type, the decontamination chamber signifies ritual purification, the "perfect" in "perfect English" hints at omnipotence, and the lab coats signify that advanced science is redemptive. Regardless of the objective nature of whatever prompted Moroney's close encounter of the fourth kind, his interpretive structure is that of the Research Scientist combined with the Celestial Savior.

Moroney reports that it took hypnotic regression to release his forgotten memories. Let's give some attention for a moment to hypnotic regression as an investigative technique. This now-common technique begins with the Betty and Barney Hill abduction of 1962 that was discussed earlier in this book. You'll recall how Boston psychiatrist Benjamin Simon employed hypnotic regression to retrieve the forgotten memories of Mr. and Mrs. Hill. Less important than the content of the Hills' report was the method for retrieving their testimony. By 1980 numerous psychologists had adopted the method for other purposes, such as uncovering forgotten memories of childhood sexual abuse and Satanic ritual abuse. In the early years of that decade, almost daily stories of child abuse made headlines. Adults realized for the first time that, as children, they had suffered from abuse either by their parents or by Satan worshippers. The method of hypnotic regression became the tool for uncovering horrid stories of torture, rape, and desecration. No such childhood abuse is reported in the Moroney case, but the method of retrieving forgotten memories is the same.

For a second illustrative case, we turn to John Mack's study of abductions, also employing hypnotic regression. Thirty-four-year-old Joe provides a more obvious example of the research scientist becoming the celestial savior. During his abduction, Joe was placed on a table by the research scientist from space. The alien touched Joe. *This guy really loves me*, Joe said to himself. Then Joe described the touching in terms of a religious experience. "He's putting his hands on my head. It's like he's baptizing me. He likes me—he's energizing me. He's blessing me. He's giving me something to help me hang in here...he's giving me strength and knowing, just knowing that I'm not alone. I'm loved, and I'm connectable with both them and on Earth."[2]

These are concrete examples. Now let's turn to a more abstract analysis of the celestial savior and the ETI myth.

THE ETI MYTH

There is one way to describe the dominant conceptual set at work in both our wider culture and in our scientific subculture: We live within an ETI myth. It does not look like a myth because it is cast in scientific language, yet it still works like myth because it provides the unquestioned assumptions within which we interpret strange experiences such as UFO experiences. The myth is virtually invisible for those of us who live within it, just as the water in a fish bowl is virtually invisible to goldfish.

What is the ETI myth? In short, it is the belief that extraterrestrial intelligent beings exist; that at least some extraterrestrial beings are more advanced in evolution and technological progress; and that when ETI share their advancements with us, on Earth we will be healed and improved and made better. It is a belief without any direct empirical evidence to support it. Yet, it is such a potent belief that it motivates space research and our interpretation of the UFO phenomenon.

Now, where did this myth come from? How did it arise? This should be no mystery. Ask yourself how often you have thought—or have you heard someone say—extraterrestrials must be more advanced than we are. This idea is so common that we seldom ask what it presumes and implies.

The logic seems so plausible. Here on Earth we have been able to fly for only a century, and able to leave our planet's atmosphere in rockets for only a half century or so. We still cannot ferry human astronauts to other planets or moons within our solar system, let alone to an exoplanet elsewhere in our galaxy. Our technology is not advanced enough. But, if ufonauts can make it here, they must have a more advanced technology. In fact, their science and their technology must be far superior to ours.

How did the spacelings get ahead of us? Perhaps they had more time to advance. Perhaps they had millions or billions of years of more time to evolve, progress, develop their intelligence, and accomplish technological feats that would blow our minds. We imagine that UFO crews have gained control over gravity or propel their craft at speeds exceeding that of light. Perhaps their scientific and technological evolution has attained levels of perfection that await us if we could borrow it or receive its benefits. In short, evolution throughout long periods of time brings progress, genius, and advancement.

Model III: The Celestial Savior

We cannot overestimate the formative role that the concept of evolution plays among scientists as well as the wider culture. Do not be misled by the controversy involving creationism, intelligent design, and atheism. This controversy notwithstanding, evolution has become so integrated into our culture that we all think from within an evolutionary paradigm. "The story of cosmic evolution [is] the metanarrative of educated people," observes sociologist of religion Robert Bellah.[3]

The concept of evolution is by no means restricted to speciation among living organisms as it was for Charles Darwin. Now, it encompasses all that is real. It is cosmic. According to Steven Dick and James Strick, "The idea of cosmic evolution implies a continuous evolution of the constituent parts of the cosmos from its origins to the present...the entire universe is evolving...all of its parts are connected and interact, and...this evolution applies not only to inert matter but also to life, intelligence, and even culture."[4]

The key to understanding the concept of evolution is progress, the belief that evolution in nature has a built-in direction or purpose that guides living things toward increased complexity and intelligence. "Everything evolves," is a cardinal SETI doctrine.[5] A corollary assumption is at work: The more highly evolved, the higher the moral value. Social Darwinist Herbert Spencer based his ethics on this assumption: "The conduct to which we apply the name *good*, is the relatively more evolved conduct; and that *bad* is the name we apply to conduct which is relatively less evolved."[6] Evolution implies progress and progress implies moral advance. So the logic of evolution as a cultural concept goes.

The ETI myth tells a story about evolution and places both earthlings and spacelings within the big history. Although the origin of life remains unknown to science, the history of past life-forms appears to be knowable, and so does the future of life. The plot of evolution's story is a movement from the simple to the complex, from pre-intelligence to intelligence, from the stupid to the smart, from religion to science, and from evil to good. In short, within an evolutionary worldview we place our faith in progress, and progress promises a future salvation through science and technology. This underlying set of assumptions focuses, frames, and forms the way we look at outer space, especially the prospect that someday we might make contact with off-Earth living creatures. These assumptions are not themselves scientific, but they disguise themselves as scientific in order to inflate what is brutally empirical into a full-blown worldview complete with a doctrine of salvation. The ETI myth in its scientific form posits the existence of advanced ETI on exoplanets, while the UFO extension of the myth adds that ETI are already visiting us.[7]

Author Albert Harrison spells out what "more advanced" could mean. It means evolution leads us to a state of international peace, beyond war:

A fundamentally positive picture emerges when we extrapolate from life on Earth: there are trends toward democracies, the end of war, and the evolution of supranational systems that impose order on individual nation-states. This suggests that our newfound neighbors will be peaceful, and this should affect our decision about how to respond to them.[8]

The proper decision, of course, will be for earthlings to welcome their new space neighbors, because the spacelings may bring us gifts from our heavens. Such a soteriological belief constitutes an eschatological myth. Author Huston Smith remarks, "The signature of myth is always its happy ending."[9] In short, the ETI myth relies upon the Celestial Savior model, a savior produced by evolutionary progress.

Cornell's Carl Sagan and SETI's Frank Drake embrace the ETI myth, including the hope for salvation coming to Earth from the skies. In their 1975 *Scientific American* article, they wrote that contact with extraterrestrials "would inevitably enrich mankind beyond measure."[10] Still, Sagan recognized that this hope is based on speculation rather than sufficient empirical evidence to deem it to be scientific:

Model III: The Celestial Savior

I would guess that the Universe is filled with beings far more intelligent, far more advanced than we are. But, of course, I might be wrong. Such a conclusion is at best based on a plausibility argument, derived from the numbers of planets, the ubiquity of organic matter, the immense timescales available for evolution, and so on. It is not a scientific demonstration.[11]

The ETI myth is at best a scientific hypothesis, not yet the product of empirical knowledge.

What Sagan knew is that evolutionary biologists repudiate the idea that biological evolution is progressive, and they repudiate the idea that evolving life on an off-Earth planet would follow our path to intelligent beings. Biologists with no less stature than Harvard's Ernst Mayr and Stephen Jay Gould or Presidential Medal winner Francisco J. Ayala denounce the ETI myth for its failure to work with the dominant understanding of evolution within accepted science. The problem, as these scientists see it, has to do with contingency and statistics. In each chapter of the evolutionary story, we find a long concatenation of contingent if not unique events. We find millions of random mutations and environmental circumstances—all points at which the history could have taken a different turn. The probability of a repeat of this history is so low as to be virtually nil. The evolutionary process would produce a different outcome every time it got going. Ernst Mayr puts it this way: "At each level of this pathway there were scores, if not hundreds, of branching points and separately evolving phyletic lines, with only a single one in each case forming the ancestral lineage that ultimately gave rise to Man."[12] Or, to say it more colloquially: If we replayed Earth's evolutionary tape, it would never play the same way twice. If this is the case, we have virtually no reason to expect an evolutionary sequence on an extraterrestrial planet to develop intelligent life like ours, let alone advance beyond ours.

It is so important to make the observation that the concept of cosmic evolution within the ETI myth is not scientific. It is rejected by the scientists most in the know. Still, many scientists work with the ETI myth as their conceptual set. This is curious, to be sure, but myth is beating right in the heart of the space sciences.

Physicist turned astrobiologist Paul Davies provides an example of how the ETI myth turns from science toward religion. Presuming evolutionary advance, Davies speculates about the spiritual superiority of our more advanced extraterrestrial colleagues:

> *It is clear that if we receive a message from an alien community, it will not have destroyed itself...it is overwhelmingly probable that the aliens concerned will be far more advanced than us...we can expect that if we receive a message, it will be from beings who are very advanced indeed in all respects, ranging from technology and social development to an understanding of nature and philosophy.*[13]

Davies proceeds to engage in theological speculation based upon his assumptions regarding extraterrestrial superiority due to their more advanced stage in evolution. "It is a sobering fact that we would be at a stage of spiritual development very inferior to that of almost all of our intelligent alien neighbors."[14] Within the logic of alleged scientific thinking about life on other planets, we see at work a conceptual set that posits somewhere in our heavens a civilization more advanced than we earthlings in intelligence, science, technology, medicine, morality, and religion. This vision, as hopeful as it may appear, is extra-scientific. I call it myth. It reveals the implicit dimension of religion built into the scientific mindset, so it is easy to see how it might appear as well within the UFO mindset.

Like a leech riding on a swimmer in a swamp, another doctrine draws life from such a myth. The leech doctrine is this: science saves. Science is our true savior, say the apostles of transhumanism, who give voice to what so many of the rest of us assume. Simon Young, an author of a transhumanist manifesto, preaches that we should place our faith in science: "Science and technology increasingly offer us the chance to overcome the limitations of the human condition. Therefore, let us believe in science."[15]

Model III: The Celestial Savior

This doctrine that science saves is by no means intrinsic to science per se. Rather, it is promulgated by *scientism*, an ideology piled on top of science. Scientism dresses naked science in a faith system. Atheist Michael Shermer makes it clear that scientism requires faith and thereby picks up religious freight. Scientism "is a secular religion in the sense of generating loyal commitments (a type of faith) to a method, a body of knowledge, and a hope for a better tomorrow."[16] What we see happening in our social economy is that science is buying out religion, but science continues to sell religion's products, such as salvation. Before the ETI myth can tell us what is actually happening on off-Earth planets, it provides us with a set of telescope lenses that frame our observations in terms of evolutionary progress and scientism.

Douglas Vakoch, a communications expert at SETI, and Albert Harrison, a consultant to NASA's space station program, lay down a challenge when they state that "myths require attention because of their great potential for influencing interpretations of extraterrestrial civilizations."[17] Here, in *UFOs: God's Chariots?*, we are giving attention to the way the ETI myth influences "interpretations of extraterrestrial civilizations."

POST-RELIGIOUS SPIRITUALITY

Many in our modern and emerging postmodern society like to think that they have graduated from religion—at least from institutional religion. They like to think of themselves as post-religious but still spiritual. Institutional religion seems narrow, dogmatic, absolutist. A post-religious spirituality, however, is attractive because it calls forth the experience of transcendence without the trappings of traditional dogma. "I am spiritual but not religious" has become a functional mantra. We might abbreviate "spiritual but not religious" as SBNR or, more affectionately, as SaBeener.

What I am calling the "religious dimension" of the UFO phenomenon is in its own way a form of SBNR belief. When working out of the conceptual set we've identified as Model II: the Research Scientist, we in our own minds have left institutional religion and replaced it with science.

Yet, curiously enough, we import religious sensibilities back into our science and dress our space visitors in SBNR clothing. This is all subtle. In what follows I will try to identify the subtle components comprising Model III: the Celestial Savior.

We will follow three steps. Our first step will be to look at a sample UFO experience in which the religious sensibilities are obvious, right up front where we can see them. Our second step—in the next chapter—will be to isolate four unmistakably religious components: transcendence, omniscience, perfection, and redemption. This will yield to our third step, a look at the contactee phenomenon and UFO cults. These selected phenomena within the larger UFO phenomenon will draw a map so that we can see the direction that religious sensibilities are taking us.

Recall that our method here is phenomenology. In phenomenology we look both at the object perceived and the subject doing the perceiving. The conceptual set the subject takes to the experience influences greatly how the subject interprets what is happening. In fact, the interpretation *is* the experience. The objective component, which interests the UFO investigator, must be abstracted from the experience. What is concrete is the object with its subjective interpretation, so to look at the object apart from the interpretation requires the investigator to abstract it from the experience. There is nothing wrong with this, of course. My only point is that what is concrete is the experience replete with interpretation, and this is where I'd like us to begin.

Within the broader field of phenomenology, our method here might be more narrowly described as a hermeneutic of secular experience. I get this from one of my favorite professors at the University of Chicago, the late Langdon Gilkey. The *Hermeneutic of Secular Experience* attempts "to see what religious dimensions there may be...in ordinary life...which will uncover what is normally hidden and forgotten."[18] The term *hermeneutic* (coming from the Greek god Hermes who delivers messages) refers to interpretation; so this phenomenological method interprets other interpretations. Specifically, we will interpret our interpretations of UFOs.

Model III: The Celestial Savior

What it seeks is to uncover...are those aspects of daily experience which the secular mood has overlooked...there are levels latent in secular life of which our age is undoubtedly aware but about which it is unable to speak or to think intelligibly. These elements are the dimension of ultimacy presupposed in all our interaction with the relative world, and the presence of ambiguity within our freedom and creativity, of the demonic and the despairing in life as well as the joyful, with both of which secular experience is suffused.[19]

We will look at some specific UFO encounters as well as the more generic beliefs within the UFO movement, especially at the UFO variant of the ETI myth. What we will find are powerful religious sensibilities coming to expression in sublimated or disguised form. We will show how the UFO phenomenon expresses "in technological idiom certain religious needs and supernatural themes otherwise lost in a secular age," to borrow Bullard's words.[20]

As I stated on the previous page, the philosophical term *hermeneutics* is derived from the Greek god of communication and miscommunication, Hermes. We know him as the wing-footed Mercury in Latin. Messages delivered by Hermes are not literally true. Rather, they come in symbolic and multivalent form. Hermes's messages require interpretation; hence, the field of hermeneutics is the field of interpretation.

We must pause a moment to contrast Hermes with another Greek god, Apollo. What Apollo wants to do is find the literal meaning of things. He wants rational and final explanations. Apollo wants univocal meaning, not equivocal meaning. But, when it comes to the UFO phenomenon, can Apollo get what he wants? No. At least not right now. Despite Apollo's rule over the minds of most ufologists and debunkers, Hermes reigns over the UFO phenomenon in its comprehensive scope. UFOs are subtle, equivocal, resonant, and multivalent, and they require interpretation.

"The proverbial landing on the White House lawn in a flying saucer wouldn't be Hermes style, which is much more suited to appearing as suggestive blips on radar," observes author Keith Thompson. "Whereas Apollo insists on single meanings, clear and straight like an arrow, communication under the sign of Hermes borrows from twisted pathways, shortcuts, and parallel routes, it makes many round trips and ends up sometimes in meaningful dead ends."[21] The UFO phenomenon cannot be reduced to the nuts and bolts used in manufacturing a space craft. It will take a hermeneutical phenomenology to understand the multiple levels of UFO meaning.

What the hermeneutic of secular experience uncovers is this: the religious interpretation of the UFO is by no means simply an afterthought. It is more often than not built right into the compact UFO experience itself. The UFO experience can be a spiritual or even mystical experience in its own right. This is certainly the case in the Andreasson affair, to which we turn as an example of the obvious religious component.

The Andreasson Affair

The immensely complex Andreasson affair begins with an experience of alien intrusion during the evening of January 25, 1967. From her kitchen window in South Ashburnham, Massachusetts, Betty Andreasson could see a pink light getting increasingly brighter, pulsating, and turning to reddish-orange. She told her seven children to "be quiet, and quick, get in the living room." Everything became still. "It seemed like the whole house had a vacuum over it," she reported to Harold J. Edelstein under hypnotic regression. Into the kitchen came Betty's father, Waino Aho, who was startled to see what he called "Halloween freaks" in the backyard. The creatures had gray skin and large, pear-shaped heads with mongoloid faces, and were wearing pants with a tuck-in–type shirt. Then, to the observers' surprise, the group of four or five alien entities marched right into the Andreasson kitchen. They came through the door—a door which was closed. The intruders walked with a jerky motion, leaving a vapory image behind. It was a misty and mystical experience all at once.

What Mrs. Andreasson was thinking at this point is important: "I'm thinking they must be angels," she reports, "because Jesus was able to walk through doors and walls and walk on water.... And Scriptures keep coming into my mind where it says, 'Entertain the stranger, for it may be angels unaware.'"[22] Betty Andreasson was a devout Christian with fundamentalist leanings. This means she was working with a religious conceptual set along with a worldview imbued with the Christian symbol system. Her natural tendency was to interpret this exceedingly strange and powerful experience in terms of the symbols she knew well, such as the biblical symbols.

The leader telepathically communicated to Betty that his name was Quazgaa. Curiously enough, Quazgaa knew Betty's name even though they had not been introduced. "He just knew it."[23] When Betty offered them some dinner, Quazgaa replied cryptically, "Our food is tried by fired." What seemed to be at work was the underlying notion that the space angels enjoyed a hard-won, purified knowledge. Perhaps they were omniscient, or at least very knowledgeable.

The entities approached Betty as Jesus approached those who would become his disciples, saying, "Follow us." The alien visitors reported that they had come to "help the world...because the world is trying to destroy itself." These angels from space were our celestial saviors.

The visitors took her to their waiting spacecraft, a circular ship parked on struts on a hillside. A door opened, as if from nowhere. One could not discern where the door was until it opened, so perfect was the seal. Revealed by the opening is a three-step stairway, reminiscent of the Dick Jackson case mentioned in Chapter 1. Also, parallel to the Jackson case is the experience of cleansing. Betty was placed on a platform and then immersed in brilliant white light. When Betty asked about this procedure, the entities explain, "It is just to cleanse you." This cleansing was followed by a request that Betty change her clothes and put on a white garment, which the ufonauts provide.

Included in this experience is a physical examination of the type we noted previously. Similar to the Charles Hickson account, a "big eye" or lens-like machine emerges from the ceiling and surveys her entire body. Somewhat similar to what happened to Sandy Larson, the space doctors inserted a silver needle into Betty's nostril and removed a piece of tissue. Similar to the Betty Hill case, they pressed a "long silver thing" through Betty Andreasson's navel. When Mrs. Andreasson inquired as to what they were doing, the research scientists said "something about creation," noting that certain parts are missing. Betty speculated that this might have referred to her previous hysterectomy. Yet she gets the message that they want to "measure" her for procreation. During the ordeal Betty experienced considerable pain, especially during the nostril examination. In response, Quazgaa eased her pain by putting his hand on her forehead, reminiscent of the Betty Hill incident. If this were all that happened, we could classify the Andrasson affair as an example of Model II, the Research Scientist.

However, a very dramatic event catapults this UFO case into the realm of religious experience. Following the medical examination Betty got dressed again and was guided through a series of long black tunnels. At the end of each tunnel was a vision. In one vision, Betty saw a great city beneath a green sky. It was a big city, "you know, a lot like science fiction," with many domes in the city. Then a bright light source began to move into view. This light source reflected off beautiful, crystalline structures like giant prisms. Dazzled and awestruck, Betty said, "I'm just there, before the light."

Between Betty and the light source there rises up an apparition of a giant bird, perhaps 15 feet in height. The bird looks like an eagle with its feathers fluffed out. The beautiful bright light is coming from behind the bird, as if the feathered being is protecting Betty from the full force of the light's power. Betty then begins to feel heat. She experiences a burning sensation in her hands. Next, the great, eagle-like bird undergoes a transformation. The heat consumes it. It is reduced to fire. The fire burns down and becomes embers, then ashes. From the ashes crawls a worm, and the apparition ends at this point.

Betty can now hear the voices of the space entities talking to her, asking her if she understands what she has just witnessed. "No," she responds. "I don't understand what this is all about, why I'm even here." To this they respond, as if speaking with one voice rather than many, "I have chosen you." Betty has been chosen for something, just as the Old Testament prophets were chosen by God to deliver a message to Israel.

"Are you the Lord God?" Betty asks in a near panic.

"I shall show you as your time goes by," was the equivocal reply.[24]

The space voice comforts and encourages Betty, asking here to wait patiently and to trust God. Her fear is a problem. "I can release you," says the voice "but you must release yourself of that fear through my son."

These words, "through my son," seem to have a direct impact on Betty. She suddenly bursts into unrestrained joy. Tears stream down her beaming face. Praising God and crying she says, "Thank you, Lord! I know I am not worthy. Thank you for your Son."

Unable to integrate this bizarre turn toward the religious, the UFO investigators press Betty to explain. Ray Fowler asks her, "Do you have the impression that this bird-thing was just as real as all the events leading up to it?"

"It is more real," answers Betty.

This is significant. The late History of Religions scholar, Mircea Eliade, has said that at the heart of the religious quest is "ontological thirst." This is a spiritual thirst for ultimate reality. The divine is what is ultimately real, and the reality of our ordinary, nuts-and-bolts world is dependent upon whatever the divine being grants to it. Intuitively, Betty knows this and reports this.

Just what is happening here? Symbols topple all over other symbols. Could Betty Andreasson have seen an apparition of the phoenix?[25] Let's digress for a moment to the background on the phoenix.

The phoenix belongs primarily to ancient Egyptian mythology. According to the ancients, as first reported by Herodotus (c. 430 BC), the phoenix is a bird about the size of an eagle. As the story goes, there is only one of its kind and it lives in Arabia with a lifespan of 500 years. At the end of its epoch, it builds a pyre of sweet spices and then sits on it while singing a song of rare beauty. The rays of the sun then ignite the pyre, burning both the bird and the nest. From the ashes emerges a worm, which eventually grows into a new phoenix. The first task of the newborn phoenix is to gather the ashes of its dead parent and fly to Heliopolis, the City of the Sun, in Egypt. In Heliopolis the priests bury the ashes with great ceremony. The phoenix then returns to Arabia for the next five centuries until the cycle is repeated.

Being identified so closely with the sun, the phoenix eventually becomes associated with Osiris, the dying and rising god of Egyptian myth. Osiris is an agricultural god, and his myth has to do with the natural cycle of fertility. Osiris symbolizes the annual cycle of planting and harvesting crops. After the harvest, the remaining seeds appear to be dead. At the end of the winter or dormant season, the seeds are planted in the ground. With the warmth of the spring and summer sun, they sprout to life again. Each plant does not return to life; rather, its seed replaces it with a new plant. So also with the phoenix. Each individual bird does not rise. Rather, the parent bird dies and its child, the next generation, rises to take its place.

We must note initially that this is by no means the Christian understanding of resurrection. The Christian doctrine of resurrection is quite different. On Easter Sunday, the same Jesus who was crucified on Good Friday emerges from the tomb. It is not Jesus' progeny. Nor is there any commitment to the annual fertility cycle in Christianity. Resurrection is a once-for-all-times event. This applies not only to the Easter Jesus but also to those of us who have faith (1 Corinthians 15). We will be resurrected just as Jesus was. It applies as well to the vision of the new creation which, significantly enough for our present discussion, has the holy city, the new Jerusalem as its symbol (Revelation 21-22). In the new Jerusalem we find the tree of life, usually represented by the color green. What we need to note here is that resurrection and the new Jerusalem belong together in Christian symbology.

Despite the differences, there is a point of overlap between the Egyptian phoenix and the Christian tradition on the matter of resurrection. During the Middle Ages in Europe a number of books known as *beastiaries* were published. They were simply books on nature, describing the various animals. Frequently, moral or theological lessons were tied to these descriptions. The phoenix was assumed to be a genuine member of the animal kingdom, not a myth. After describing the bird, the typical beastiary would ask the reader: "If the phoenix has the power to die and rise again, why, silly man, are you scandalized by the word of God?" In sum, through time the phoenix became incorporated into Christian vocabulary as a kind of natural analogy that represents the resurrection of the dead.

Let us now return to Betty Andreasson. When being interviewed and asked to report her UFO experience, she does not initially enunciate Christian doctrine. Rather, she struggles for the words to articulate her encounter of overwhelming emotional and intellectual impact. What she is undergoing in the experience is communication at the level of symbol prior to its explanation in cognitive discourse. She does not have to know how to explain everything in order to have communicated to her the meaning of what is happening. According to the clues and symbols we can reconstruct some of what is going on.

Although the symbol is obviously that of the phoenix, what is not immediately obvious is the idea of resurrection. Rather, the phoenix seems to be the vehicle of a more general event of revelation or enlightenment. What Betty is undergoing is a more basic theophany. The revelation of Moses and the burning bush comes to mind here has a precedent (Exodus 3). The presence of the fire and light is common to both. Light, of course, always symbolizes purity, knowledge, and truth. Also, for both Moses and Betty, we recognize a symbolic cleansing in preparation: Moses removes his shoes, while Betty is vacuumed by light. Moses is told about the promised land "flowing with milk and honey," while Betty is given a vision of the equivalent of a new Jerusalem. Most significantly, both stand in awe before the overwhelming presence of the Holy One and both are called to a divine task, that is, to be a prophet.

The chief clue to the association with Moses, I think, is the remark by the spaceling, "I will show you as your time goes by." This recalls the very name of God—actually a non-name—given to Moses by the voice in the burning bush, יהוה, or *Yahweh,* in Exodus 3:13–14. But Moses said to God, "If I come to the Israelites and say to them, The God of your ancestors has sent me to you, and they ask me, 'What is his name?' what shall I say to them?" God said to Moses, "I AM WHO I AM." He said further, "Thus you shall say to the Israelites, 'I AM has sent me to you.'" The NRSV version of the Bible translates the Hebrew into English as "I AM WHO I AM." But the Hebrew, *ehyeh asher ehyeh,* can just as easily be translated in the future tense, "I will be who I will be." This connotes the ongoing mystery of God as well as the ongoing steadfastness or faithfulness of God.

The Andreasson experience, I submit, is a basic theophany similar to that of Moses. "I really believe it was God that spoke to me," Betty sums it up. "I don't feel as if that bird was God. I feel as if the light in the back of the bird was the radiation of God. I could not see God. All I did was hear his voice, and that was it. I could not see any form, and I don't think I even wanted to look upon the form, if there was such a form." Moses was not permitted to see the face (or form) of God. Neither was Betty. Yet both knew it was God who was present in the fire and light and spoke through the medium of the word.

After noting the similarities with Moses at the more obvious level, there is a difference that may take us back to what is less obvious, namely, resurrection. In the case of Moses, the burning bush was not consumed by the fire. The phoenix was, however. Once burned, the bird ceased to exist. The ashes gave birth to a worm and the worm to another generation of the phoenix, but the fire did its damage amidst glory. Perhaps at an even more subconscious level, therefore, the symbol of resurrection is at work in Betty Andreasson's UFO experience. She does not actually say so, but the connotations seem to take us in this direction. The dark tunnel is a classic symbol of the dark grave. To emerge from the blackness of the tomb into the light of day represents the passing from death to new life. It was after traversing such a tunnel that Betty saw the beautiful new city and the rise of the phoenix. The emotional release of joy and confidence which is the resulting impact of the entire phoenix apparition, could be due to the pre-reflective communication of the message in Ephesians 2:5–6: "Even when we were dead through our trespasses, [God] made us alive together with Christ—by grace you have been saved—and raised us up with him and seated us with him in the heavenly places in Christ Jesus."

THE INVESTIGATORS AND THEIR OWN CONCEPTUAL SETS

In an attempt to grasp what is happening, Ray Fowler draws upon something akin to the theory of conceptual sets with which we are working here. He seems to recognize that we tend to interpret new and strange experiences in light of the conceptual framework that is already familiar to us. In the case of Betty Andreasson, that conceptual set consists of Christian doctrine, so one would expect her to make religious sense out of what is happening. Fowler writes: "Could Betty's encounter with the huge bird best be described as an intense *religious* experience? One is tempted to propose that the stimulus for the event was Betty's strong religious background."[26]

It would be best if Fowler resisted the temptation to say that Betty's religious background constitutes the "stimulus" for the experience. The stimulus comes from the UFO, from the encounter with what is *unidentified*. The religious background provides the conceptual set, the interpretive filter, so to speak, through which Betty tries to comprehend her experience. Yet, it is more than a filter. We cannot actually get to the raw experience itself apart from the symbolism that means so much to Betty. The religious symbolism belongs intrinsically to the UFO phenomenon proper. Fowler seems to understand this a bit more clearly—yet skeptically—in a later passage: "The very concepts of UFOs and extraterrestrial life had no place within the confines of fundamentalist Christianity. Perhaps, heightened by the effects of hypnosis, Betty's subconscious mind accommodated and reinterpreted the troubling elements of her UFO encounter. The result? A vivid, relived compensatory dream."[27] Just a compensatory dream, eh?

Even though I credit Fowler for recognizing that Betty's own religious conceptual set is likely to be a factor in interpreting her strange encounter, I wonder if investigator Fowler fully recognizes the problem created by his *own* conceptual set. Fowler simply cannot accept the fact that there is a religious event occurring. He wants to assume that the UFO is strictly objective and machine-like in nature. He can work with the Research Scientist model. An objective or nuts-and-bolts spacecraft could pass through the filter of his own conceptual set. The report of a religious apparition, however, is too strange for Fowler. So he finds he has to expunge it by consigning it to Betty's subjectivity. He does so by dubbing it a "compensatory dream."[28]

There is marked growth in the investigative interpreting found in Fowler's second book on this case, *The Andreasson Affair: Phase Two*. During the late 1970s, Betty Andreasson divorced her first husband and got remarried to a man named Bob Lucas. Her name became Betty Ann Lucas. Her new husband has had similar UFO experiences, and the UFO tie contributed in an uncanny way to both their meeting and their marriage. Fowler's follow-up book records hypnotic regressions of both Bob and Betty that deal with multiple encounters. During a series of interview sessions in the spring of 1980, Betty reports an event in 1950 that parallels the 1967 account. These interviews exhibit the same strong religious overtones we have already noted. One dialogue between Betty and Fowler's colleague, Fred Max, demonstrates the initial resistance on the part of the investigators to take the religious component seriously:

> **Fred Max:** *...to convince more people of your legitimacy, could you kindly give us something that is not yet known that we could use to accept this more fully?*
>
> **Betty:** *Your faith is lacking.*
>
> **Fred Max:** *It is not necessary from my faith that I am asking this question. But that many others would believe your message if you could convince them that you had something superior to offer.*
>
> **Betty:** *We do not make deals. It is a free gift to accept or reject.*[29]

It appears that Fred Max wants to approach the subject from the position of the uninvolved or scientific observer, whereas for Betty Andreasson it is a matter of responding existentially to the call of faith. Her faith is integral to understanding the very UFO experience itself. Apart from the eyes of faith, its essence cannot be revealed. Mr. Max seems to miss this.

When commenting on this interchange, one can see the light beginning to dawn on Ray Fowler. He struggles to take into account Betty's conceptual set while still wondering if there could be a religious dimension to the phenomenon proper. "Everyone in the room was dumfounded by this strange story. It seemed as if Betty was superimposing her personal belief structure over the encounter. The alternative was that her belief structure and the UFO phenomenon *were* intimately connected. Personally, I am trying to keep an open mind to all of this."[30] That's the right idea, Ray, keep an open mind![31]

UFO THEOLOGY

In cases that fit the Celestial Savior model, we frequently find conversations or even speeches that enunciate a philosophy or even a theology. In the Andreasson affair, Betty is eventually returned to her home where she finds the rest of the family in a sort of suspended animation. Upon her arrival things return to normal. Just prior to the departure of the space intruders, Quazgaa and another alien named Joohop provide Betty with some brief teachings. The overriding theme of these teachings is that the space entities "love the human race." Because of this love they are coming from the heavens to Earth in order to help us. They have a "technology that man could use..." but "unless man will accept, he will not be saved." In Quazgaa's farewell address he says, "We are coming to the earth. Man is going to fear because of it. We love the human race. We have come to help the human race. We do not want to hurt anybody, but because of great love we cannot let man continue in the footsteps he is going. It is better to lose some than to lose all. It is through the spirit, but men will not search out that portion."[32]

During one of the hypnotic sessions in which Ray Fowler and David Webb are interviewing her, Betty claims to receive direct transmission from the space spokespersons. She is in direct telepathic communication with entities in the celestial realms. Part of Betty's speech at this moment seems to be in an unknown foreign language, perhaps glossolalia. Betty has gone through her initiation rite, received the divine call, and is now functioning as the prophet.[33] Included in the transmission is a theological anthropology that describes the human predicament on Earth. "Man seeks to destroy himself. Greed, greed, greed, greed. And because of greed, it draws all foul things. Everything has been provided for man. Simple things. He could be advanced so far, but greed gets in the way."[34]

Why do we earthlings not love one another? Joohop answers, "Because man has separated himself; he has become dual. Separation, duality.... In love there is not separation."[35] We humans on Earth should live according to truth, freedom, and love, but instead we give ourselves over to greed and eventually to self-destruction. The UFO aliens have entered our state of alimentation to help us. They are our celestial saviors.

How can they help us? They can save us by stimulating in us right understanding, by granting us the right knowledge, the saving gnosis. We are told, "Know yourselves."[36] When the UFO investigators press Betty as to what this "right knowledge" is, she answers, "The truth." They then ask her, "What is the truth?" just as Pontius Pilate did once before (John 18:38). To this Betty answers, "Jesus Christ is the truth. He is the answer for mankind. He's the only answer."[37]

CONCLUSION

Despite their best intentions and thoroughness, the investigators found Betty Andreasson's account baffling. They were bewildered in part because they were ill-equipped to interpret Betty's symbolic discourse; they were thwarted by her multivalent language and images. The ufologists kept looking for a secular explanation for a religious experience. The entanglement became confusing.

Model III: The Celestial Savior

Perhaps our next task should be to systematize just how symbolic discourse is working in the UFO phenomenon. To that task we turn in the next chapter.

9

Unmasking Symbolic Meaning

Let us now turn to the more general structure of the Celestial Savior model. In the specific case of Betty Andreasson, the interpretive symbols are obvious. We find natural symbols such as fire and light, we find biblical symbols such as Jesus Christ, and we find other mythological allusions such as the phoenix. Symbols belong to first-order discourse, to the very language within which we have primary experience. If we abstract to second-order discourse, we can put Betty's symbols, along with those we find in many other UFO reports, into categories. We'll call these categories "families of symbolic meaning." Here are four families of symbolic meaning that we will discuss: transcendence, omniscience, perfection, and redemption.[1]

1. TRANSCENDENCE

UFOs convey a sense of transcendence. This is due to their association with the sky, with heaven, and with the mathematical infinity of outer space. Infinity fills us with a sense of awe and holiness.

Lie on the beach on a clear day and look at the horizon. Meditate. Allow yourself to be impressed by what you see: a sky that is high, majestic, immovable, and powerful. The sheer immensity of its inexhaustible distances makes you feel minute and insignificant in comparison. The awareness of great height communicates transcendence. Simple contemplation of the celestial vault provokes religious sensibilities; it creates in us a sense of awe in the face of the infinite and holy. "Most high" spontaneously becomes an attribute of divinity. Christians open their Lord's Prayer, "Our Father, who art in heaven."

Almost every archaic culture has a belief in a god of the sky who created the Earth and who sustains it by pouring out the life-giving rain upon it. The African Ewe tribe says, "There where the sky is, God is too." The name given to the supreme divinity of the Maori peoples is *Iho*, which means "elevated, high up." The ancient Chinese word *T'ien*, means both "heaven" and the "god who rules in heaven." The mighty warrior gods such as Zeus, Thor, Baal, and Indra were gods of the sky. In the Old Testament the Hebrew God is often referred to as El-Elyon, "The Lord Most High." At Jesus' birth the angels sang, "Glory to God in the highest."

The "high" is something inaccessible to us mortals. Thus, the heavenly realms so far beyond our reach become invested with the divine majesty of the transcendent, of absolute reality, of everlastingness. Heaven naturally belongs to superhuman powers and beings. The late University of Chicago scholar Mircea Eliade wrote, "Even before any religious values have been set upon the sky it reveals its transcendence. The sky symbolizes transcendence, power and changelessness simply by being there. It exists because it is high, infinite, immovable, powerful."[2]

Despite all of this, of course, we modern people endowed with the scientific approach to reality have fooled ourselves into believing that we need not think of the sky as holy. We earthlings have conquered the sky. We watch weather reports on our televisions or computers. No matter how frequently the forecast for our sky may turn out to be wrong, we continue to think that the heavens are not capricious but rather subject to human calculation and prediction. In addition, we have built subsonic and even supersonic jet passenger planes that cruise about at will, as if the heavens have become our backyard. What was previously the holy heaven for premodern people has shrunk in our modern consciousness. We now think of the sky as a thin envelope of atmosphere containing our little Earth. We cannot believe in gods such as Zeus or the Father of Jesus if they rule such a puny and vulnerable heaven as our local atmosphere.

However, just as we moderns thought we had conquered the sky, something unexpected happened. Another sky appeared behind the first one, namely, outer space. The virtual infinity of outer space was hiding in the darkness, and once revealed, it engulfed us in an even more awesome realm of transcendence. The commonly used adjective "astronomical" connotes the mind-boggling mathematics that accompany our awareness of the immense and unconquerable distances that separate galaxy from galaxy, which separate us from the rest of reality. Outer space provides a new sense of infinity, a new sense of our minuteness and dependence upon what is so much greater.

One of the interesting byproducts of the U.S. space program has been a stimulation of religious consciousness among the astronauts. Frank Borman, who was on the first orbit of the moon in 1968 and then became an aviation executive, said that in the vast regions of space he saw "evidence that God lives." Former astronaut James B. Irwin claimed his visit to the moon constituted a "spiritual awakening" of such intensity that in 1972 he founded an evangelistic organization known as "High Flight." William R. Pogue, one of the three crewman of Skylab 3, which set a record in 1973 of 84 days in space, eventually resigned from the space program to join the staff of High Flight. The new sky, outer space, continues to perform the task of revelation described in Psalm 19:1: "The heavens are telling the glory of God; and the firmament proclaims his handiwork."

This is where the UFO picks up its religious baggage, where it begins to bear the message of transcendence. In the popular mind, belief in flying saucers is almost synonymous with belief in extraterrestrial and even extrasolar visitation. A subtle or covert logic is at work. We believe that beings capable of traversing such unfathomable distances are slightly more advanced technologically and radically advanced than we are. We rank such beings with Zeus or Thor. The UFO has mastered the sky, conquered infinity. The UFO is mysterious and majestic. It humbles us by reminding us of our earthbound limitations, of our inadequacies, of our finitude.

As mentioned earlier, *Close Encounters of the Third Kind* is one of the rare films that accurately reflects the mood of the UFO phenomenon as it was actually experienced. This is because Steven Spielberg has the sensitivities of a genuine artist. He admitted that when he began the project he was intending to produce a sci-fi blockbuster. But as he began to research the matter, he discovered that it was a religious phenomenon. So, he portrayed it as such. In this movie, the sky symbolism and communication of transcendent power is overwhelming. The space visitors do not merely fly in our Earth's sky, they control it. They make the clouds foment, lightening flash, and thunder roar. In the Spielberg masterpiece Zeus and Thor have returned in the form of technological deities visiting us from a mystifying realm transcendent to our world of comprehension. The sky behind the sky—outer space—has brought the dead gods to life again.

This means, among other things, that the extraterrestrial hypothesis is an indispensible ingredient in the emerging UFO variant of the ETI myth. This is a point missed by Jacques Vallée in his book, *Dimensions*. Vallee simply underestimates the significance of the extraterrestrial hypothesis. On the one hand, Vallée recognizes that UFOs have religious power. But, on the other hand, he fails to see why. By identifying UFOs with previous experiences involving fairies who live under rocks, Vallée is looking in the wrong direction. He is looking down. He should be looking up. It is their association with outer space that evokes in us the response that gives UFOs their religious potency.

This point can be illustrated in a revealing confessional statement offered by Jenny Randles, director for the British UFO Research Organization (BUFORA). She asks her fellow investigators:

Be honest with yourself. If it could be proven beyond any shadow of doubt that UFOs were not alien...would you still pour all that time, money and effort to investigate these things?.... Some people would answer yes. They are involved in the UFO field for altruistic reasons. But I suspect that the vast majority, even when they deny it thrice until the cock crows, really have an inner longing to see their belief vindicated that UFOs are advanced alien visitors who have come here, will change the world and maybe help us get out of the mess we are in. When I am honest with myself I know that's true of me.[3]

Randles is working with the celestial savior model as her conceptual set. It is this which inspires her to pursue her work as a UFO investigator. It is the driving force behind UFO research in general. It is this which makes UFO investigation important, worthwhile. Implicit here is that the extraterrestrial hypothesis connotes, even when below the surface of recognition, the hope of redemption from a transcendent source.

2. OMNISCIENCE

As we previously discussed in Chapter 1, how did the spaceman know Dick Jackson's name? How did Quazgaa know Betty Andreasson's name? There had been no formal introductions. The alien astronauts just seemed to know.

This brings us to the second salient symbolic structure of UFO encounters, omniscience. In classical theology *omniscience* refers to God's ability to know all things. Much debate rages over whether this includes divine knowledge of future events before they happen, but virtually every theologian agrees that God knows all that can be known. Betty Andreasson testifies that the ufonauts who visited her had this high quality of knowledge as well.[4]

There are two ways in which the ufonauts are knowledgeable: technologically and personally. The logic of the developing UFO variant on the ETI myth is that there exists an extraterrestrial civilization which is further advanced than ours on Earth. Accepting the theory of evolution with a built-in idea of progress, this advanced civilization is simply further along on the same linear time scale we apply to ourselves. In a sense, the ufonauts represent our own future, dipping back into the present. They bring with them technological advances we can only project but not yet manufacture. Extraterrestrial knowledge in matters of science and technology is so far superior to ours that they might as well be omniscient.

With these technical abilities, the ufonauts can learn a great deal about life on Earth through electronic surveillance. Note a slight equivocation here: on the one hand, the aliens already know; on the other hand, the aliens are here to learn. In the latter case, the research scientists are visiting Earth with their advanced technology to learn more about us earthlings than we know about ourselves.

I have had numerous conversations with Charles Hickson, one of the two Pascagoula fishermen abducted in 1973. During one of those conversations, Mr. Hickson told me that the space aliens have placed in his body an electronic transmitter that allows them to monitor his every activity. Even our interview conversations were being overheard by astronauts somewhere in orbit. Like the angels of yesterday, today's ufonauts know Mr. Hickson's every move. They watch over him.

Yet, there is more to omniscience than mere technological prowess. The extraterrestrials also know the human mind. They understand the wisdom of the ages. They even understand us. They are now faced with the task of communicating to us, of teaching us. But this proves difficult, because what they have to teach we cannot quite comprehend. They are too far advanced for our more primitive level of comprehension. Thus, the alien intruders quiz Betty Andreasson frequently, asking her if she understands. Not quite, she tells them, and asks for further clarification.

A quality of intimacy is tied to omniscience. John Mack reports an abduction case he investigated. The abductee was a man named Ed. A female alien with "a small mouth and nose" and "intense large dark eyes," looked at him. Ed reported, "I had this uncomfortable feeling that every time she looked at me she could see right into me."[5] Another of Mack's cases is Scott, who similarly said, "They know everything about me.

There are no secrets."[6] Still another, a woman named Jerry, says, "It's like someone just crawled right inside you and knew everything about you."[7]

These accounts remind me of Saint Augustine, a fifth-century African patriarch of Christian doctrine. Augustine said that "God is closer to me than I am to myself; hence, God knows me better than I do." Not only do the celestial saviors know our names, they know our needs and inclinations.

Whitley Strieber, author of *Communion*, writes of omniscience when describing what he felt when looking into the eyes of one of his UFO abductors, a female alien. "It was as if every vulnerable detail of myself were known to this being. Nobody in the world could know another human soul so well, nor could one man look into the eyes of another so deeply, and to such exact effect. I could actually feel the presence of that other person within me—which was as disturbing as it was curiously sensual. Their eyes are often described as limitless, haunting, and baring the soul. Can anything other than a part of oneself know one so well?"[8] Strieber seems to develop his own philosophy through the description of this encounter, affirming a supra-personal oversoul or psychic unity among beings. Nevertheless, what we see in Strieber, as we saw in Spielberg, is this: A religious sensibility is evoked when thinking about visitors from outer space.

We have said that the forms of knowledge most frequently exhibited by extraterrestrial engineers are scientific, technological, and personal. When we turn to the Hybridizer model, this list will add sexual knowledge. David Jacobs describes the abductees he interviewed as being subjected to a "Mindscan." The alien researchers seem capable of scanning the human mind, knowing our thoughts. While scanning the mind, another form of knowing gets added: sexual knowing. "The aliens will induce rapid, sexual arousal and even orgasm in women as part of their Mindscan procedures."[9] Somehow, knowing us and sexual arousal get associated. How?

Jacobs seems to be unaware of the biblical understanding of "knowing" that is being elicited here in camouflaged form. In ancient Israel, to know a woman is to know her sexually. Knowledge and intimacy converge. The verb for copulation is the verb "to know." For example, the conceiving of Cain by Adam and Eve is a form of knowing. Genesis 4:1: "Now the man knew his wife Eve, and she conceived and bore Cain." Alien knowledge is multi-faceted; aliens are equipped for scientific knowledge, technological knowledge, personal knowledge, and even sexual knowledge.

The natural symbol for all knowledge is light, sometimes fire. The flame at the tip of an oil lamp is found on the coats of arms of many universities. It identifies knowledge and wisdom. When we turn on the light in a room, things get illuminated. We can see them. Our word *enlightenment* signifies that we can now see what was previously enshrouded in darkness. Light and truth belong together. In a religious experience the light is so bright it is blinding, signifying that the truth being revealed is so glorious that we partially blind humans are not fully able to comprehend it.

Dazzling light is so common to close encounters that one could cite cases almost endlessly. When Charles Hickson entered the hovering craft near the Pascagoula River, he told me the light inside was so blinding that his eyes hurt. When he came to visit me at my office (then in New Orleans), he asked his son to drive since he was waiting for his eyes to heal. The radiant revelation from God witnessed by Betty Andreasson was so blindingly bright that the phoenix had to stand in the way, providing a protected area so that she could perceive a form and receive at least a partial communication. In Spielberg's movie depiction, the UFO witnesses were constantly cowering and covering their eyes, so bright was the light.

In sum, the UFO contactee or even abductee is like a shaman or a prophet, that is, he or she ascends to the heavenly realm—in this case to the hovering space craft. In the sky he or she learns from heavenly omniscience, and then returns to Earth with previously secret knowledge. In many cases, the contactee or abductee becomes the *axis mundi*, the center where heaven and Earth come together.

3. PERFECTION

The shape of Dick Jackson's flying saucer was round. Betty Andreasson's was global in shape.[10] Roundness or circularity naturally connotes perfection. That is why medieval artists painted halos over the heads of saints.

Could it be that Mr. Jackson was subconsciously wishing for God to come into his life? Because he could not believe in God, he could only accept something that communicated divine perfection minus the divine label. Betty Andreasson was different. She welcomed the coming of the divine, once she could be confident that it in fact was God who was speaking to her. In both cases, perfection was communicated in symbolic if not sublimated form.

The space emissary spoke to Jackson in "perfect" English. Once Jackson had accepted the invitation to enter the realm of the circle, he underwent sterilization. So did Betty Andreasson. Both use the metaphor of being "vacuumed" clean. A baptismal rite of cleansing is necessary to prepare one to stand in the presence of the holy, the wholly perfect. In some Christian traditions, the baptismal rite includes a washing in the waters of regeneration along with the donning of a new garment, a gown "white as snow," much as Betty did upon entering the circular room in the star craft.

As we mentioned previously, many UFO believers and speculators operate with the confidence that the aliens who fly these inter-planetary machines come from a civilization that is markedly more than advanced over ours. Assuming the concepts of evolution and progress, the extraterrestrials are pictured as having achieved insuperable technological marvels. When Betty Andreasson looked at the landed spacecraft, she could see no seams outlining the door until it opened.[11] So perfect is extraterrestrial engineering! So advanced are the Planethites beyond the present stage of Earth's development, the aliens told Dick Jackson that we earthlings look primitive in comparison.

At this point, the growing UFO myth makes an unwarranted jump in logic. We begin to think: If the spacelings are so far advanced technologically, perhaps they are equally advanced morally. Perhaps they have lived through the era of atomic weapons, yet they have learned how to live in peace. Perhaps they have a moral perfection which we lack. We here on Earth will need to draw on this moral perfection if we are to have a long future. This brings us to the quality of eternity. Only moral perfection deserves to live for eternity. What is sinful or evil should, by definition, be slated for, at best, temporary existence and then die. Evil is temporary. Virtue is eternal.

Eternity is a quality of perfection. In the dialogues that appear in the Andreasson affair, the relationship between time and eternity is mulled over frequently. "The future and the past are the same as today for them," Betty says.[12] This is what enables the ufonauts to see the future. Vallée shows how in so many cases we find time lapses and other anomalous reports that lead him to conclude that UFOs are not governed by the same time-space constraints we are. For them time does not seem to pass. They transcend our condition.[13]

The concern for eternity comes up repeatedly in UFO accounts as concern for age. It is assumed that technological advances in medical science have enabled these extraterrestrials to greatly extend their life span. The spacemen who visited Dick Jackson told him they were much older than they looked. Whitley Strieber is fascinated by his female abductress, about whom he has the distinct impression "that she was old. Not just aged, like an elderly person, but *really* old."[14] R.L. Dione, mentioned among the UFO theologians in the previous chapter, believes the extraterrestrials have discovered how to live forever through medical science.[15]

Closely tied to eternity is resurrection. We rise from death into eternity. If eternity is subject to technological manipulation, then perhaps what we want is Dione's medical triumph, which will permit us to live forever. But what occurs is usually a bit more subtle than this. In the Andreasson case, resurrection to eternity is revealed to Betty in a visionary moment of suspended time.

Spielberg communicates eternity and longevity in *Close Encounters of the Third Kind* during the closing and climactic scene. When the landed

UFO spits out a number of Earth people who had formerly been abducted, some as long as 30 years earlier, the watching crowd is amazed. The abductees have not aged. The UFO is the fountain of youth.

Finally, and most importantly, the sense of perfection is communicated indirectly through the equivalent of the kingdom of God. The new world offered to Dick Jackson by the space visitors will be perfect in ways that our present world is not. In that extraterrestrial civilization we will find a society with no war, no competition, no disease, and no meaningless labor. It is no accident that Jackson described it to me as "heaven."

In order for us primitives at our stage of evolutionary development to enter this world of future advanced perfection, we must undergo a fundamental change. In the Dick Jackson case, we must leave everything behind and adopt totally new ways. We cannot even take our buttons with us. The old world of impurity and profanity cannot be carried over into the new and more perfect realm.

4. REDEMPTION

The celestial saviors offered Dick Jackson and others the equivalent of salvation or, in the words of many religious studies scholars, the means for "ultimate transformation."[16] For Jackson himself it comes in the form of transcending his mortal destiny: the cure of all his deadly diseases. For everyone else who makes the trip to the new world, it comes in the form of participation in the realm of perfection. Anxiety over striving for the necessities of life or from the inner striving to compete for superiority will be overcome. There will be absolute security, wealth, and cooperation. The *transportation* to the new planet will include a *transformation* of the very nature of human living. Psychic tension will be relieved in a world of such harmony. The vale of tears known here on Earth will be replaced with the bliss of a new heaven created by technology.

The vale of tears is usually defined by the UFO visitors in terms of the threat of war, especially nuclear war, and more recently the threat of ecological disaster. The threat of nuclear war gave urgency to the message of the contactees in the 1950s, who urged earthlings to cease nuclear weapons testing. This wreaked havoc on our conscience. No one in the West could clear his or her conscience by simply blaming the Soviet Union for what might result in total world destruction. First, the United States was already on record as the only nation to use atomic weapons against human beings; and second, any confrontation at all would have a no-win consequence because both sides would meet the same fate. The populace felt overwhelmed by the prospect that the bombs we invented might actually go off. We were caught in a giant demonic system that was our own doing. Global anxiety was high, and it has not yet abated. What we need is salvation not just from destruction per se, but from *self*-destruction. We need redemption from our own sin. The time is ripe for a celestial savior to appear.

Thus, the abiding theme of the contactees, which we will illustrate in a later chapter, was an ethical mandate delivered to us by our benevolent visitors from the sky: We earthlings must put away our nuclear weapons of war and cultivate a planet-wide brotherhood consisting of mutual understanding and love. It is out of heaven's love for us that the space messengers have come to our fallen realm in order to deliver this teaching. Certainly this is what Betty Andreasson learned from Quazgaa. Heaven's heavy heart over our dilemma is reflected in what we might call "flying saucer poetry," a poem delivered by a space brother named Hukar to John C. Hoffman in 1958.

> *Our reason for coming is to try to recover*
> *from old Mother Earth, our dear long lost Brothers...*
> *There are many things of value,*
> *Some of which the eye can see.*
> *But the priceless gift that we offer you,*
> *Is the Redeemer's love for free.*

As Hukar expresses it, the celestial saviors seek our redemption as a gift of grace descending to us from heaven.

A Vatican spokesperson, Monsignor Corrado Balducci, sums up the hope we place in the Celestial Savior model: "It is desirable [that the extraterrestrials exist] because if they are better than we are, they are going to intervene, then they are going to help us."[17]

Hope for redemption from a transcendent source is perhaps the driving force that generates the vitality we know in the UFO movement. When faced with the anxiety that arises from the fear of personal or even global destruction, we yearn for a supraterretstrial power that can save us from ourselves. When the bright shiny flying saucer zooms up within the framework of our horizon, we take it as a hint. Perhaps there does exist an extraterrestrial technology that can do it. Perhaps it will descend upon us and share its glory.

Spielberg capitalizes on this hope for redemption and the image of perfection in *Close Encounters of the Third Kind*. The dramatic finalé of the movie could have been taken directly from the closing pages of the Bible. The UFO encountered atop Devil's Tower is no ordinary flying saucer. It is a gigantic city, a celestial metropolis. It descends upon Earth with the majesty and opulence befitting the prophesied New Jerusalem. Revelation 21:10–11: "And in the spirit he carried me away to a great, high mountain and showed me the holy city Jerusalem coming down out of heaven from God. It has the glory of God and a radiance like a very rare jewel, like jasper, clear as crystal." The film's color and drama offer an apocalyptic phantasmagoria portraying our hoped-for supraterrestrial redemption.

Conclusion

What we have outlined here are identifiable components of the symbolic structure endemic to the religious dimension of the UFO phenomenon. This structure is often covert, masked under scientific or technological language. What we have done is employ the method of phenomenology—the hermeneutic of secular experience—in order to unmask the religious meanings that are often only implicit in a UFO encounter as well as in the broad cultural picture of what UFOs are. This has been a descriptive, not a prescriptive, procedure.

I have not as yet rendered any theological evaluations or commitments. I have made the point that the naturalistic constrictions of the Western scientific mindset have functioned to repress our religious sensibilities so that they often come to expression in distorted or sublimated ways. What is healthy about the UFO phenomenon, culturally speaking, is that it provides a medium through which these repressed sensibilities can still come to expression. UFOs provide an escape valve from the self-imposed constrictions of scientism.

Theologically speaking, however, I do not recommend that anyone begin to formulate his or her spiritual practices around the UFO myth. I do not recommend that we make an emotional investment in UFO saviors, pinning our hopes on them to descend upon Earth and save us from self-immolation. If we are tempted to do so, we make ourselves ripe for idolatry. In this case, we may call it "ufolatry."

Ufolatry would consist, frankly, in the creation of gods in our own image, that is, in the image we like to apply to our best selves. We have learned throughout the last century to place a great deal of trust and confidence in technology to solve our practical problems. There is a constant temptation to elevate technology, to view it as the solver of our moral and spiritual problems, as well as the practical. What the UFO phenomenon does is conflate—conflate with tension, to be sure—our technological reverence with our deeper religious sensibilities. UFOs present our imaginations with the possibility of a supraterrestrial technology dedicated to meeting all our political and moral and even spiritual needs. How we wish they could end war, stimulate love and brotherhood, provide peace on Earth. But these are problems concerning the relationship between the human heart and the divine will. They can be solved only through God's work of grace in our lives. No technology can do it, whether it be terrestrial or extraterrestrial technology. To place one's trust in UFOs is like building a house on sand. In the final analysis, God and only God is worthy of such trust. God and God alone is capable of saving us from, and for, ourselves.

10

Contactee Theology

In this book I am testing the hypothesis that even though we in our modern era have been enlightened by the discoveries of science, to the extent that we feel we have outgrown the mythological world view of the ancient religions, the same spiritual needs that found expression in those ancient religions are still with us. These needs press through to expression in almost unrecognizable ways. We have the deep need to be assured that we are not alone, to be given courage in the face of anxiety over impending catastrophe, to be comforted that there is divine forgiveness and salvation for us even when we have sinned, and to know that the standards of right and wrong are not floating with whims of desire but are grounded in ultimate reality itself. When the ancient mythological worldview, which included spirits and angels along with prayer and a picture of heaven in the sky, was replaced with the scientific worldview, our religious feelings had to find another conceptual language for expression. Ufology is one way this has been done.

I am also testing a second related hypothesis, which I will call the *global anxiety hypothesis*. Perhaps the growth of UFO interest can be attributed in part to the kind of fear or anxiety that a soldier feels in a foxhole under fire. That notion is reminiscent of the famous saying from World War I: There are no atheists in foxholes. We note a noticeable correlation—though certainly not a totally positive correlation—between UFO flaps and international tension. In the United States, for example, flying saucers zoomed into the public eye at the close of World War II and with the growing fear of the Soviet Union in the late 1940s. Between 1947 and 1952, the world underwent the Berlin blockade, the Korean War, Senator Joe McCarthy's anti-Communist hearings, and the development of the H-bomb. Another major flap occurred during the economic recession of 1957, the year Khrushchev said "We will bury you" and the Soviet Union sent two Sputniks into orbit. The rash of sightings between 1965 and 1967 coincided with the national turmoil over the war in Vietnam, and the flap of 1973 occurred during the anxious months of the Watergate scandal. It might be an overstatement to say that political tensions caused all these sightings, but the relationship between UFO experiences and anxiety cannot be dismissed. In the minds of at least some people, UFOs represent an unconscious or semiconscious desire for a celestial messiah who will save us from self-destruction, or, more likely, for a gnostic redeemer who will give us the knowledge (gnosis) to save ourselves.

Carl Jung advanced the global anxiety hypothesis in his 1959 book *Flying Saucers*. Jung argued that the UFO phenomenon has the characteristics of a collective vision with just such a psychic cause.[1] Although Jung stands neutral on the question of whether or not UFOs exist as a physical phenomenon,[2] he maintains that the worldwide scale of this visionary rumor makes it an important concern. Its psychic base is found in an emotional situation common to all of us. "The basis for this kind of rumor is an emotional tension having its cause in a situation of collective distress or danger, or in a vital psychic need. This condition undoubtedly exists today, in so far as the whole world is suffering under the strain of Russian policies and their still unpredictable consequences."[3]

In addition to the tensions of the Cold War, Jung suggests that the prodigious increase of the world's population and the growing awareness of insufficient resources to support everyone also contribute to this emotional tension. "Congestion creates fear, which looks for help from extra-terrestrial sources since it cannot be found on earth."[4] Might Jung have been prescient regarding the global eco-crisis of the 21st century? Regardless, Jung's version of the global anxiety hypothesis posits that such psychic tension issues in the unconscious call for a messiah to deliver us from our impending catastrophe. Jung writes, "The present world situation is calculated as never before to arouse expectations of a redeeming, supernatural event."[5]

In regards to UFOs as fantasies, two Boston psychiatrists, Lester Grinspoon and Alan Persky, say the increase of attention to UFOs "is to some extent a consequence of the increasingly anxious times in which we live."[6] And a study by J.A.M. Meerloo stresses "the anxieties of the nuclear age and man's resorting to magical interpretations of his observations...betraying the desperate need to be saved."[7] These analysts recognize the implicit need for a celestial savior, but Meerloo's identification of UFOism with "magical interpretations" (let alone fantasies) may overlook the definitely scientific mindset of so many UFO believers. If there is in fact fantasy involved, then it is a kind of scientifically oriented fantasy. It is not a simple reversion to primitive magic. As I believe should be obvious from von Däniken and most UFO theologians, the messiah Jung points to would certainly not be supernatural but rather super-technological. In sum, contactee theology is Celestial Savior theology, according to which UFO gnosis is redemptive.

EARLY AND CONTEMPORARY CONTACTEES

If we are to confirm or disconfirm the global anxiety hypothesis, then reviewing the scientized theologies of the contactees provides a fitting starting point.[8]

The standard contactee account seems to follow a particular structure, not unlike the career of the prophet in the Old Testament. The biblical prophet was chosen by the Lord and given a revelation in the form of an oracle; similarly, the contactee is very mysteriously singled out by the crew of a flying saucer to be the recipient of saucer secrets. Often the revelation is communicated telepathically rather than linguistically, which certainly carries overtones of meditative prayer and inspiration. (To "in-spire" means to put the spirit within.) When the contactee delivers this revelation to others at the Rotary Club or, on occasion, to a packed auditorium, he or she is liable to be called a kook or charlatan for presenting such a preposterous story. But this is interpreted as a form of persecution, much like that endured by the chosen prophets of old.

Some of the contactees who made it big on the lecture circuit in the 1950s were George Adamski, Orfeo Angelucci, Truman Bethurum, Gabriel Green, Howard Menger, and George Van Tassel. Some, like Daniel Fry and George King, developed full-fledged religious organizations around the new revelation. In more recent decades devoted cults formed around Ernest and Ruth Norman and Raël. Each contactee functions as an *axis mundi,* and disciples are bound together by a worldview replete with redemptive UFOs. After examining the careers of some of the contactees, David Jacobs affirms the global anxiety hypothesis:

> *The Adamski, Bethurum, Fry, Angelucci, and Menger stories all contained similar concepts. They defined the contactee literature genre and illustrated the contactees' anthropomorphic style of thinking. These concepts possibly reflected the contactees' anxieties about post–World War II American society and, more specifically, the prospect of atomic war, the role of religion in a technological society, the yearning for peace and harmony in the Cold War political climate, and the possibility of extraterrestrial visitation. An analysis of these themes is at least essential for understanding why the contactees became so popular.*[9]

Along with von Däniken and the ancient astronaut theorists, the contactees have tapped a widespread feeling or sensibility in people. Looking at the contactees may help us to look at ourselves.

FROM VENUS WITH LOVE

The most famous contactee of the 1950s was George Adamski. Adamski resided and worked in a restaurant in Palomar Gardens, California, and engaged in some amateur astronomy. He had no association with the staff of the Hale Observatory atop Mount Palomar, but through his 15-inch telescope he was able to see flying saucers on the surface of the Moon, which were never reported by those looking through the 200-inch scope in the observatory.

In the book he coauthored with Desmond Leslie, *Flying Saucers Have Landed,* Adamski describes himself as being led by hunches and feelings to drive out into the California desert one day to make contact with an alien spacecraft. On November 20, 1952, George and some friends made the trip and UFOrtunately, a flying saucer flew down to greet them. Suddenly Adamski found himself face to face with a man from Venus. Adamski's friends stood and watched from afar as the two conversed for an hour. The Venusian was Caucasian but with high cheekbones, about 5-feet 5-inches tall and 135 pounds. "The beauty of *his form* surpassed anything I had ever seen," writes Adamski. "And the pleasantness of his face freed me of all thought of my personal self."[10] The alien's countenance had the innocence of a child yet gave the sense of great wisdom and love. He had long hair that danced in the wind, and his clothing consisted of a one-piece garment. The description of beautiful long hair and a one-piece garment would certainly fit the image of Jesus sung about in so many gospel songs.

Conversing through mental telepathy and sign language, the space traveler explained that he was from the planet Venus and was quite worried about the explosions of atomic bombs on earth. This was dangerous not only for earthlings, but radioactive forces from our bombs being tested could potentially contaminate others living in space. But he did not speak with resentment or judgment toward earthlings. "His expression was one of understanding, and great compassion; as one would have toward a much loved child who had erred through ignorance and lack of understanding."[11] Later Adamski concluded, "...their object is to help us and perhaps to protect us from even ourselves." At one point in the conversation the sophisticated visitor, seeking to express himself, drew the outline of a mushroomshaped cloud and said, "Boom! Boom!"

Suddenly, the thought occurred to Adamski to ask his Venusian colleague if he believed in God, the "creator of all." The spaceman said, "Yes." He went on to point out that we Earth people really know very little about this creator. Our understanding is shallow because we worship in the temples of materialism. On Venus, he said everyone obeys the laws of God.

Adamski also asked the spaceman about death. The man from Venus said that bodies do die, but—pointing to his head—the mind or intelligence does not die. It goes on to live again. In fact, our visitor from Venus had once lived on Earth, presumably in a prior incarnation.

After an hour's conversation, Adamski walked the visitor back to his waiting flying saucer. As the scout ship began to ascend, Adamski overheard two occupants talking together, "and their words were as music." Were they the voices of angels?

In Adamski's *magnum opus* published in 1955, *Inside the Spaceships*, he describes how he was picked up in a Los Angeles hotel on February 18, 1953, by a Martian and a Saturnian, and driven to a deserted spot where a flying saucer was waiting. He was then taken for a ride. The scout ship that picked him up eventually took him to a 2,000-foot-long mother ship floating in space. There, after sipping water in a cocktail glass in the company of two "beautiful" spacewomen, Adamski was introduced to a great teacher, referred to as the Master. The Master unctuously referred to Adamski as "my son" and explained to him the meaning of what was happening.

Drawing upon the metaphysics of Madame Helene Blavatsky and the Theosophical Society, Adamski was able to construct a worldview that could explain inter-planetary relationships. The advanced development of extraterrestrial civilizations was due to their scrupulous adherence to the laws of nature and the laws of All Supreme Intelligence, he said. Both the laws of nature and the laws of God seemed to collapse into a single scheme called the "Universal Laws." The mission of the Master was to bring an understanding of the Universal Laws to those on Earth who were thirsting for greater understanding.

In reading the words of the Master the image of the Buddha comes to mind. Buddha traversed the road to enlightenment, and, once enlightened, he turned back to lead others down the path. The Master told Adamski, "There is a growing desire on the part of many on Earth who seek sincerely for greater understanding. We who have traveled the path you now are treading are willing to help and to give of our knowledge to all who will accept it...we feel it our duty to enlighten you if we can."[12]

The Master's message is an urgent one. Earth people will have to learn to embrace the all-inclusive life of brotherhood and cooperation found in the other worlds, rather than the selfish, individualistic life found on Earth today. With atomic weapons, life on Earth cannot continue in the future as it has done in the past. If things are not changed soon, earthlings will either be destroyed or stopped before they endanger life on other planets. Adamski was asked to share this message with his fellow earthlings as other messengers had done before, one of whom was named Jesus.

Unmasking the symbolic meaning in Adamski's case takes little effort. By claiming to have made contact with beings like Jesus, Buddha, and extraterrestrial beings aboard a spaceship high in Earth's sky, he is claiming his role as shaman, as *axis mundi,* as having brought to Earth transcendental knowledge. Adamski brings us redemptive truth. This heavenly truth Adamski dispenses to his followers has the potential of saving Earth from self-destruction through nuclear warfare.

As a teenager growing up in the Detroit area, I remember Adamski coming to the motor city to lecture. He spoke at the Masonic Temple on March 28, 1954, to a crowd of 4,000, about the same number who heard the von Däniken lecture I attended in 1976. Adamski told his listeners that the saucer people are here to warn us to change our ways before we disturb the entire solar system by destroying Earth in one powerful atomic explosion.

He admitted that many would not believe him and would persecute him as a crackpot. One skeptical letter to the editor of the *Detroit News* on April 2, 1954, declared, "The only flying saucers seen in the vicinity of the Temple, Sunday, were the coins of those who paid to hear that rubbish." The letter was signed, "A Venusian." While enduring this persecution, Adamski was probably comforted by the encouraging words of a space Master who had told him, "My son, do not be discouraged if you meet with ridicule and disbelief on your earth."Adamski told a Detroit newspaper reporter, "The type of persons who did not believe Marconi, Edison and Columbus are the same type who do not believe me."[13] Signs of the pseudoscientist?

Not everything George Adamski said has passed the test of critical review. Journalist Frank Edwards said that one of Adamski's purported photographs of a Venusian scout ship could have been the top of a canister-type vacuum cleaner manufactured in 1937. J. Allen Hynek pointed out in 1966 the close resemblance between Adamski's photograph of a UFO and that of a chicken brooder he found in a Sears Roebuck catalog. Space probes sent to Venus in the 1960s convinced scientists more than ever that the planet is too hot to have the water necessary for life as we know it. The landings of Vikings I and II on Mars in 1976 discovered no signs of an interplanetary civilization. Adamski also made the mistake of reporting that in his alleged spaceship ride he was shown that the Moon has an atmosphere, and that on the back side of the Moon there are UFO bases, lakes, rivers, vegetation, and life. During the decades since Adamski began having these experiences, the United States has sent astronauts in multiple Apollo command modules around the Moon taking pictures of the lunar surface, front and back. Earthlings have even walked on the Moon. Sorry, George, there are no UFO bases, vegetation, or living creatures there. However, a friend of a friend of George Adamski told me that Adamski died in 1965 still affirming all he said was true.

BETHURUM'S BEAUTY AND MENGER'S MELODY

Truman Bethurum was a general maintenance man employed with a road crew on Highway 91 in Mormon Mesa, California during the summer of 1952. One Sunday night in late July he decided to take a relaxing snooze in his truck. He claims he was awakened by eight or ten small uniformed men who took him into their landed flying saucer (called a "scow") to meet the captain. To his pleasant surprise, the captain turned out to be a beautiful woman named Aura Rhanes. "So this queen of a woman was the lady captain!" he exclaimed.[14]

Bethurum asked her questions about the solar system and her religion. She told him that in her world they worship the Supreme Deity who sees, knows, and controls all. This must have been consoling to Bethurum, for he wrote, "Immediately I got the idea that these people are *very* religious, understanding, kind and friendly and also certainly trusting. But the time came when she let me know that they are also cautious and took no chances of being fired upon, captured and detained by our warlike earth peoples."[15]

Captain Rhanes came to visit every few days or so, and Rhanes and Bethurum had a total of 11 conversations during that time. She told him that she and her crew came from the planet Clarion, a planet invisible to Earth astronomers because it is always behind the moon. Clarion is quite a place. The people there do not age; they do not even die. There are no taxes, no illness, no rushing, no weeds, no poverty, no divorce, and no adultery. "Boy," exclaimed Bethurum, "Clarion sure sounds like heaven."[16]

Much like the Venusian and the Master in the Adamski adventures, Aura Rhanes expressed concern over atomic testing on Earth. She said the Clarionites were worried that earthlings might accidentally blow themselves up, setting loose considerable confusion in the space around.[17]

Because Mrs. Bethurum would not believe the stories of her husband's contact with the space people, Captain Rhanes wrote her a letter.

In the letter she said the Clarionites were Christians and that the Christian faith on Earth was retrogressing due to the pressures of a dreadful paganism gnawing away at the moral fabric of modern societies. The letter recommended a reaffirmation of the values of faithfulness in marriage and family unity. "But, above all," she wrote, "learn to place your faith in God."[18]

Bethurum was pleased when word of his experiences eventually led to an invitation to visit George Adamski, who said he believed Bethurum's story.

Like Adamski and Bethurum, Howard Menger claims to have had a series of contacts with UFOlks, mostly from Venus. In Menger's case, however, it was a lifelong association. His first contact was with a "beautiful" spacewoman in 1932 when he was 10. She appeared to be 25 but eventually told him that she was more than 500 years old. As we have mentioned, these claims regarding agelessness hint at perfection in the form of eternity. Because of the "beautiful" woman, Menger becomes the vehicle by which the rest of us have access to longevity, if not eternity.

Menger, like most shamans and prophets, was drafted into the celestial messenger service and asked to spread the astral philosophy of life to other terrestrials. In this case the laws of nature and the will of God are collapsed into a single rule to live by called the "Universal Laws." The universal laws prohibit killing and war and promote the fatherhood of God and brotherhood of humanity. Menger was charged to form groups and to teach them. He was also warned not to take the assignment if he lacked the courage to face almost certain ridicule and persecution. He accepted the challenge.

To carry out his mission he was given certain gifts or talents by his space benefactors. The first gift was the power of teleportation, that is, the ability to decompose his physical body in one location, travel to another location via his thoughts, and then recompose his original body.

A second gift was music. While on a spaceship in the fall of 1956, he was introduced to a pianist from Saturn. Menger had never played the piano. After the Saturnian had played his concert, he guided Menger to the piano bench. "From this time on you will be able to play a piano whenever you are moved to do so, and not only this tune, but any melody you wish," Menger was told.[19] And he played. The music became part of his lecture program and he eventually recorded an LP album.

Coming from the mouth of his wife, Marla, Menger's saucer theology absorbs a curious combination of Hinduism and the occult. We on Earth live on the wheel of karma, Marla tells us. As our minds lose themselves in material and physical things they take on a debilitating reality and imprison the spirit within us. Jesus understood this when he said, "Know the truth, and the truth will make you free." Marla warns that those who die on Earth without becoming enlightened by the truth will be reborn—reincarnated—on this planet and not leave it. They are bound to the wheel of karma.

Those who die knowing the truth, however, will be reborn on another planet, such as Venus. Venus is a veritable heaven compared to Earth. Menger himself is the reincarnation of someone who used to live on Jupiter. Now, his mission on Earth is to make people aware of the truth that will set them free. (Note: The average temperature on Venus is around 860-degrees Fahrenheit. This makes it a good deal warmer than we would expect heaven to be. In fact, it much more resembles the other place.)

In symbolically arrogating to himself the role of *axis mundi* connecting heaven and Earth, Menger claims he was taken by scout ships to both Venus and the Moon. On both places he saw dome-shaped buildings. The Moon, he claims, does have an atmosphere conducive to good farming, and he had a potato allegedly grown on the Moon analyzed by a Philadelphia laboratory, which purportedly revealed an unusually high proportion of protein. The center of his book *From Outer Space* includes a number of photographs of flying saucers that closely resemble George Adamski's chicken brooder. Sorry, Howard!

UFOs: God's Chariots?

FRY'S FANTASTIC FOURTH

As another example of the celestial savior masked as scientized religion, let me mention Understanding International, Inc., and its president, Daniel Fry. Fry was an electronics engineer with a suspicious PhD from an unknown university who claims to have taken a ride in a flying saucer while working at the White Sands Proving Ground near Las Cruces, New Mexico, on July 4, 1950. His book *The White Sands Incident* is an account of the telepathic conversation between Fry and a spaceman, with an actual photograph of the spaceship included.[20] The interplanetary messenger, a Martian whose name is A-lan (or Alan for short), is quite concerned about international tensions on Earth, now that we have developed weapons for atomic warfare. Of course, Alan comes from a celestial society at an advanced stage in the evolutionary process where they have learned how to live in perfect peace and brotherhood:

> *We are not here to assist any nation to make war, but to stimulate a degree of progress that will eliminate the reasons for wars on Earth, even as we, some thousands of years ago, have eliminated the reasons for conflict and misunderstanding among our own people.*[21]

Do we have here a secular or utopian vision of the kingdom of God at work? Does Alan really come from what we used to call heaven? Will space benefactors make the Lord's Prayer come true? The religion scholar Robert Ellwood reports hearing a speech by Dr. Fry in which he expounded his scientific eschatology. Fry projects a utopian "human future—now enjoyed by the saucer people—in which man, freed from the face of the planets, will live generation after generation on great self-sustaining ships in space, swigging as whim directs them from one world to another."[22] Fry's role as contactee is to provide Earth with redemption.

In *The White Sands Incident*, Alan congratulates earthlings on their advances in the area of material science that have produced such powerful nuclear weapon systems, but he warns us that if we do not quickly make equal advances in the science of the human spirit we may destroy ourselves before the future utopia can include us in its blessings. Note that this is not simply an escapist theology. Our astral messiah is informing us as to how we can save ourselves; he is not doing it for us. The great commandment that Alan delivers is this: Human beings on Earth should understand more about themselves and about God. It is through increased understanding that earthlings will achieve the "one world" about which our politicians so glibly talk. Alan encourages us: "Your greatest era, your Golden Age, lies just before you. You have only to go through the proper door. When you increase your understanding, you will speed up the time when that Golden Age will be reached."[23] The Golden Age will bring us redemption.

Alan even says that our English versions of the Bible have mistranslated St. Paul's great passage from 1 Corinthians 13, "So faith, hope, and love abide, these three; but the greatest of these is love." Alan claims that instead of "love" the original text reads "understanding." The New Testament was originally written in Greek. Being a professor of Greek, I thought I would double-check the word in question. That word in 1 Corinthians 13 is *agape*, which can only be translated as "charity" or "love." It seems Fry's martian friend needs to study his Greek a bit more thoroughly.

Fry has been chosen by Alan to spread the gospel of understanding. He is warned that he may be persecuted for propagating this celestial revelation, a fate shared by the great prophets of the Old Testament and even by Jesus himself. Through his organization, Understanding International, Inc., which has its headquarters in Oregon, Fry traveled the country on speaking tours trying to show how flying-saucer enthusiasts are ahead of the times and what we must do to save ourselves.

What I find interesting is that this message is one whose central theme is understanding (gnosis?), rather than love or brotherhood directly. This suggests again the attempt to mask religious sensibilities behind a scientized mentality. Qualitative sensitivity for the spiritual depths of life seems to have been neatly quantified into a manageable pool of understandable information. Our sensitivity to omniscience is evoked, but here the spiritual dimensions of life become flattened to look like the study of sociology or computer repair. Alan's basic injunction is that we are to get on more rapidly with the job of understanding this information.

MASTER AETHERIUS

An even more fantastic amalgam of UFOs, life on Venus, belief in Jesus, Hindu metaphysics, the occult, and celestial super-saviors is found in the Aetherius Society. The Society contends that there exists an Interplanetary Parliament anxious to help our world, and that some spacecraft are being sent into Earth's atmosphere to make a "metaphysical survey" and to absorb the harmful effects resulting from atomic radiation.

The Society's founder and mystical prophet was George King, DD. An Aetherius Society publication explains how, as a child growing up in England, Dr. King had profound religious leanings, but as time passed he could no longer adhere to the limitations of orthodox Christianity. He began a serious study of psychic phenomena along with the practice of yoga and spiritual healing. "Thinking of nothing but his self-appointed task to relieve some portion of the burden of man's suffering, he had prepared himself for another great step forward."[24]

George's first contact with beings from outer space came on a Saturday morning in March 1954. An audible but disembodied voice told him, "Prepare yourself, you are to become the Voice of Interplanetary Parliament!" Not fully understanding the significance of this command, Dr. King apprenticed himself to an Indian guru who taught him how to enter the state of samadhi trance at will. This, along with his compassionate disposition, fully prepared him for mental rapport with the great beings who inhabit the other planets of our solar system.

Early the next year he was contacted by Master Aetherius from the planet Venus. Aetherius (after whom the society is named) designated George King as the "Primary Terrestrial Mental Channel." On Venus there is a highly developed civilization with other Great Masters such as Jesus and a saint named Goo-Ling. After his resurrection and ascension, Jesus went to live on Venus, where in the company of other religious founders such as Buddha and Ramakrishna he continues his concern for the enlightenment of earthlings. Jesus is *one* of the Great Masters and not the sole son of God.

Beginning in 1954, Dr. King would go into trances before larger and larger crowds at Caxton Hall at Westminster in London to deliver the wisdom and instruction that he received telepathically from the Venusian Masters to the people of Earth. A small but loyal group of disciples formed around him in London to carry out the cosmic directives. The Aetherius Society grew so large that it established chapters in Detroit, Sydney, and Los Angeles. I interviewed Dr. King at his Los Angeles headquarters.

Dr. King tells us that most of the planets in our solar system are populated, and each planet represents a different level of spiritual advancement. Saturn is more spiritually advanced than the others, while Earth (referred to by the term "Terra," which shares the Latin root with "terrestrial") is one of the most materialistic and spiritually dead places in the universe. Aetherian cosmology recognizes that the whole universe is a battleground between the opposing and incompatible forces of good and evil. The battles are fought on both the astral and physical planes. The opposing armies advance from planet to planet via spaceships and teleportation. Because Terra is so underdeveloped spiritually, it could become easy prey and fall to an all-out assault by the forces of evil, led by a group with the ominous sounding name of the "Black Magicians." What saves planet Earth from destruction is the constant and repeated intervention on her behalf by the space Masters, sometimes referred to unabashedly as the "Three Saviors."

One of the most dramatic, perhaps even bizarre, episodes reported by the Aetherius Society is the Cosmic Initiation of Earth on July 8, 1964. George King's book *The Day the Gods Came* is a step-by-step account of a cosmic battle telepathically communicated to him by a being named "Mars Sector 6." Evidently the Black Magicians had decided to wage a war against Earth. Discovering the plot in the nick of time, the celestial saviors intervened and soundly defeated the powers of blackness. The entire battle was fought on the astral plane, which is why it went unnoticed by the U.S. Air Defense Command and the *New York Times*. Nevertheless, the Society contends, it was the greatest event in the history of the world.

The saviors or Masters do not expect to save the world all alone. They request the help of the beings on Terra. In times of crisis, earthlings are called upon to join in a "Spiritual Push." Borrowing from the Hindu concept of *prang*, wherein all physical life-forms are believed to be animated by an underlying metaphysical spiritual power, the Spiritual Push represents an all-out attempt to tap this power for the purposes of doing good. Because Terrans have allowed their capacity to use this power to atrophy, outside assistance is required. This aid comes from a gigantic mile-and-a-half-long spaceship known as "Satellite Three," which is positioned in tight orbit around the Earth. While in orbit it covers itself with a radiation-absorbing screen that prevents its detection by Earth's radar surveillance. Satellite Three acts as a base to focus the Push of vital spiritual energy.

Members of the Aetherius Society assist in the Push through various spiritual rituals and, most important, through prayer. However, they do not pray to any sort of spiritual or volitional being such as an angel or a god. Rather, they pray to a battery that is "recharged" by prayers, much as other batteries are recharged by electricity. Society members gather at scheduled times and pray their prayers into the battery, and the amount of spiritual power stored is measured in prayer-hours. In times of crisis, the power is "discharged," and human input is enhanced by the space dwellers. As much as 700 prayer-hours can be stored in a small container and released in less than one hour. This concentrates prayer energy and enhances its effectiveness hundreds of times over.

It is important to charge mountains as well as batteries. The mountain at Holdstone Down in North Devonshire, England, was charged by Master Jesus himself on July 23, 1958. A rock from Holdstone Down is available for sale; it is embossed in the center of a handsome 5 1/4-inch-high cross, crafted of black walnut, hand rubbed and oiled. The price is $30 per cross.

On the night of January 19, 1959, George King's mother, Mary King, met with Master Jesus aboard a spacecraft. She was picked up in a flying saucer and taken to a larger vehicle orbiting Earth for the prearranged rendezvous. In a blessing ceremony, Jesus said that her son, George, was "The one whom Thou didst choose to be a leader among men of Earth in this their new age." The captain of the spacecraft told her that in a previous incarnation she had been a close friend of Jesus, which accounts for her devoted love of him in this life. Some followers of the Aetherius doctrine asserted that Mary King, in an earlier incarnation, had been the biblical Mary, the mother of Jesus, thus making George King a form of the second coming of Christ. The modesty of Dr. King has led him to deny that this is the case, but, even so, Dr. King has become our *axis mundi*, connecting heaven with Earth.

What about redemption? The Aetherius Society is looking forward to a new and higher level of physical and spiritual existence. The new era looks a great deal like Dr. Fry's future utopia and the Bible's kingdom of God. Our guardian Masters from space have already begun the long arduous task of bringing this new Aquarian age into being. In the words of Dr. King: "Religious writings of the past have prophesied a great event, when through a stupendous Spiritual renaissance, the Kingdom of Heaven would be manifest upon the Earth. The inspired ancient Sages have foreseen a time when all matter would be quickened—a time when the God respecting would inherit a shining world upon which evil, as we know it today, could no longer exist."[25]

Dr. King and the Society are calling humanity to make a decision on behalf of this new and imminent age of utopia. It will be preceded by the coming of an avatar—a Hindu version of divine incarnation—following the pattern of Jesus, Buddha, Krishna, and others in the past. This majestic being will come into our world dressed in the one-piece suit typically worn by intelligences from other planets. The avatar will teach truth, peace, and spirituality. Those who do not learn from this great teacher and enter enlightenment will find themselves stuck on the wheel of karma. Those who do follow the lead of the avatar will be ready to enter the Golden Age. "Mankind should spare no efforts to help prepare the way for the next great cosmic event for the next Master, who will come!"[26]

It appears that the Aetherius Society developed as a response to the tensions of the Cold War, general uncertainties about outer space, the popularity of flying saucers, and an inner need for an experience with the sacred in a mystical manner. One commentator, J.A. Jackson, says, "Neither the teachings of the Churches nor the wisdom of science could give authoritative answers to the new range of questions which people were asking about space."[27] The Society seems to provide an outlet for mystical expression and gives a small group of people an important role to play in the redemption of humankind.

CONTACTEES VS. ABDUCTEES

War consciousness is built right into space consciousness, especially for the contactees. The planet hungered and thirsted for peace, and the contactees prophesied that peace was just around the corner. This characteristic is under appreciated by some historians of the UFO phenomenon, especially those who do not like the contactees. "The new UFO organizations were horrified at the contactees and spent large amounts of time and energy trying to dissociate themselves from them."[28] This is the observation of historian David Jacobs. Jacobs, however, is more than a historian. He is also specialist in UFO abduction research. He has an agenda, namely, to fence off the domain of UFO research over which he rules. We will meet him again in a later chapter dealing with Model IV: the Hybridizer.

Jacobs tries to build a fence between the contactees and the abductees:

Major differences exist between the contactees and the abductees. Contactee claims were deeply rooted in the popular science fiction of the period, and their tales were bounded by their knowledge of science. However, the abductee claims contain events that include exact and minute details of procedures known only to a few UFO researchers.... Furthermore, while contactees talked of utopian worlds and compassionate Space Brothers, abductees describe aliens who use them as specimens. They feel violated and victimized.[29]

In short, contactees are frauds while abductees are authentic.

Let me make two points: First, it is inaccurate to say the contactees were influenced by science fiction. They certainly appear to be emissaries of Klaatu in *The Day the Earth Stood Still*. However, this movie does not belong in the science fiction genre, a genre that overworked the theme of an alien invasion—an interplanetary war—requiring a terrestrial defense. However, it is one of only two movies that are authentic to the UFO phenomenon (*The Day the Earth Stood Still* of 1951 and *Close Encounters of the Third Kind* of 1977). Yes, the contactees mimicked Klaatu, but this is not science fiction. What the contactees said may have been incredulous, but they were not giving voice to science fiction.

The second item is Jacobs's attempt to fence off the utopianism of the contactees from the alleged anti-utopianism of the abductees. Yes, of course the contactees were utopian. It is the utopian promise of a redeemed Earth that places them within the Celestial Savior model.

Because Jacobs wants to emphasize the negativity of the abduction experience, he excoriates the utopian hopes welling up from underlying spiritual sensibilities. Jacobs wants to put a lid on religious expression, especially religious hope. He wants to pound it down. Snuff it out. Therefore, Jacobs is willing to go to great lengths to separate his abductees from contactees. This emphasis among those who dealt with UFO abductions after the mid-1980s has led me to formulate an additional model, the Hybridizer. The Hybridizer cannot be reduced to the Celestial Savior, so it seems. Jacobs wants to make certain this does not happen. In the meantime, none of this negative abduction talk has discouraged the contemporary generation of contactee cults, especially the Unarians and Raelians.

UFOs: God's Chariots?

THE UNARIANS

One of my favorites among the more recent UFO cults is The Unarius Society and its former shaman, Ruth Norman, who gave herself the modest moniker of Archangel Uriel. On one occasion, Mrs. Norman invited me to visit her at her center near San Diego, and she provided me with warm hospitality. Dressed in her elegant white robe and sitting on her cosmic throne, she answered all my queries like a queen speaks to her servants. She has since passed into her next incarnation, but her worldview consisted of a savory metaphysical soup of ancient and contemporary tastes. Who are the Unarians?[30]

The Unarius Academy of Science denies that it is a religion. In fact, its members don't like the word religion; they like the word *spiritual*. The worldview of the Unarians is replete with an impersonal God that is the author of all intelligence, a story of evolution in which life progresses toward increased intelligence, karma, reincarnation therapy, mental telepathy, space travel, and the arrival of a new age of advanced consciousness accompanied by world peace and prosperity. Founded in 1954 and led by Ernest and Ruth Norman well into the 1990s, this non-religion reinterprets the texts of ancient religions to uncover the presence on Earth of visitors from outer space. These ancient astronauts are our ancestors. Relying on the concept of progressive evolution, Unarians say we human beings who have begun our upward climb toward higher intelligence need coaching and even aid from our more advanced extraterrestrial benefactors.

The ancient astronaut theology is alive and well among the Unarians. The Unarius mission statement includes the following:

> *Countless ages ago, millions of advanced spiritual beings, living in the timeless-ageless inner dimensions, were able to look into the future history of the earth world and to accurately plan what may best be described as a life-saving mission. They realized that without certain aid and assistance the people of such an earth world could only advance in their evolution to a certain point.*[31]

What is that point? Are we there?

As if reading from the script for *The Day the Earth Stood Still,* the Unarians warn us: We earthlings face a crisis. Atomic weapons threaten our very existence. The testing of these weapons threatens our health because of the radiation poisoning. Ufonauts travel a great distance to teach us to put away our experiments and to eliminate our weaponry. "We astronauts have traveled great distances, from more highly evolved and varied planets," to save you earthlings from self-immolation.[32] The celestial saviors plan to bring to Earth not only peace but also spiritual growth.

How do we go about spiritual growth? The Unarians affirm that the infinitely intelligent God has placed within each one of us a divine spark. Our spiritual task in this world is to fan the spark into a blazing flame, to realize the divinity that lies within us. "The Unarius concept of life is to reawaken the individuals to their inner spiritual higher self. Each person is a reflection of an Infinite Creative Intelligence whose purpose is to evolve positively."[33] Extraterrestrials, who are more highly evolved than we earthlings, are visiting our planet to aid us in pursuing an expansion of consciousness and realizing our higher self. The Unarians provide Exhibit A among examples of the gnostic redeemer myth among the modern UFO cults and religious movements.

THE RAËLIANS

Most of the cults of the 1950s and even those of the 1990s are effete if not non-existent. However, one group remains robust, energetic, and advancing. The most potent of the contemporary UFO religious groups is the International Raëlian Movement (IRM), with 60,000 members at the time of this writing. The IRM began with the equivalent of a prophet's call vision or a shaman's flight on December 13, 1973. Race car driver Claude Vorilhon was visited by a descending flying saucer in the Clermont-Ferrand Mountains in France. The spacelings invited Vorilhon to a six-day Bible study. The Bible has been misunderstood by religious traditions, he was told. It requires re-interpretation in light of modern science. The space travelers were actually scientists from their own extraterrestrial civilization, and referred to themselves as the *Elohim*. Hebrew scholars are familiar with this term. It refers to God in Genesis 2 and later chapters. Actually, it is a plural form, and could be translated as "gods." The true extraterrestrial Elohim are not gods in a religious sense; however, they are celestial scientists who, as told in the Bible, created the human race on Earth. Using their own extraterrestrial DNA, they created human life in their image and set us on the long evolutionary path toward progressive development.

When the race driver became the shaman, the *axis mundi*, the Elohim changed Vorlihon's name to Raël. The new name comes from *Israel,* and means that this chosen one will become "the Elohim bearer of light." The Elohim instructed Raël to become a teacher, to demystify Bible readers and substitute the literal truth—the truth of science and technology. We are the creatures of celestial science, not of celestial gods. In addition, prophet Raël should warn earthlings of a coming apocalypse, an apocalypse we will bring on ourselves with nuclear weapons. To avoid self-destruction and to usher in a millennial paradise, we must disarm ourselves and embrace the materialist philosophy being taught to us by the Elohim.

You will recall that shamans travel to heaven and return with heaven's message. This heavenly ride confirms the shaman's authority. It certainly worked for Raël. The Elohim took Raël to one of their home planets and instructed him on the details of genetic science. By our genes we will evolve, improve, and progress. In 1997 Raël founded a company, CLONAID, selling cloning services at $200,000 per child. Through cloning, personality and memory are transferred, or so Raël claims. Therefore, cloning a clone in sequence means one's life continues indefinitely through one clone after the other. Cloning "will enable mankind to reach eternal life," says Raël.[34] Immortality through genetic science, not through resurrection, is the promise of Raëlian salvation. An immortal human clone will become a member of the Elohim.

On the list of IRM goals is planetary salvation, a salvation beyond individual immortality. Before the Elohim will return to Earth, the

Raëlians must accomplish two tasks: spread the message and build an embassy where the space emissaries can meet with all Earth's heads of state and the media. As New Religious Movements scholar Susan Palmer observes, the "postmillenarian Raelians anticipate gradual progress toward the realization of Heaven on Earth. This will be achieved through their own work of reforming, improving, and educating humanity. Only when human society has succeeded in cleaning up its act will the Second Coming" [second coming of the Elohim] take place.[35] The worldview developed here combines a myth of origin with a chiliastic anticipation of a coming new age, a new age guided by a select gnostic prophet and his loyal disciples armed with celestial knowledge. That celestial knowledge is shot through and through with what Raëlians think is science, especially genetic science. It is scientized religion supported by a scientized myth, a myth not unlike that which supports establishment scientists searching the heavens for a more advanced science.

One thing New Religious Movements scholars find again and again among UFO believers is a trust in the future, an eschatological future that will bring from the skies a scientific and technological salvation. What the celestial saviors will bring, among other things, is a new religion. We on Earth will be confronted with a decision to stick with the old traditions or abandon them for the new. The new will be tempting. The new religion "will be a religion of love in the most profoundly intimate and biotechnological sense of the word, and a religion without death, and it will have come not from Heaven but from the heavens."[36]

NEW AGE GNOSTICISM

The mystical mood of the Aetherians, Unarians, and Raëlians carries over into spirituality. For some reason or another, UFOs are being identified with occultism, astrology, channeling, and self-realization. Perhaps this is due to the intersubjectivity that some resort to when explaining the weirder dimensions of the UFO phenomenon. This seems to have been the path followed by John Mack. The "expanded use of the self relies on empathy and is, in essence, intersubjective. Within this framework, hypnosis, shamanic journeys, meditation, Grof breathwork, vision quests, and other modalities, which are called in the West 'non-ordinary' states of consciousness, become natural investigative allies. For they involve, by definition, the opening of the psyche to the deeper realms that lie behind the rational or observing mind."[37] Mack further observes that "abductees seem to feel increasingly a sense of oneness with all beings and all creation."[38]

Evolution and spiritual advancement have converged in the mind. "Our notions of the Divine, like everything else, seem to grow along with the evolution of our consciousness," writes Mack.[39] Seemingly, New Agers have taken the emerging UFO myth and are adapting it to their otherwise gnostic ascent of the self up through the planes of physical and spiritual existence toward cosmic consciousness. The role UFOs with their extraterrestrial pilots play is that of celestial guides, which aid in our ascent.[40] When UFOs become incorporated into New Age metaphysics, redemption seems to await just around the corner.

REDEMPTION FROM A MESSIAH OR A GNOSTIC REVEALER?

I am in basic agreement with Carl Jung on the global anxiety hypothesis; I think that, to some extent, belief in UFOs is an expression of insecurity or anxiety and the need for salvation. Logic dictates that there are two basic ways to gain salvation: either do it yourself or have someone else do it for you. The concept of the Messiah in the Hebrew language, or "Christ," coming from the Greek, is the latter for Christian theology: Out of his gracious love the Almighty God stepped into human history, incarnated himself in Jesus, and, through a hideous death and glorious resurrection, won for humankind eternal salvation in the divine kingdom. The dominant atonement motif is that of the victorious warrior, *Christus Victor*, who defeats the enemies of sin and death, in order to hand over forgiveness and eternal life to us as a trophy. The Messiah as victorious warrior gives us salvation by his grace alone, free of charge, because God loves us.

But there is another, less orthodox motif for understanding salvation. This alternative involves a good deal more cooperation and striving on the part of the sinful human being. It is the Gnostic revealer. The gnostic revealer comes from heaven to deliver the revelation to Earth. Nevertheless, once we receive the divine message we must work to conform our minds and our lives to it.

As we have already pointed out, the word *gnosis* means knowledge. The typical gnostic myth tells of a divine being who descends from the realm of light and truth in the heavens down to the realm of darkness and ignorance on Earth. Only those who are initiated into the cult can share in the knowledge of what was revealed. At the center of every tightly organized cult is the shaman, the *axis mundi,* who claims to possess the saving gnosis.

The gnostic redeemer, much more than the gracious Messiah, seems to fit the method for attaining salvation in contactee theology. Our martian in Daniel *Fry's White Sands Incident* waffles between these two positions. Alan has come from Mars to aid in the salvation of Earth; yet, the method of preventing nuclear self-destruction requires human action. The human action consists of spreading the saving gnosis in the form of understanding. Alan says there is a "free choice of the race" and tells Dr. Fry, "Your race and your culture, however, are not doomed to extinction." Nevertheless, we may choose self-obliteration. From Alan we hear what we heard in Klaatu's speech: "The choice, you see, is yours."

Alan challenges Fry and the rest of us: "Whether or not your children have any future to look forward to, will depend largely upon the success or failure of your own efforts."[41] According to this contactee theology the celestial savior delivers the knowledge of redemption to us earthlings through the contactee; then it is our responsibility to make the choice and take the action to prevent self-destruction. Our redemption may depend upon UFO omniscience, but our redemption also depends upon our choice of action.

In the last analysis, then, our UFO theologians have expressed a need for a savior but have not really found one other than ourselves. The buck still stops at home. The actual content of what the space travelers tell our UFO prophets is not all that new. Skeptics would say it is not new because the contactees fabricated it or dreamed it themselves. But it is sufficient to note that sensitive artists, the clergy, and other moral leaders have been giving us the exact same message: Either we make the decision to live in brotherhood or we risk unnecessary self-destruction. Salvation is to be achieved only through the works of righteousness.

The UFO-based religions and theologies have not yet heard or comprehended the Christian gospel. They certainly do know God's law, that is, they know we should love God and love our neighbor. But the gospel is something different. The gospel begins when we discover that we have failed to live according to the mandate to love. It begins when we discover we have sinned.

The message of the gospel has two parts. First, God offers forgiveness of our past sins and an opportunity to start over brand new. Second, God offers us eternal salvation in spite of the fact that we have failed to earn it through works of righteousness. This is where the Messiah or the Christ comes in. Through the death and resurrection of Jesus, God has declared that salvation is through his grace alone. Someday, he plans to destroy the present reality and recreate it anew. You and I are invited to join him in the new creation, and he offers to carry us there by his power. This is a piece of good news that has yet to reach the ears of our contactee theologians.

CONCLUSION

I am not alone among scholars who try on the global anxiety hypothesis or to analyze the UFO myth. Diana Tumminia describes the UFO myth as a postmodern phenomenon:

> Postmodern myths, such as flying saucers, extraterrestrial deities, and alien abductions, express pluralistic collage-like symbolism of relatively recent origin. With the dawning of the rational technological age, social scientists expected secularization and science

to wipe out superstition and magical religions. This has not happened. Instead, a magical enchanted worldview subverted the scientific paradigm into an animistic account of space being that was readily available for our mass consumption. That condition now pervades in our popular culture.[42]

Note that in her description, Tumminia suggests that the UFO myth subverts the scientific paradigm by reintroducing magic.

The magic item is debatable. I would simply like to point out that when we look at the ETI myth, we see no obvious magic. We see only science in a very speculative form. It is not the return of magic that defines the ETI myth or even its UFO variant; rather, it is the belief that the gnosis for self-salvation comes to Earth from the heavens, from outer space.

11

Model IV: The Hybridizer

For the most part, the UFO phenomenon today is virtually the same as it was six or seven decades ago. We've added many new names, dates, and places to the list of UFO experiences, but the nature of the UFO phenomenon has been consistent since 1947. When I wrote the first edition of *UFOs: God's Chariots?* in the mid 1970s, I could get along with the first three models to account for a large portion of the phenomenon.

However, one startling new component was added in the late 1980s: abduction accounts where abductees are mistreated, abused, and even raped by the occupants of flying saucers. In some cases, abductees report that involuntary sex aboard the spacecraft has resulted in hybrid children with heritable traits from both heavenly and earthly parents. To organize the reports and evidence associated with such abduction accounts, I am introducing a fourth conceptual model, Model IV: the Hybridizer. The Hybridizer overlaps with the Research Scientist and Celestial Savior models, but its distinctive characteristics warrant a new and separate model for interpreting the scenarios.

As mentioned earlier, some ufologists use the category "Close Encounter of the Fourth Kind (CE-IV)" from which to work in the hybridizer model. C.D.B. Bryan summarizes what a CE-IV looks like:

UFOs: God's Chariots?

Personal contact between an individual or individuals is initiated by the occupants of the spacecraft. Such contact may involve the transportation of the individual from his or her terrestrial surroundings into the spacecraft, where the individual is communicated with and/or subjected to an examination before being returned. Such a close encounter is usually of a one-to-two-hour duration.[1]

As we have seen in earlier chapters, Hynek's CE-III category works just fine for what Bryan describes. However, the key to distinguishing the CE-IV, if we are to use the category, is the purpose of the abduction: creating a race of hybrid children. "All this leads to the unwelcome speculative inference that...hybrids of some sort...are being produced by a technology...superior to ours," says author Budd Hopkins.[2]

I date the rise of the Hybridizer model to the mid-1980s and to the publications of four ufologists: Whitley Strieber, Budd Hopkins, David Jacobs, and John Mack. These four musketeers mutually influenced one another during gatherings in New York City, and subsequently each published widely read books and became popular on the speakers' circuit. The abductee accounts they report are dated much earlier, to be sure, but the accounting itself dates from this period and represents an augment to the pre-existing UFO phenomenon.

Prior to the mid-1980s, the UFO reports of contact portrayed an image of ufonauts as celestial saviors, as beings visiting Earth with a more advanced science and a compassion aimed at teaching us to transform ourselves into a just and peaceful global society. Then, things changed. Skeptic Robert Sheaffer describes the change: During the 1980s the "alien abductions became more sinister, their intention frankly more sexual."[3] Certainly there was continuity between abduction reports prior to the 1980s and after; however, the later accounts shift away from benevolent images of our space visitors and toward those of abusers and rapists.

Despite the claims of abuse, the hybridizer model does not require malevolence on the part of our abductors from space. Rather, the perpetrators of these abductions seem to be short on feelings, short on empathy. Perhaps they lack the mirror neurons we *Homo sapiens* are said to have. Or, to say it another way, the space visitors behave as the stereotypical scientist: apparently feelingless because they try to avoid personal bias. The purpose of these abductions is not to traumatize or injure earthlings. Rather, the purpose behind these abductions has to do with extraterrestrial science. The spacelings are conducting a breeding experiment. In the words of Budd Hopkins, "An ongoing genetic study is taking place—and...the human species itself is the subject of a breeding experiment."[4] What abductees experience as abuse is a byproduct of feelingless science. Abductees are treated as lab animals by their abductors. Hence my label for this model, the Hybridizer.

Two Scenarios: Celestial Savior Versus the Hybridizer

We have two scenarios to compare. The old scenario prior to the 1980s is familiar to us: a close encounter with a UFO, missing time, partial loss of memory, retrieved forgotten memory, and unusual marks on the body. Through hypnotic regression the abductee reports a Close Encounter of the Third Kind. The space visitors appear as extraterrestrial scientists coming to Earth to perform experiments on the body of the abductee. In addition, the abductee interprets the UFO experience in a positive manner, almost as a religious or life-transforming event. The ufonauts are scientized saviors, so to speak, coming from the celestial spheres with their advanced science to transform life on our planet.

The new scenario, the post-1980s scenario, overlaps with the first old one with some noticeable differences: an abduction from one's bedroom, repeated abductions from childhood through adulthood, missing time, partial loss of memory, retrieved forgotten memory through hypnotic regression, giving birth to hybrid babies, implants that are invisible to investigators, and such. Although the model of the Research Scientist remains constitutive, its redemptive or salvific dimension is replaced by confusion and dread.

It is important to note that the method of retrieving forgotten memories through hypnotic regression was developed during the first scenario. This now-common technique begins with the Betty and Barney Hill abduction of 1962, which was uncovered by Boston psychiatrist Benjamin Simon in 1965. Doctor Simon employed hypnotic regression to retrieve the forgotten memories of Mr. and Mrs. Hill. He was not persuaded that what the Hills reported could be objective. He placed their account on the subjective side of the ledger. But, curious to him was the fact that the Hills corroborated each other's traumatic account. If a delusion was at work, it would have to be a shared delusion. So, Simon coined the phrase *folie à deux,* which we described in an earlier discussion of Model II: the Research Scientist. This phrase *folie à deux* escaped the UFO fold and became widely used in the field of psychiatry. In fact, in the 1980s, two professional therapists from San Francisco moved to the Napa Valley and named their winery *Folie à Deux.* The point here is this: The method of hypnotic regression for retrieving forgotten memories has wandered from its UFO home into other lands where therapy is practiced.

A cautionary note: Neuroscientists and other researchers these days have low confidence in human memory, regardless of how forgotten memories are retrieved. In fact, scientists observe, we can remember events that never happened, and we can even elicit false memories in children. Elizabeth Loftus at the University of California at Irvine, for example, avers that "memories can be manufactured," so "she has been investigating the possibility of using those memories to modify behavior."[5] Without jumping to any conclusions regarding investigator claims about UFO abductions, we should simply note that the veracity of abduction claims should be open to general growing knowledge about how the human memory works. In the meantime, our observation here is that retrieval of repressed memories is no longer restricted to the field of ufology.

By the 1980s, numerous psychologists had adopted the method of hypnotic regression for other purposes, namely, uncovering forgotten memories of childhood sexual abuse and Satanic ritual abuse. In the early years of that decade, almost daily stories of child abuse made headlines. Adults discovered for the first time that as children, they had suffered from abuse either by their parents or by Satan worshippers. The method of hypnotic regression became the tool for uncovering horrid stories of torture, rape, and desecration. Might there have been a cultural cross-over between forgotten memories of childhood abuse and forgotten memories of UFO abductions?

ABDUCTION: THE NEW NEGATIVITY

In his best-selling book, *Communion,* New York City journalist and fiction writer Whitley Strieber reports that while asleep during a vacation at his country cabin, he was abducted by a group of gray-skinned creatures that moved in an insect-like manner. Strieber was taken aboard some kind of craft, and then returned to his bedroom before awakening. He adds that he had been contacted frequently throughout his entire life by aliens. As Strieber reflected on these alleged experiences, he considered two possibilities: the aliens may come from the outside (from space), or they may come from inside (from within his own terrestrial consciousness). He did not suggest that UFO abduction accounts are fiction. Rather, he suggested that a form of higher consciousness is communicating with us through such contacts.[6] In Strieber's writing, lines seem to get blurred between fact and fiction, between objective and subjective, between a UFO experience and metaphysics.

Some critics accused Strieber of making up his story about alien abductions and selling it as fact. Strieber denied dishonesty and went on to publish a second similar work, *Transformation.* No one could prove malfeasance. "No definitive evidence emerged to invalidate any of these theories or responses—as usual in the universe of ufology," comments Thompson.[7] Still, we might note here that Whitley Strieber and Budd Hopkins wrote their books, *Communion* and *Intruders,* simultaneously. They communicated regularly. Strieber even attempted to get the publication of Hopkins's book delayed so as to avoid competition with his own book's sales. The point is this: The kind of abduction described here was in the making, so to speak, during the mid 1980s.

When we turn to Budd Hopkins the mood turns menacingly negative and away from religious or spiritual speculation. Hopkins investigated abduction cases, employing hypnotic regression to retrieve memories of what happened during missing time. Not uncommon is for an abduction to occur during the night while one is sleeping. The abductee is taken from his or her bedroom and, after one or two hours aboard a spacecraft, returned to bed. While aboard the spacecraft, extraterrestrial scientists manipulate the earthling's body, usually with a special interest in his or her reproductive organs and related biological matters. Some female abductees claim to have been taken multiple times. During one abduction the woman is impregnated. During a later abduction the growing fetus is removed. During a still later abduction she is given her own hybrid baby to rock, fondle, feed, and love. It appears that the feelingless extraterrestrial scientists want to learn just what terrestrial affection looks like. Women abductees

> have either had dreams or normal recollections of having been shown, at later times, tiny offspring whose appearance suggests they are something other than completely human...that they are in fact hybrids, partly human and partly what we must call, for want of a better term, alien.... An ongoing and systematic breeding experiment must be considered one of the central purposes of UFO abductions.[8]

As I have been emphasizing, according to Hopkins's interpretation these experiences are negative. Hopkins comments frequently this way: "I have observed this sort of free-floating apparently unreasonable dread in many people who have undergone consciously unremembered yet traumatic UFO abduction experiences."[9] What accounts for this negativity? Are the ufonauts malevolent? Do they deliberately perpetrate harm? No, says Hopkins. "In none of the cases I've investigated have I ever encountered even the suggestion of deliberate harm or malevolence."[10] The space visitors are not malicious. The negativities are the effect of the disruptive trauma.

Are spacelings abusers? Rapists? Not exactly. The aliens in question are not lusting after the daughters of Earth. "I know of no case in which a female abductee has ever reported an act of intercourse. Above all, in none of these cases involving either men or women do we have what can be called a basically *erotic* experience. The descriptions are invariably of a detached, clinical procedure instead, even if some of them result in a more or less involuntary ejaculation."[11] The aliens are scientists, not rapists. At least in regard to Earth's women. With Earth's men, it might be different. "So far I have been involved in the investigation of four UFO abduction cases im which men have described acts of intercourse with apparently alien females."[12] Whatever is going on, it has to do with reproduction and not sexual abuse.

Hopkins deliberately removes this hybridization model from the celestial savior model. "Abductees are not believers in some religion of outer space, they are not seeking publicity or other rewards, and they are, at heart, confused and frightened."[13] The hybridizing aliens, according to Hopkins, are scientists preparing a mixed race of post-human beings. Aliens are not here to redeem us.

In an earlier chapter, we distinguished between Apollo and Hermes. The disciples of Apollo are looking for a prosaic explanation of the UFO phenomenon, a nuts-and-bolts explanation of textured and nuanced experiences such as abductions. The disciples of Hermes, in contrast, would be satisfied with something less than an explanation. They would be satisfied with merely discerning the meaning of the abduction experience, even if abduction cannot be fully explained. It appears to Thompson that Hopkins is a disciple of Apollo, not Hermes:

The absence of ambiguity and ambivalence in Hopkins' portrayal earned him a loyal following among close encounter witnesses weary of having their experiences dismissed as fantasy, hoax, or delusion. At the same time, Hopkins became something of a role

241

model for mainstream UFO investigators, many embracing his 'master narrative' (Hopkins believes aliens have come to search for human genetic material to restore their dying race).[14]

ABDUCTION AND PTSD

At the 1988 Mutual UFO Network (MUFON) annual symposium, David Jacobs, retired historian at Temple University and director of the International Center for Abduction Research,[15] described abductions in strictly negative terms. Abductions do "not improve their lives, give them mystical or psychic powers, or put them in touch with the all-inspiring Infinite. In fact, the majority of abductees wish that their experiences had never happened, and most of them live in fear that it will occur again."[16] Researchers in the fields of psychology and psychotherapy put abductees into the category of persons suffering from post-traumatic stress disorder (PTSD).

Like Strieber, Hopkins, and Mack, Jacobs published books on UFO abductions during this same definitive period. "By the late 1980s the phenomenon had begun to yield some of its secrets," he wrote. "The abductions, once considered the fringy stepchild of the UFO phenomenon, were irrevocably changing UFO studies."[17] The abduction accounts retrieved by Jacobs through hypnotic regression led to a leap forward in our understanding of UFOs, Jacobs claimed. Separate accounts from separate individuals converged and melded into a single, often-repeated scenario. Jacobs learned that alien transportation is supra-physical; that is, the abductees are transported through walls or ceilings. Communication is telepathic, not linguistic. Evoking the Research Scientist model, Jacobs writes that "the Small Beings are quick, efficient, and focused. They target specific anatomical sites for poking, feeling."[18] When the smaller lab assistants have finished gathering data, a taller ufonaut takes over. The taller being may address the abductee with something like, "You are very special to us" or "This is very important and you are helping us."[19]

We saw machines in the research scientist model. So does Jacobs. "The variety of machine examinations is great, although the exact purpose of the machines is unknown. Most abductees think they are recording devices, much like X-ray equipment. Somehow people know that the machines are scanning them."[20] According to Jacobs, the aliens seem like extraterrestrial scientists going about their work with little or no feeling, while the abducted earthling is being traumatized to the brink of despair.

Jacobs took the MUFON podium again at the 2013 annual symposium. He drew a picture of systematic multi-generational ufonaut abductions of earthlings for the purpose of creating hybrids of interplanetary beings. What appears to us to be abusive rape is in fact extraterrestrial science at work in genetic experimentation.

In the early 1980s, researchers found that abductees consistently described not only a single event in adulthood but also remembered fragments of abductions when they were children. Eventually there was a substantial body of evidence supporting the intergenerational nature of abductions: abductees are abducted throughout their lives; their children also have abduction experiences; and abductees indicate that their mother and/or father have had unusual experiences, such as seeing ghosts or religious figures or having puzzling missing time episodes.[21]

In short, the gray aliens along with their insectoid and reptilian partners wreak havoc on human lives from youth through adulthood. Aliens are not here to save us; they are here to monitor us, and we translate it as harassment.

Negativity dominates. Jacobs's investigation into abductions "has led to profound apprehension for the future. The abduction phenomenon is far more ominous than I had thought...the alien agenda is primarily beneficial for them and not for us."[22] Like Hopkins, Jacobs directly repudiates the celestial savior model in favor of the research scientist model, and then he draws the research science model into the hybridizer model.

What accounts for this negative turn? Thompson offers an explanation: the good abductors are more highly evolved, while the bad abductors are less evolved. "Some UFO beings appear to be more evolved than others, that is, beneficent in both action and intent, while others—especially those who kidnap humans and hold them against their will—behave more like terrorists than gracious spirit guides."[23] I think I must dismiss this attempted explanation, because Thompson offers it from inside the ETI myth rather than in critical analysis of the myth. The tacit faith in evolutionary progress simply fails to make it onto a list of credible scientific assumptions. The doctrine of evolutionary progress leading to goodness is a secularized sublimation of the religious hope for redemption, as I tried to show when explicating Model III, the Celestial Savior.

ABDUCTION: THE NEW SPIRITUALITY

The new negativity described by Hopkins and Jacobs is like a venetian blind: light slips through between the slats. In a very revealing statement, Jacobs tells us how the abductees "prefer to think of their experiences as fantasies or dreams. They want the phenomenon to be benevolent and insist, against all evidence, that it is."[24] Within the abductee account there seems to emerge a thrust toward hope, toward an interpretation of the space visitors that is positive. The abductee wants to see the ufonaut as beneficent. Jacobs wants to keep the blinds drawn so that everything is dark, but enough light peeks through to demonstrate a connection between the Hybridizer model and that of the Celestial Savior.

When we turn to the work of John Mack, we will see that the darkness in the abduction experience is latticed by spiritual light. And Mack is going to separate the blinds to let even more beneficent light in.

Mack wrote a blockbuster book in 1994 titled *Abduction*. He followed this up half a decade later with a second book, *Passport to the Cosmos*. Via hypnotic regression Mack provided the reader with story after story of earthlings finding themselves, against their will, inside spaceships and undergoing abuse. (Or what appeared to be abuse.) In time, the "abuse" turned out to be passage through a spiritual gate into a magnificent sublime reality.

As with Hopkins and Jacobs, the abduction cases Mack reports fit a paradigm, a consistent pattern. The pattern includes: (1) a series of abductions from ordinary life, usually from sleep in one's bedroom; (2) ascent into a hovering spacecraft; (3) interaction with ufonauts, usually with the grays but on occasion with the more frightening insectoids or reptilians; (4) physical probing, with the grays showing particular interest in human reproduction; (5) sperm or egg removal; (6) involuntary sexual intercourse, something that differs in the Mack accounts from the Hopkins accounts; (7) the birth of a hybrid baby accompanied by repeated abductions to aid in caring for the baby; (8) all of the above, leading the abductee to a new and deeper appreciation for the sacredness of the natural realm. Despite the harassment, abuse, rape, and kidnapping, abductees pass through a stage of dread into a stage of affirmation and spiritual advance.

As I have mentioned, I found myself disturbed at Hopkins' *Intruders* and some of the surrounding literature. It appeared to me that Mack's first book on the topic, *Abduction,* functioned to extend this negative paradigm. It seemed to deviate too radically from what I had interpreted as the Celestial Savior model, and I felt I needed to study the matter more thoroughly. Had I missed something important? Had Mack missed seeing what I thought I was seeing? Should we have a conversation about this?

Mack and I agreed to meet in early October 1994 in Boston at the office of PEER (Program for Extraordinary Experience Research). When a colleague and I arrived, we found that John Mack had prepared for a serious interaction. In addition to his PEER staff, he had invited his Harvard colleague and renowned theologian, Harvey Cox. All listened carefully while I reviewed the back story of abductions and their reported experiences. I stressed that the new negativity seemed inconsistent with the precedents set during three-plus decades. Despite the traumatic power of these experiences, I stressed that abductees reported saving gnosis, redemptive knowledge.

Mack was surprisingly non-defensive. He thanked me for pressing these points. He also reminded me that I might have missed seeing the light between the dark slats in *Abduction.* He proceeded to restate that the clients whom he had interviewed did report traumatic experiences with devastatingly negative repercussions. But, Mack added that over time, his clients mellowed, reinterpreting their UFO experience and finding positive meaning that had not been present at first. In his future writings, Mack said, he would try to make this more clear. As I reread *Abduction* in addition to his follow-up writings, I could see that Mack's description differed from that of Hopkins and Jacobs on these points. Mack's own view comes closer to the Celestial Savior model, even though it belongs primarily in that of the Hybridizer.

The aliens in Mack's abduction accounts remain primarily in the Hybridizer model, because the alien agenda includes "...some sort of genetic or quasi-genetic engineering for the purpose of creating human/alien hybrid offspring."[25] Why? Mack learned the answer from a patient named Joe. "The purpose of the hybridization program was evolutionary, to perpetuate the human seed and crossbreed with other species on the ships and elsewhere in the cosmos."[26] Genetics, evolution, progress, and the decisive role of science in improving our reality all come together in this UFO package. Certainly an abduction experience could be dramatic and even traumatic, but in itself this does not make it evil.

Despite what Mack calls the "ontological shock" associated with the UFO experience, the experience is not exclusively negative. The effects "are traumatic and disturbing, but they can also be transforming, leading to significant personal change and spiritual growth."[27] Mack goes on:

> *Yet the abduction phenomenon is not simply traumatic. Experiencers may be left with fears, nightmares, and other...stress.... [But] virtually all abductees with whom I have worked closely have demonstrated a commitment to changing their relationship to the earth, of living more gently on it or in greater harmony with other creatures that live here. Each seems to be devoted to transforming his or her relationships with other people, to expressing love more openly, and transcending aggressive impulses.*[28]

Model IV: The Hybridizer

The result of the abduction is greater love and higher consciousness. "Consciousness expansion and personal transformation is a basic aspect of the abduction phenomenon."[29] In fact, the abduction events precipitate a new resolve to pursue higher concerns, especially spiritual concerns. "Many abductees begin to pursue a more explicit spiritual path as they open themselves to the depth and meaning of their experiences."[30]

The spiritual path of the UFO abductee follows the road toward the higher self, toward mystical union with the inter-subjective world.

The UFO abduction experience, while unique in many respects, bears resemblance to other dramatic, transformative experiences undergone by shamans, mystics, and ordinary citizens who have had encounters with the paranormal. In all of these experiential realms, the individual's ordinary consciousness is radically transformed. He or she is initiated into a non-ordinary state of being which results, ultimately, in a reintegration of the self, and immersion or entrenchment into states and/or knowledge not previously accessible.[31]

Note the emphasis here on knowledge. This is not scientific knowledge. Rather, it is esoteric knowledge. It is the kind of knowledge that re-realizes the unity of subject and object, a supra-rational knowing of the self in relation to nature. It is gnosis.

It is worth recognizing here that a change takes place, a change in the perspective of the abductee due to taking the time to interpret the meaning of the event. The rather feelingless gray spaceling gradually becomes someone worth loving, worth respecting and caring for. "The frightening and adversarial quality of the relationship gives way to a more reciprocal one in which useful human-alien communication can take place and mutual benefit is derived. The abductees may even experience a profound love for the alien beings."[32] This change is not instant. It takes time. "Over time they may come to see [the grays] as odd spirit guides, closer to the ultimate creative principle or Source than humans, even as emissaries from the Divine."[33] The abductors become partners or, better yet, teachers.

The particular terrestrial concern on the minds of the space teachers is ecology. Planet Earth is approaching an ecological crisis, approaching self-destruction due to short-sighted human behavior. Anthropogenic climate change and pollution will soon make Earth uninhabitable for intelligent species. The spacelings are here to warn us, much as the prophets warned ancient Israel, and much as Klaatu warned earthlings about nuclear warfare in 1951. "Information about ecological disaster with powerful apocalyptic imagery is also commonly transmitted by the aliens to human subjects."[34]

Mack enthusiastically observed how the UFO phenomenon is attuned to religious sensibilities. However, Mack feared that the metaphysics of the emerging worldview would not be acceptable within traditional religions. Similar to other New Agers, the mysticism is said to be antithetical to whatever traditional religions are being taught. "There can be little place, especially within the Judeo-Christian tradition, for a variety of small but powerful homely beings who administer an odd mixture of trauma and transcendence without apparent regard for any established religious hierarchy or doctrine."[35] As Mack formulates his own UFO theology in the final 10 pages of *Passport to the Cosmos,* it appears he would be comfortable joining the choir of SBNRs.

ABDUCTION INVESTIGATORS

Important to our treatment here is the mindset of UFO investigators: They believe they are pursuing science. They adhere to self-imposed standards of research and embrace intellectual rigor. Although most abduction reports can be dismissed as less than *real* (the term *real* is employed by the UFO investigators themselves), abduction reports are still worth investigating. The criteria that make an abduction report worthy of scientific investigation are specific: "multiple witnesses testimony, missing and being actively searched for, credible evidence that is deemed anomalous by qualified scientists, and conscious recall of at least part of the abduction by a credible witness, according to Kathleen Marden."[36] We dare not miss the point that ufologists see themselves as pursuing science, regardless of what other scientists or skeptics may say about them. Regardless of what side of a controversy one finds oneself on, we all stand under a single umbrella of appreciation of, if not faithfulness, to science.

The Abduction Research Team of MUFON has attempted to identify "the commonalities that alien abduction experiencers share."[37] Among their findings is that more women than men claim to have been abducted. Also, "the majority of abduction expierencers believe they have been taken repeatedly over a number of years or throughout their lifetime generally starting when they were children...[and they] reported that they had been the victims of childhood abuse."[38] The study found a connection between childhood abuse and negative or abusive abduction experiences.

On the list of commonalities are paranormal phenomena. "Abduction experiencers consistently report being transported through solid surfaces, telepathic communication, light orbs that expand into non-human entities, poltergeist activity in their homes (soon after a contact experience), and new psychic abilities."[39] But, the researchers say, they find this "perplexing and troubling to investigators."[40]

The investigators are unable to pursue research into this paranormal dimension of the UFO phenomenon. Why? Because "MUFON is a scientifically oriented UFO investigating group that does not investigate these phenomena."[41] This self-understanding is very important for us to observe. Because MUFON is a "scientifically oriented" organization, it is unable to conduct research on paranormal phenomena. This self-understanding of UFO investigators tells us something significant, namely, they see themselves as obeying the canons of science and assume that their subject matter, UFO reports, can be understood in scientific terms. Science belongs to the wider culture, not merely to those wearing white coats in laboratories.

We might ask: What defines *science* as science? Is it the content or the method? Marden seems to assume it is the content, the materialist assumptions regarding the world the scientist studies. But, if it is the method that makes science science, then openness to wherever the evidence leads would require that Marden consider the "psychic" evidence too. Regarding abductions, Mack remarks, "The abduction phenomenon... manifests itself in our physical space/time world but is not *of* it in a literal sense."[42] What if Mack is correct? Would Marden be in a position to study the psychic scientifically? Or, would she have precluded it because of her assumptions?

Science must be judged by still higher science, according to UFO chasers Stanton Friedman and Kathleen Marden. If establishment scientists refuse to look impartially at all the evidence, then they are not practicing the best science. Because UFO investigators are open to evidence excluded by establishment scientists, the former are practicing better science. Even with this, the matter of abduction accounts elicits caution. So much caution, that UFO researchers prefer to study the abductees rather than the abductors. Friedman and Marden write that

> the primary focus of academic investigations is not upon alien abduction per se, but psychological explanations based upon the a priori belief that alien abduction is highly improbable...social researchers therefore have viewed alien abduction as a psychological aberration, not a physical experience. Boundary deficit disorder, fantasy-proneness, hallucinations, sleep anomalies, confabulation in hypnosis, false memory syndrome, and cultural mythos have all been offered as psychological explanations for alien abduction.... Academia seldom examines the scientific evidence that suggests some abductions by extraterrestrial beings could be real.[43]

Among the abduction investigators, Hopkins and Jacobs stand out as the experts we all listen to. However, they have garnered critics who dub abduction reports as hoaxes. In her critique of alien abduction investigators, Carol Rainy contends that

*the marshy ground of alien abductions is afloat in hoaxes and par-
tial hoaxes.... What Hopkins and Jacobs claim as 'the powerful evidence' for alien abductions and hybrids among us is based primarily
on the powerful, hypnotic repetition of their own proclamations—
and the public's gullibility in believing whatever unfounded theories
these star paranormal investigators punt down the field.... Unless
they're to become quickly obsolete, alien abduction experts are expected to deliver the goods: newer, fresher, stranger, and ever more
strange reports.... It's my personal belief, knowing both Jacobs and
Hopkins, that they are trapped, like Br'er Rabbit in Tar-Baby, by
the very phenomenon they attempt to confront. They can no longer
extricate themselves from the surreal, richly imaginative blend of
fantasy and reality that is generated around anyone who is deeply
involved in paranormal research.... I believe now that these abduction investigators are sometimes trapped by their own deeply held
beliefs into becoming the victims of hoaxers.[44]*

Whether hoax, fact, or a mixture of both, the abduction phenomenon provides us with the information we need to understand what is
going on in our culture, namely, the presence of the ETI myth and a
yearning for contact with a scientifically advanced reality in the heavens.

SEXUAL ABUSE AND SATANIC ABDUCTIONS

Let us pause to note carryovers between ritual abuse and the hybridizer. The first carryover is: hypnotic regression. It should not go
unnoticed that a transfer has occurred from the UFO phenomenon
to the ritual abuse phenomenon. The method of hypnotic regression
instituted by Benjamin Simon in the case of Betty and Barney Hill established a precedent; it continued to be employed by UFO investigators such as Leo Sprinkle, James Harder, and countless others within
ufology down to the present time. This practice of hypnotic regression
also became the method employed by therapists to retrieve the horrific
accounts of childhood sexual abuse and abuse by Satanic cults. Both

the courts and the anti-anti-Satanists exposed therapists for leading their clients. Hypnotic regression undeniably yokes the UFO and the ritual abuse phenomena.

The second carryover is negativity. This negativity is remarkable because of what I have pointed out frequently: Early positive accounts of abductions get replaced in the 1980s with negative accounts. Why? The negative abduction accounts belonging to the Hybridizer model explode on the UFO scene shortly after publicity over ritual abuse. Does this not warrant the question: What might be the connection, if any?

We must pause to assess the possible influence of another backstory. A tidal wave of fear splashed over North America during the first half of the 1980s. It took the form of a fear that our preschool children were at risk for abduction, sexual abuse, and ritual abuse at the hands of unscrupulous worshippers of Satan. Anxiety-filled parents suspected preschool workers of complicity in these perverted and horrid practices.

The phenomenon began in 1980 thanks to the publication of *Michelle Remembers*. The authors, Michelle Smith and Lawrence Pazder, recounted the early life of Michelle, who grew up in a family that participated in Satanic ritual practices during the 1950s on Vancouver Island. Michelle was the victim, and Lawrence Pazder was her psychiatrist who retrieved her forgotten childhood horrors through hypnotic regression. Because Michelle was unable to remember consciously what had happened to her, hypnotic regression became the method for reconstructing her past. Smith and Pazder went on a nationwide book promotion tour in 1980, and again in 1985 to promote the paperback edition.

During that time, the media familiarized the public with multiple personality disorder (MPD). According to this diagnosis, the victim of childhood trauma experiences personality splits. He or she actually becomes multiple persons, and some of the resulting personalities immunize themselves from the trauma of childhood abuse. The victim has forgotten the abuse, so the goal of the therapist is to retrieve all alternative personalities and reintegrate them. In the case of Jenny in Judith Spencer's book, *Suffer the Child,* the therapists found they had to deal with more than 400 such personalities. Clients lined up at therapists' doors to retrieve their forgotten abuses. An epidemic of MPD broke out among adults, and therapists quickly trained themselves to employ hypnotic regression to help them.

Meanwhile, a second epidemic broke out. Thousands of parents sought to protect their young children by demanding the arrest and prosecution of preschool staff workers. They filed complaints that preschools were fronts set up to lure innocent children into secret dens of sexual perversion and Satanic worship.

The McMartin Preschool trial provides an illustrative example. Located in Manhattan Beach, California, the preschool owners—Raymond Buckey and his mother, Peggy McMartin Bucky—were charged with 52 counts of child molestation. The charges were based on children's testimony describing robed adults, chanting, animal sacrifice, babies cooked and eaten, and forced participation in kiddie-porn movies. The trial began in August 1983 and concluded on January 18, 1990. At the time, it was the most expensive court case in American history. It degenerated into a circus of charges, countercharges, precedents, and influences. The event began when the mother of a two-year-old boy complained to Los Angeles officials that her son had been abused by McMartin employees who had worn masks and capes, taped the boy's mouth shut, stuck a tube in his rectum, made him ride naked on a horse, jabbed scissors and staples into him, stuck his finger in a goat's anus, and made him drink blood from a murdered baby.

Included among the accusations was the fact that the children had been taken to a cave underneath the school. In this cave the children were forced to participate in Satanic rituals. As one might expect, an inspection of the premises proved that there never had been any cave at this location. Videotaped interviews with the children showed how the therapists had led them to construct the Satanist story. Rather than listening to the children, the therapists were leading the children's testimony. The actual charges had been based on the images drawn by the therapists while leading the children to tell a particular story. Once this became clear to the jury, the verdict decision became easy. In the end, none of the 52 counts of child molestation were sustained, and the school's owners were acquitted.

The daily publicity regarding the McMartin trial spawned copy-cat cases. In the months following the beginning of the McMartin trial more than 100 similar cases were prosecuted. Seldom was a guilty verdict rendered.

In my analysis of the Satanic ritual abuse phenomenon in the 1994 publication of *Sin: Radical Evil in Soul and Society,*[45] I divided those engaged in this controversy into three groups: the Satanists, the anti-Satanists, and the anti-anti-Satanists. The first group, the Satanists, was probably very small. Satanists existed, to be sure, but their size and influence were blown out of proportion by the beguiling urban legend.

The group of anti-Satanists was made up primarily of Evangelical Christian psychotherapists who were employing hypnotic regression to retrieve forgotten memories. The lurid details of childhood ritual abuse were passed from therapist to therapist, so they would know what to look for in their respective clients. These therapists became key witnesses for the prosecution in many of the court cases.

The group of anti-anti-Satanists was made up of skeptics and social scientists who were out to expose the anti-Satanists. The anti-anti-Satanists accused the anti-Satanists of scapegoating the Satanists.

David Bromley offers one of the most illuminative attempts to explain what happened during the 1980s: The shocking and hideous descriptions of sexual and ritual abuse so prevalent during this time were due to an urban legend. Why this particular urban legend? The root cause is a social tension created by the increased number of professional women working outside the home. The percentage of mothers leaving the home to go to work jumped from 39 percent in 1970 to 56 percent in 1988. This meant that many more families required the services of preschools; and a new and large market for preschools developed overnight. Beneath this social and economic change festered an anxiety: Should we abandon our family responsibility and pay professionals to raise our children? Have we lost our control and influence on our children? Are we guilty of failing as parents? This anxiety led to parental anger against oneself, and then it was projected outward toward the preschool professionals.[46] Indeed, the preschool staffs became the scapegoats of this urban anxiety.

The evangelical therapists had their own motives for complicity. Their own contorted logic seems to have gone like this: If we can convince the larger public to believe in Satan, then it will be easier to persuade the public to believe in exorcism and the power of the gospel. In short, therapy for abused children became a method of evangelism.

Now, perhaps you find what I'm describing here outrageous. Perhaps you think I'm making sweeping generalizations that are too speculative and perhaps lacking in respect for those involved. Perhaps I am. Nevertheless, this discussion is relevant to understanding Model IV: the Hybridizer.

If we ask about a possible connection, arrows fly. Jacobs finds he must hold up a shield so that arrows flying his way from childhood sexual abuse or Satanic ritual abuse don't poke holes in his abduction theory. One arrow bears this question: Might a UFO abduction account actually convey a retrieved memory of childhood abuse in camouflaged form? Jacobs puts up his shield: "There are serious problems with this explanation," he avers. "Most abductees do not claim to have been sexually or physically abused as children (at least not by humans)."[47] Jacobs's response here begs the question, because we would only be interested in a *forgotten* memory of childhood abuse, not a consciously *remembered* trauma. Having deflected this shot, Jacobs lifts his shield a bit higher: "Because the abduction phenomenon is ongoing, the memories are of events that happened in the very recent past, not screen memories of childhood when the abuse would have taken place."[48] Again, Jacobs may be dodging two arrows. Jacobs's own abductee interviewees report childhood kidnappings, and childhood abuse is frequently serial, similar to the kind of abductions Jacobs studies.

Jacobs announces with a tone of triumph: "To date, neither researchers nor therapists have found a single abduction case that is unequivocally generated from sexual or physical abuse."[49] Jacobs feels safe behind his shield. He shouldn't. I don't believe this arrow can be so easily deflected. The issue is not the fact of childhood abuse; rather, what is at stake is the role the therapist plays in drawing out the forgotten memory of the abuse. A more accurate question would be this: Is the abuse a memory or a fabrication? Did the memory come from the victim or the therapist? Might this apply to both childhood abuse and to UFO abductions? In sum, the question of connection between childhood abuse and the UFO hybridizer deserves more detailed attention.

Jacobs would defend his position by observing that, "most abductees refuse to be led."[50] If this turns out to be the case, then Jacobs's shield would adequately defend him.

CONCLUSION

If any single feature of the Hybridizer model for interpreting UFO abductions stands out, it is ambiguity. Such abductions cannot mean only one thing. They are multivalent. This is why I hesitate to give them a restrictively negative interpretation.

Is a marriage between heaven and Earth taking place? This would seem to be the case in the Hybridizer model. In fear and trembling, Jacobs warns us: "I have come to the conclusion that human civilization may be in for a rapid, and perhaps disastrous, change not of our design and I am all the more uncomfortable because the reason for this change is the *least* acceptable to society—alien integration."[51] Jacobs approaches "alien integration" with xenophobia, fear of the outsider. Yet, might there be other earthlings, xenophilic earthlings, who would welcome hybrids descending from the heavens?

Because of their association with outer space and with our own sky, UFOs connote transcendence. They connote heaven. In archaic agricultural societies, myths of sky gods included their impregnation of the earth mother goddess. By dropping their sperm in the form of rain, the gods of the heavens consorted with Gaia to give birth and nourishment to the crops that supported the tribe. This archaic agricultural symbolism might have been at work in city-state religion, where we find myths of gods copulating with humans. Such fertilization of Earth by heaven led to incarnations.

Might this symbolism be at work here in disguised form? Thompson thinks so. "Aliens *crossbreed* with us, one of the oldest myths of all: gods and goddesses coupling with mortals, resulting in the birth of a hero (Jesus, Confucius, and Achilles, among many others)."[52]

I hesitate to press the connection as far as Thompson does to include incarnation. Nevertheless, the marriage between heaven and Earth does seem operative in the Hybridizer model. Might it be the light shining between the slats of abduction negativity?

12

Astrotheology and UFO Spirituality

As we have seen in the previous chapters, the UFO phenomenon vibrates with spiritual intensity. The *unidentified* nature of unidentified flying objects arouses a sense of mystery. The association of UFOs with the sky awakens our curiosity about transcendence. And the association of UFOs with cosmic space beyond the sky conjures our inner attachment to infinity. Our hearts palpitate at the prospect that other beings like us or even unlike us have mastered the unfathomable distances and are inviting us to join them in a cosmic intimacy.

In addition, UFOs precipitate a blurring of what were previously impervious categories: objectivity vs. subjectivity; matter vs. spirit; normal vs. paranormal. The dualistic division between subject and object in the Enlightenment became midwife to the birth of modern science, which, now in its energetic adolescence, is sewing its wild oats. Modern science has put away childish toys such as subjectivity and now plays only with objective knowledge about the physical world. Our modern scientized worldview with its presupposed materialism has bullied and bruised traditional religion as well as superstition, occultism, magic, and especially personal meaning in life. No one can counter the scientized bully. But with UFOs we can join the bully at play and smuggle some subjectivity back into the scientific toy chest.

Like a child undressing a doll, our hermeneutic of secular experience has uncovered the dimension of ultimacy hidden beneath political and scientific rhetoric. Beneath secular talk is religious feeling. Beneath scientific investigation is spiritual searching. Beneath the objective pursuit of the UFO mystery is the subjective pursuit of ultimate meaning.

In this book we have been looking at UFOs, and we have been looking at the persons who look at UFOs. This is what phenomenology does. It analyzes. Now, we turn from analysis to synthesis. We turn from observation to reflection on observation. We turn to theology and offer some reflections on the UFO phenomenon.

INTRODUCING ASTROTHEOLOGY

By this time it should be clear that I am not a disciple of the Ancient Alien Theology; I'm not a follower of Contactee Theology; nor do I sympathize with any of the other UFO theologies. In contrast, I embrace Astrotheology.

What's Astrotheology? Astrotheology is that branch of theology which provides a critical analysis of the contemporary space sciences combined with an explication of classic doctrines such as creation and Christology for the purpose of constructing a comprehensive and meaningful understanding of our human situation within an astonishingly immense cosmos.[1]

In the earlier edition of *UFOs: God's Chariots?* I had used the term *Exotheology* at this point in the book. I have changed the vocabulary because NASA changed its vocabulary. As mentioned earlier, Carl Sagan had coined the term *Exobiology* in the 1970s to refer to the study of life off-Earth. By the 1990s NASA had elected a different term, *Astrobiology,* as the label for a broader field to deal with both the possibility of microbial life within our solar system plus the possibility of intelligent life on exoplanets. I have elected to use the term *Astrotheology* in large part because I wish to place theologians into dialogue with astrobiologists and other space scientists.

In addition to engaging astrobiologists and other space scientists, I encourage astrotheologians to examine carefully the UFO phenomenon. Analyzing the UFO phenomenon provides considerable illumination regarding the human psyche at work in our wider culture as well as within the scientific subculture. The UFO movement gives voice to the human hope for a better future, a redemptive future.

I must admit at the outset that I have no patent on the term, *Astrotheology*. Others use this term and mean something quite different by it. One alternative use ties astrotheology with traditional astrology. Allegedly, looking to the skies inspired our ancestors to worship the impressive phenomena of nature, especially the stars and the planets. Today's astrology-astrotheologians of this brand study ancient myths and petroglyphs to recover lost wisdom, allegedly suppressed by organized religions such as Christianity.[2] Astrologer-theologians are mythicists, reviving the pre-religious myths that allegedly led to the rise of the historical religions.[3] A certain anti-establishment tone accompanies this version of astrologer-theology, a tone common to the new religious movements of the late-19th and 20th centuries.

My use of the term *Astrotheology* is completely divorced from this alternative usage in the occult. Astrotheology incorporates scientific knowledge into a critical and constructive theology of nature. Now you might ask: Is an alliance between theology and science reasonable? Yes, if the astrotheologian incorporates science into a *theology of nature*, or, more rarely, if the two fields engage in *creative mutual interaction* (CMI). The two fields—theology and science—bring distinctive resources to any interaction. More than mere complementarity, I recommend we pursue both a theology of nature and, when fitting, a creative, mutual interaction between Astrobiology and Astrotheology.[4]

ASTROTHEOLOGY MEETS ETI

In this the final chapter I will try to address two questions of a particularly theological character. The first question has to do with whether or not belief in the existence of extraterrestrial life is consistent with belief in

God. It seems to be assumed by skeptical scientists, at one extreme, and by reactionary fundamentalists, at the other extreme, that these two are mutually contradictory. One must either be a Christian and reject ETI, or else one must reject Christianity to affirm ETI. This, in my judgment, commits the fallacy of false alternatives. In the next few paragraphs, I hope to demonstrate that there is compatibility between Christian cosmology and the possibility of other worlds with intelligent life.

The second question is the one posed by the ancient alien theologians discussed in an earlier chapter: Is the God in whom we believe actually a space alien? It appears to me that there are two answers to this question: no and yes. In pursuing these answers, I wish to alert the reader to the much deeper issue: idolatry. We might call UFO idolatry *ufolatry*. My maxim will be: Let us not place our hopes on false gods or idols. Once this maxim is understood, then we will be ready to appreciate the relative value of UFO revelatory experiences and their messages regarding peace on Earth.

CAN CHRISTIANS AND JEWS AFFIRM ETI?

On at least four occasions I have been interviewed by reporters writing for the *National Enquirer* regarding the same question. Knowing I am both a theologian and a UFO researcher, they ask: Don't you think that if we were to get incontrovertible proof that ETI exists, it would destroy the Christian religion? When I first heard the question I was dumbfounded. I had not really thought this way before. So I asked, "Why is this a question?" The interviewer would then reveal the logic behind the question: "Well, if Christians assume that man is the center of God's universe, and if we find a higher form of life than man in the universe, then this would prove the Christian belief wrong, wouldn't it?"

I was flabbergasted. Despite decades of theological study, I had never heard that Christianity teaches "man is the center of the universe." Medieval Christians thought in terms of a hierarchy of being in which angels were considered both extraterrestrial as well as superior to the human race. And to my knowledge, Christians have always taught that

God is the center of reality, not humanity. I was finding it difficult to get a hold of what the issue at stake here might be. I surmised that despite the interviewer's formulation, perhaps there was some sort of preconceived model of a Copernican revolution in the reporter's mind, supposing that a revolution in contemporary experience might render an ancient religious tradition outdated. The chauvinism of modern scientific thinking was at work again. I did not know whether I should simply tell the reporter his question was hopelessly naïve, or, given the possibility that I had been missing something all along, whether I should beg for time to research the matter and think it over. I avoided making an insult and chose the latter.

What I found in pursuing this research is most intriguing. I began with this question: What has been said about the question of ETI by theologians who are recognized as authentic spokespersons for the Christian tradition? If the reporters from the *National Enquirer* were correct in their assumptions, then I would expect to find a uniform rejection of ETI by our best theologians. But I found no across-the-board rejection. In fact, I discovered two things: first, the subject seldom comes up; second, when the subject does arise, our theologians are, at minimum, flexible and, in many cases, positive in their embracing of the possibility of other worlds with intelligent creatures of God's making. Some theologians even greet the prospect with enthusiasm. This is the case whether the theologian be Protestant, Roman Catholic, or Jewish. This is the case whether the theologian be conservative, liberal, or middle of the road. This is the case whether the theologian be ancient or modern. There is no reason to think that the biblical tradition is vulnerable to falsification by making contact with extraterrestrial beings.

Still thinking about how I should answer these reporters from the *National Enquirer,* I telephoned my friend and colleague Rabbi Hayim Perelmuter. Dr. Perelmuter is former president of the Chicago Board of Rabbis and a professor at the Catholic Theological Union in Chicago. He is one of those renaissance people who covers the waterfront: he is an author, a scripture scholar, knowledgeable about the history of intellectual thought, experienced in Jewish-Christian dialogue, up to date on the politics of Israel, and most apt to know the broad sweep of current Jewish thinking. I described the issue on which I was working. His response was forthright and clear. Contemporary Jewish theology would have no difficulty whatsoever in accepting new knowledge regarding the existence of extraterrestrial life. In fact, it would simply broaden the scope of our understanding of God's creation. Then he added a note of tragic humor, "We Jews have had to adjust to all kinds of things in history, including Nazi Germany and the difficulties with Israel. I am sure we could adjust to space beings emerging from flying saucers as well."

When I reported my findings to each *Enquirer* interviewer in turn, I received a faint though polite "thank you." To this day, I have not seen any of my findings reported on the pages of this publication. I have the impression that the answer I gave was not the one that the interviewers wanted to hear.

THE PETERS ETI RELIGIOUS CRISIS SURVEY

Sensationalist supermarket newspapers such as the *Enquirer* were not the only ones to spread this rumor that ETI would provoke a religious crisis. So did some academic scientists. Paul Davies provides a salient example. Religions seem to be fragile, breakable, says Davies. "The existence of extra-terrestrial intelligences would have a profound impact on religion, shattering completely the traditional perspective of God's special relationship with man."[5] Or, "undoubtedly the most immediate impact of an alien message would be to shake up the world's faiths. The discovery of *any* sign that we are not alone in the universe could prove deeply problematic for the main organized religions, which were founded in the pre-scientific era and are based on the view of the cosmos that belongs to a bygone age."[6] Religions are fragile and vulnerable to dissolution because their beliefs were formed in a pre-scientific age, and scientific knowledge regarding extraterrestrial intelligences could not fit into out-of-date religious worldviews. It appears that Davies and the *National Enquirer* agree on this point. Yet, it seemed to me that they must be mistaken. Could I prove this?

Astrotheology and UFO Spirituality

I set out to confirm or disconfirm the hypothesis: Confirmed contact with extraterrestrial intelligent beings would precipitate such a crisis among traditional religions that these religions would collapse. Along with my Berkeley research assistant, Julie Louise Froehlig, I devised a survey, the Peters ETI Religious Crisis Survey.[7] The survey received more than 1,300 responses worldwide from individuals in multiple religious traditions. It became clear that the vast majority of religious believers, regardless of religion, see no threat to their personal beliefs caused by potential contact with intelligent neighbors on other worlds. In short, what the *National Enquirer* and Paul Davies assumed could not be confirmed.

Let me provide a small sample of the survey's data. In figure 1 (Question 3), note the consistency of the dominance of the third bar, "disagree/strongly disagree." The short bars are "strongly agree/agree" and "neither agree nor disagree." This shows how Roman Catholics, Orthodox Christians, evangelical Protestants, mainline Protestants, Mormons, Jews, and Buddhists right along with the non-religious fear no threat to their personal beliefs.

Q3. Official confirmation of the discovery of a civilization of intelligent beings living on another planet would so undercut my beliefs that my beliefs would face a crisis.

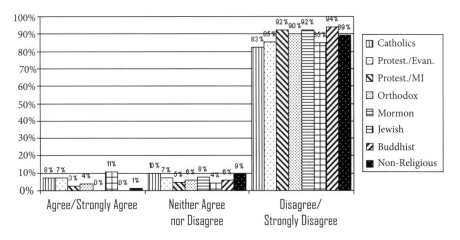

These are the numbers. The additional comments illuminate the numbers. Yes, some responders are concerned about a possible religious crisis. One self-identified evangelical Protestant admits that confirmation of ETI would provoke a crisis but, curiously, not if ETI were a long distance away: "The actual interaction with advanced extraterrestrial life would create a crisis for my belief system. Finding some extraterrestrial life form in a far away planet would not." Another respondent, self-identified as a non-denominational Protestant, associates alien beings with Lucifer. "I believe that all extra-terrestrial beings are fallen angels (demons, if you will). And whatever traits they have can be traced back to Lucifer." These comments came from the "Agree/Strongly Agree" pillars.

But the dramatic news, I think, is that the vast majority spoke positively about potential interactions with ETI. Among those who Disagree/Strongly Disagree we hear a Muslim state, "Islamically we do believe that God created other planets similar to Earth." An evangelical Protestant sanguinely reports: "I can't see why the discovery of other life would affect our belief at all. God has made our world—and can make millions more, I suppose. Is Jesus the savior for all of them too, or did God do things very differently in those places? I'd be fascinated to find out, but not at all disturbed by it." A Roman Catholic foresees no crisis: "My religious viewpoints and practices would remain unchanged. The same God who made me is also capable of making extraterrestrials. His message of faith, hope and love of neighbor goes beyond the borders of the known universe."

Does this indicate a mere grudging adaptation? No, much more. Many religious responders are ready to put out a welcome sign for space visitors. A mainline Protestant hopes that ETI would actually strengthen faith: "If life were discovered elsewhere in the universe, I think my faith in the absolutely mysterious and grace-giving God would actually be more confirmed than it is now. I would have to believe that God is involved not just on our planet, but in the universe in its entirety." So also does an evangelical Protestant: "Traditional Christian understanding teaches there are other intelligences in the universe who are more powerful than humans. Discovery that this teaching is confirmed strengthens Christianity, not weakens it." Another mainline Protestant said, "I'd gladly share a pew with an alien."

The Peters ETI Religious Crisis Survey did not test directly for geocentrism or anthropocentrism. Yet, these two items appear repeatedly among the voluntary comments offered by respondents. A Buddhist takes a stand against geocentrism: "I believe that anything is possible including life on other worlds. To think that in the infinity of the universe that we are the only intelligent life form in existence is ludicrous. I would only hope those beings would exhibit more wisdom than humans have in how they relate to their world and fellow beings." Another respondent self-identified as non-religious says almost the same thing: "I believe that we are not unique in the universe (it would be sheer hubris on our part, not that we are not a completely narcissistic species) but the universe is so large that contact among advanced civilizations is limited to neighboring planetary systems; and we may not have very advanced neighbors."

It is important to note how opposition to geocentrism and anthropocentrism dominates, regardless of tradition. One Mormon exclaims: "Our universe is huge. So astonishingly huge that I find it absurd to think we are alone in this universe as a sentient life form." A Roman Catholic trumpets, "The world is too vast and wonderful and God's power is so limitless, that there must be more than little old us." One mainline Protestant explicitly rejects anthropocentrism: "God is God of all creation and all that is within it. The only way this should be a religious problem is if the true (though unstated) center of our worship is humankind." A Muslim similarly chastises anthropocentrism: "Only arrogance and pride would make one think that Allah made this vast universe only for us to observe."

Does ETI Exist?

What is the verdict? Does such a thing as ETI exist? The jury is still out. There is only circumstantial evidence that life on other worlds is possible. A 2013 poll conducted by Troy Matthew found 37 percent responding yes to the question: Do you believe in the existance of extraterrestrial life? Twenty-one percent answered no, with 42 percent not sure. Religious affiliation adds an interesting accent: 55 percent of those self-identifying as athiest/agnostic answered yes while only 30% of Christians gave the affirmative answer. Between these two we find Muslims at 44 percent; Jewish at 37 percent; and Hindu at 36 percent.[8] Note how the question asks whether responders believe in the existence of ET. This is an empirical question to which the verb "believe" has been applied.

To the empirical question as to whether or not there is such a thing as ETI, Astrotheology brings no privileged resources. It is an open question. The answer is most likely to come from the explorations of science, not from the speculations of the theologian. What the theologian can do is consider the meaning and importance of finding that we are not alone in the cosmos, but the theologian must permit actual experience to discern the relevant facts.

There are some who try to preempt the search by appealing to biblical authority. ETI is not mentioned in the Bible. However, just because the Bible does not mention the existence of something is insufficient reason for denying that it exists. The Bible never mentions the existence of Chevrolets or fresh frozen orange juice, for example, yet these are undeniably part of my everyday reality. The authors of biblical times could not be expected to know about discoveries and inventions that would occur centuries into their future. Similarly, we cannot expect them to have anticipated the importance of the question of ETI. The Bible was not meant to function as an exhaustive inventory of everything that has existed or will exist in the history of God's creation. What the Bible does is deliver to us the message of God's gracious work of salvation. This is enough. Let us not ask of the Bible something it was not intended to deliver.

We might still ask: Should we hope that ETI will be found to exist and, further, that our extraterrestrial neighbors will turn out to be our celestial saviors? Should we expect that the God in which Christians and Jews have placed their trust throughout the centuries will turn out to be a space alien?

No, God Is Not a Space Alien

God is not an alien in the von Däniken sense of a misperceived or misinterpreted UFO occupant, nor does the ancient astronaut theory provide a viable theology. And further, even though some UFO theologians seek salvation from a God-substitute, they reveal they have not yet heard that salvation has already been offered by God through Jesus Christ.

The first commandment given to Moses indicates that God is not spatial. And if God is not spatial, the divine ought not to be confused with anything terrestrial or extraterrestrial. We are able to make graven and conceptual images of the people we know because each one possesses a particular spatial form or profile. Objects in space, whether on Earth or in cosmic space, are finite in character.

God is infinite. God transcends space as well as time. This does not mean God is divorced or separate from the space in which we live. He is present with us every moment. He is omnipresent. He is not absent from any point in space. Transcendence does mean, however, that God is not present in space. Though present, God is not limited by space, even the wide-open spaces of the multi-galactic universe.

The forming of an image consists in dividing up space. As soon as you draw a line you in effect divide all space into two parts; the space on one side of the line is separated from the space on the other side of the line. The drawing of a form consists basically in distinguishing one section of space from all the rest. To draw or carve an image of a person is to say that person is here, not there or anywhere else. His or her image is contained within these lines.

The first commandment in Exodus 20:3-4 reads "You shall have no other gods before me. You shall not make for yourself an idol, whether in the form of anything that is in heaven above, or that is on the earth beneath, or that is in the water under the earth." This means that images of God are impossible, and that if we insist on making one we end up with only an idol. Even if we divide space into two parts by the lines of an image, God is still on both sides of each line. He cannot be conceived as "here but not there." He is omnipresent and transcendent. No image can contain him and separate him from the rest of space.

Furthermore, the God believed in by Hebrews and Christians is the creator of this majestic universe. As the author of all things he comes prior to all things. God ought not to be confused with the things he has made. The creatures ought not to be confused with their creator. The being of God, his aseity, is not dependent upon the being of other things.

Many of us recall the familiar medieval proof for the existence of God known as the cosmological argument. One form of the argument begins by recognizing that everything or every event in the world is caused. Everything we know is the effect of a prior cause. But each cause in turn is the effect of a cause prior to it. And that cause has a still prior cause. Is there an uncaused cause that first brought the world into being? Yes, answers Thomas Aquinas, and that first cause is God.

Everything in the universe is contingent. Its being depends on the being of other things. Is there a necessary being, upon whom everything else depends but who is himself independent? Yes, answers St. Thomas, it is God, the creator of the world. The point of retracing these arguments here is not to prove to the atheists of the world that they should believe in God. Rather, by examining these arguments we can see that traditional Jewish and Christian conceptions affirm that God is the creator of the universe and therefore ought not to be confused with any creature in it.

We have raised the same kind of argument with regard to the chariots of the gods. If it is true, as von Däniken argues, that the creators of human intelligence on Earth came from another planet, we may still ask from where did they get their intelligence? If the extraterrestrial astronauts are "gods" for you and me on Earth, do those astronauts in turn have their own creator gods? If so, who created that set of gods? And so forth. Unless we allow for an infinite regress, the buck must stop somewhere.

Somewhere or sometime there must be a first creator of all intelligent beings. It is that first creator, not an already created, that corresponds to the God worshiped by Jews and Christians.

Von Däniken recognizes the need to understand God as the transcendent and infinite creator, and he makes this abundantly clear in the last chapter of *The Gold of the Gods*. Following George Gamow's big-bang theory of the creation of the universe, he asks about the origin of the compressed gas prior to the big bang. Even the theory of evolution takes us back to a creator of all things. Von Däniken crudely names that creator IT. Christians and Jews should give up their "familiar and well-loved fairy stories," he says, and stop worshiping misinterpreted space travelers in favor of contemplating the indefinable IT. In his incredible naiveté and astounding ignorance of religious history, von Däniken believes he is the first to suggest that we worship an infinite deity rather than finite human forms.

Moses did not make this mistake. If he had any understanding whatsoever of the first commandment that he delivered to the Israelites, he knew he was worshiping the creator of human beings and not human beings themselves. He knew the difference between God and idols. A space traveler might possibly pass for a messenger of God (such as an angel), but an angel or a ufonaut could never be confused with God himself. Hebrews and Christians do not worship angels, even the angels of God. That would be idolatry.

We see, though, that the Bible does speak of God in human terms. There are repeated references to his "face" and his "mighty hand and outstretched arm." In more recent centuries we have become accustomed to speaking of God's "will" or the "mind of God." All such references are anthropomorphisms, that is, we interpret our experience with the divine by attributing qualities to God that are characteristic of human beings. But this does not mean we believe God to be a mere human. To speak of God's face is symbolic or metaphorical speaking; we are not saying that he has a physical face. We need to keep in mind that though the Bible is the Word of God it is still written in the words of us humans.

UFOs: God's Chariots?

Recall the function of the symbol discussed in the first chapter. The symbol uses something ordinary and of this world to open us to something extraordinary and transcendent. The mistake so often made that leads to idolatry is the insistence on interpreting symbolic language literally. Such Apollonian literalism ignores the mystery and ineffability of God, which Hermes can help us interpret.

Von Däniken and other ancient astronaut theorists refuse to recognize this symbolic dimension. They interpret the Bible literally when it requires symbolic sensitivity. And they reject what is meant literally, and replace it with their own updated words and concepts. They then apply these updated words and concepts to refer literally to human-like beings and not symbolically to an infinite God.

This method is spurious. On the one hand, they say the Bible is valid; it reports the Hebrew experience with the superhuman reality we call God. On the other hand, they say the Bible is invalid: it testifies that God is infinite and mysterious, whereas he is really finite and comprehendible in scientific terms. One would expect that literal interpreters of the Bible would simply either accept or reject what they read. But the ancient astronaut theorists do both, taking the liberty to change what they read by translating it into a new literalism. What they fail to recognize is that the heart of the Hebrew Scriptures is the Torah or Law, and this Law has as its focal point the first commandment: I am the Lord your God, have no other gods before me and do not make any images of me.

Consequently, the suggestion that Moses was using a walkie-talkie radio transmitter hidden within the Ark of the Covenant is ridiculous. It presumes that the God on the other end literally has ears and mouth, and that he is dependent for communicating upon the radio waves picked up by the membranes of Moses' ears. It makes God finite, subject to the limits of space. God would have to be in one place only, in the hovering UFO talking into a microphone. He would not be omnipresent or transcendent. For Moses to have so pictured God would have meant a contradiction of the understanding implied in the first commandment. The Hebrews did not mistakenly worship space aliens. They worshiped

God. The Hebrews would never knowingly have worshiped spacelings; they would have condemned such a practice as being idolatry. Perhaps today's UFO theologies should receive the same label.

Although God is not literally a man from another world, he has revealed himself to us in a man from this world. We speak of Jesus Christ as the incarnation of God. To *incarnate* means to "make fleshly," and in the incarnation of Christ God took on the flesh and blood of human living. Jesus Christ is the fullest expression of God's will under the finite conditions of time and space. Hence, Christians do see God in the form of a man, in the form of Jesus of Nazareth. But the finite Jesus is not the same thing as the infinite God himself.

We may occasionally refer to Jesus as the Son of God, which compares Jesus's relationship with God to a person's relationship with his or her father. But it is a comparison, a symbol. God is not literally a father. A father on Earth is to some extent a creator of his children, but God as creator of all things is much more than an earthly father.

Thus, Jesus Christ is a symbol. He is an earthly finite being, but he opens up the windows of transcendence so that we can become aware of God's presence. Jesus was a man of integrity; he spoke honestly and kept his promises. So also through him we see that God too will keep his promises. Jesus cared for victims of disease and injustice. He visited the lonely and the outcast. He showed compassion and forgiveness to those burdened by sin and guilt. Jesus behaved this way to the people who lived in his generation and in his nation. Jesus carried out his ministry at one time and in one place. Nevertheless, through him it is revealed that the transcendent and omnipresent God is at all times and places a God of love and compassion. God is always concerned about healing the sick, comforting the lonely, and forgiving the guilty. Jesus is a finite symbol through which the infinite God becomes known.

Jesus worshiped God, prayed to him, sang hymns to him, and served him daily. It would be a mistake for us, then, to worship a finite man rather than the infinite God, to worship the symbol rather than the God symbolized. But the finite historical human Jesus who walked the dusty roads of Palestine so many years ago is not the end of the story. This Jesus became the Christ, the Messiah. He was the right hand of God dipping down into human events in order to attain victory over sin and salvation for us. God loves this world—our cosmos—and he has become involved in its affairs. By "Christ" we mean God at work among us. By "Christ" we mean the finite Jesus of yesterday as well as the infinite resurrected and living Christ—the Holy Spirit—at work in our world today. Christians worship an ineffable Trinity: God the Father, Son, and Holy Spirit.

Is the God of the Bible a misinterpreted visitor from space? No. Although in Jesus God took the form of a man, God did not cease to be the God of infinity. God is much more than a apace alien could ever be.

YES, GOD MAY COME TO US AS A SPACE ALIEN

We noted that Jesus is the incarnate presence of God, that is, God has come to us in the flesh of our own world. God uses things subject to our perception and to our understanding in order to make the divine will known. God does not come to us as pure spirit devoid of any physical attachments. Any finite object on Earth may be pressed into service as a symbol, as a window opening us toward divine transcendence.

Could God use space aliens? Yes, I believe God could use them, whether they are actual alien beings or whether they are figments of human imagination. In fact, UFOs seem to be proclaiming the law of God to the people of Earth. What do we mean by the law of God? Most often this term reminds us of the Ten Commandments. The first four commands of the law of Sinai given to Moses say we should worship only the one God, and not idols; we should not use God's name in vain; and we should keep the Sabbath day holy. The last six commands say we should honor our parents and avoid killing, adultery, stealing, dishonesty in speech, and coveting the wealth of others. In the New Testament Jesus sums up the law of God in two commandments: love God and love your neighbor. And St. Paul reiterates the words of Jesus in Romans 13:10, "Love does no wrong to a neighbor; therefore love is the fulfilling of the law." If all of us were to fulfill God's law, then there would be peace on Earth as it is in heaven.

But a law of God is much more than a simple rule that demands a certain behavior pattern for people to follow. The law of God is the expression of the very heart and activity of God himself. It appears as a command to us, but it is not a command to God. It is his very way of being. It is the divine nature to love. God already loves. The law of love becomes a command only to those who fail to love. The law of love *describes* what God already does, while it *prescribes* what we as humans have yet to do. The law exists as a command only for those who live alienated from God.

In a sense, laws of our legislatures are an extension of the law of God. Laws help us to love our neighbor. Those who obey the law are in tune with God's will, and those who disobey risk serious injury and even death to other persons, a violation of both the Ten Commandments and of the peace of the community.

The commandments ask that we embody—that we incarnate in ourselves—the very love of God. Jesus Christ is the fulfillment of God's law because he is the incarnation of God's love. His life was not in contradiction to the law. It was the law in action. It was total and complete love even to the point of self-sacrifice. For us, in contrast, the law of God stands against us as a command to perform work yet to be done, namely, to love our neighbor.

In many cases, UFOs seem to be telling us to love our neighbor as well. Where God dwells fully there is love. This was true for the incarnate Jesus Christ; it must also be true for heaven. And the UFOs come not only from the heavens in the sense of the sky, but also heaven in the sense of perfection. Their very existence as perfect stands over against us as judge and commandment: "Be ye therefore perfect even as your Father which is in heaven is perfect." (Matthew 5:48, KJV)

Sometimes the ufonauts become very explicit in articulating their commands. George Adamski was told that on Venus everyone obeys the laws of God and that we on Earth need to do the same before we destroy ourselves. Alan told Dr. Fry that we earthlings should engage in understanding one another better in order to foster a worldwide sense of brotherhood. One psychic of the 1970s who claimed to be in telepathic contact with the occupants of UFOs was Ted Owens of Cape Charles, Virginia. Owens said the UFOs are working toward a change of heart in the human race, a change away from hate and corruption toward love, peace, gentleness, kindness, truth, honesty, compassion, and brotherhood. "They are working to utterly destroy war and crime and those who perpetuate war and crime, so the earth can have an age of peace and happiness."[9]

Marianne Francis of the Solar Light Center, an organization in Central Point, Oregon, claimed to have regular telepathic contacts with 12 men and 12 women from other planets. They are *Homo sapiens*, not monsters, and come from diverse planets such as Saturn, Venus, and Mars. The 24 space people are referred to as our space brothers and are presently aboard starcraft XY-7. Miss Francis said the starcraft people represent a civilization that has evolved to a more advanced stage than Earth has, spiritually, mentally, morally, and physically. The Earth is a kind of fallen planet, and all have hopes that perhaps someday it may be invited to join the stellar alliance. The messages sent to earthlings via Miss Francis are challenges for us to turn to the inner world and see the god within each of us. We need to amplify our god-consciousness.

"Regardless of the source," write two ufologists from within the Celestial Savior model, Glenn McWane and David Graham, "the messages always follow the same basic text, telling us of the need for brotherhood, peace, and urging man to overcome his greed so that he might seek the truths found at the inner levels of consciousness. While there is uniformity in the messages from space, we must also appreciate that there is uniformity in the teachings that date back to the time of Jesus, Buddha, and Krishna, and a score of other religious leaders and prophets, who also told us to seek such attributes as love and peace toward our fellow man."[10]

Could God be using the earthly image of space visitors to communicate once again what he tried to say so long ago on Mt. Sinai? Why not?

He has shown that he uses the things of the familiar world as vehicles for his message. Regardless of the reality or unreality of UFOs, when his message is presented, I think we should listen.

During the 1950s we became strikingly aware of the need for peace—worldwide peace—because of the rising threat of atomic war. We were in the process of inventing thermonuclear weapons that threatened not only to kill the enemy but to kill ourselves as well. We were investing great money and effort to create the most daring disobedience to the sixth commandment—Thou shalt not kill—in the history of the world. The only way to stop the slide downhill toward calamitous world-destruction would be a rebirth of the sense of unity and brotherhood between the competing sides. Neither side would choose to kill someone they loved. If only we could spread love fast enough we might be able to avert disaster. And because human efforts so often failed, we were ripe for accepting aid from extrahuman allies—if not from God, then from flying saucers.

In the 21st century the threat is less from nuclear war and more from climate change, but the same logic applies. Despite what we think, the threat of thermonuclear destruction has not disappeared. Actually, it is worse now than ever. More nations have the bomb. However, we may be less conscious of the atomic threat because we have grown somewhat accustomed to it throughout the last decades The threat is just as awesome, but we are a bit more adapted to living under the threat.

The ecological crisis frightens citizens in a more acute way The problems of rapid population growth and dwindling food supply were known to social scientists in the 1950s, but the widespread sense of the precariousness of our future is recent and still going strong. Recall how in this regard Carl Jung argued that the sense of "congestion creates fear" and arouses "expectations of a redeeming, supernatural event." The fear of impending ecological crisis may also revive a more primitive awareness of God's law. The crises may be slightly different, but the UFO message is the same: Unless we cooperate together in love and brotherhood we will all suffer the consequences.

Vociferous conservatives deny that the planet faces a problem and, if there were such a problem, say that we could cure it with more industrial growth. This growth remedy is impossible on two counts. First, our estimated reserves of natural resources necessary for industrialization are too small. At the present rate of use, many will last only a century. If we increase their use, we will reduce the time accordingly. Second, increased industrialization not only increases the production of goods but also the production of pollution. Massive industrialization would poison the human race to death before the job could be completed. Our ecosphere may become so contaminated that some earthlings will begin seeking a new and fresh world in space to colonize. But many other earthlings—those too poor to buy a ticket on the departing rocket ship—will be left behind to drink the cup of industrial poison. Someday, the rich may be able to discard the planet Earth as one would an empty beer can. The poor can never afford that luxury.

The gulf between rich and poor accentuates the ecological crisis and even dictates the form the solution must take. There will be no solution to the ecological problem that does not include a sharing of wealth by the rich with the poor. This forecast draws together the threat of nuclear destruction with the threat of ecological destruction. As the poorer starving masses increase in number in the coming years, they will become increasingly envious of the wealthy industrialized nations. Envy will turn to anger, and anger to violence, and violence to destruction. As atomic weapons proliferate throughout the third world the threat of holocaust will escalate. India and Pakistan now have the bomb, and all sides of the Middle East struggle are seeking it.

What stands on the horizon is nuclear blackmail. A nation victimized by poverty and hunger may demand help from an advanced nation under threat of nuclear attack. If help is denied, then a nuclear weapon will be sent to the advanced country. The rich nations may threaten to retaliate by sending nuclear warheads back to bomb the poor. But the poor can say, "So what have we got to lose?" Only the wealthy have something to lose.

In order to avert nuclear blackmail the poorer peoples must be made to feel they have an investment in the peace and tranquility of the world. They need to have security and a share of the world's wealth. If they have something to lose they will not be so reckless with their power.

But we have already said that increased worldwide industrialization is not the answer. The result of that would be the destruction of both rich and poor. The only answer, then, is some sort of redistribution of the Earth's present wealth. We need sharing. Only through sharing what we presently have can we curtail growth and bring the world economy into equilibrium. Such a program of sharing can be the product only of a widespread sense of the brotherhood and unity of all humankind. It must come from a deep desire to alleviate suffering and to achieve peace on Earth.

Thinking about the medium- to long-range future, then, has dimensions that are scientific, political, and religious. These dimensions are both spatial and temporal, both planetary and intergenerational. John Dryzek, Richard Norgaard, and David Schlossberg remind us that the challenge of climate change is global, planetary. "Climate change involves a complex global set of both causal practices and felt impacts, and as such requires coherent global action—or, at a minimum, coordination across some critical mass of global players."[11] Still thinking spatially, we may include in our vision what surrounds the Earth, not merely the Earth. Our planet fits within a larger context, a cosmic context. Boston University theologian John Hart expands our ethical context to the cosmos, thinking of a "cosmic commons" as the arena of human moral responsibility.[12]

To the threat of atomic war in the 1950s the subsequent decades have added the threat of ecological catastrophe; the threat of ecological catastrophe will in turn revive the threat of nuclear war. The UFO message remains the same: To avert disaster we must consider everyone a member of the single planetwide brotherhood; we must replace greed with sharing, relax tension, cultivate compassion and cooperation, and promote planning for the benefit of future generations we may not live to see. Is this message not a call to obey God's law?

The law of God presents us with God's desire that all people live together in peace without conflict, united not divided, in compassion without covetousness, loving rather than hating. This law stands over us as judge and as command. As judge it reminds us how far we have fallen short of God's will. As command, it encourages us and leads us toward a better future.

CONCLUSION

I wish to close with a story of irony. On Saturday, November 26, 1977, something unprecedented happened during a broadcast of the South England Television Network. Around 5 p.m., the regular programming was interrupted. A strange voice declared, "'This is the voice of Asteron." Asteron claimed to represent an intergalactic association that is deeply concerned about our welfare on Earth. He went on to warn us that we have only a short time to live. To avoid total annihilation, we must put away our weapons of war, embrace one another, and learn to live together in peace. After six minutes the transmission ended. The TV station was bombarded by its frightened audience. A mood of panic gripped the viewers. Officials at the network set about an investigation. The following Tuesday I heard a news broadcaster reporting the public statement of a network spokesman. Asteron's message that we should put down our weapons of war and strive for world peace was the result of a hoax, and the spokesman guaranteed that that *message would not be heard again* on that station.

Ironic, but sad. It was a good message, regardless of the source. If anyone on Earth tells us to embrace one another in love and strive for world peace, that person is a messenger from God. Whether UFOs are fact or fiction, real or unreal, if they bring us such a message, I believe we should listen.

Notes

PREFACE

1. Troy Matthew intervieed by Alejandro Rojas, *Open Minds*, February 7, 2013, *www.educatinghumanity.com/2013/09/ufo-poll-results-2013.html*

2. Jacques Vallee, *Passport to Magonia: From Folklore to Flying Saucers* (Chicago: Henry Regnery Co., 1969), 150.

3. Gregory L. Reece, *UFO Religion: Inside Flying Saucer Cults and Culture* (London and New York: I.B. Tauris, 2007), 3.

4. Catherine Keller, *On the Mystery: Discerning God in Process* (Minneapolis, Minn.: Fortress, 2008), 17.

5. John Haught, *Deeper than Darwin* (Boulder, Colo.: Westview, 2003), 179.

CHAPTER 1

1. Philip Coppens, *The Ancient Alien Question* (Pompton Plains N.J.: New Page Books, 2012), 288.

CHAPTER 2

1. Michael Salla, "Preface: Protocols for Future Contact," in *UFOs: How Does one Speak to a Ball of Light?*, Paola Leopizzi Harris (self-published, 2011).

UFOs: God's Chariots?

2. This set of observational categories comes first from the pioneering work of J. Allen Hynek, *The UFO Experience: A Scientific Inquiry* (New York: Ballantine, 1972).

3. Richard F. Haines, *Observing UFOs* (Chicago: Nelson-Hall, 1980). Haines, a perceptual psychologist formerly with NASA and a retired professor at San Jose State University, stresses that we need to study the UFO observer in the act of observation as well as the UFO that is observed.

4. Philip Morrison, "The Nature of Scientific Evidence: A Summary," in *UFOs—A Scientific Debate,* ed. Carl Sagan and Thornton Page (Ithica, N.Y.: Cornell University Press, 1972), 285.

5. Jacques Vallée, *Anatomy of a Phenomenon: UFOs in Space* (New York: Ballantine Books, 1965), 92–95.

6. Edward U. Condon, *Final Report of the Scientific Study of Unidentified Flying Objects* (New York: E.P. Dutton & Co., 1969), 11, 45.

7. *Flying Saucers* by the editors of UPI and *Look* (New York: Cowles Communications, Inc., 1967), 12.

8. Donald Keyhoe, *Flying Saucers from Outer Space* (New York: Henry Holt, 1953), chapter 5; the government reports are available in *Project Bluebook*, ed. Brad Steiger (New York: Ballantine Books, 1976), chapter 6.

9. Condon, *Final Report*, 158.

10. Keith Thompson, *Angels and Aliens* (New York: Fawcett Columbine, 1991), 28.

11. Condon, *Final Report*, 391.

12. Ralph and Judy Blum, *Beyond Earth* (New York: Bantam Books, 1974), 109–121.

13. Ibid., 117.

14. Leo R. Sprinkle, "Hypnotic and Psychic Implications in the Investigation of UFO Reports," in *Encounters with UFO Occupants,* Coral and Jim Lorenzen (New York: Berkeley, 1974), 285.

15. UPI report in *Skylook* (March 1976), 11.

16. *The National Enquirer* (11 May 1976), 4–5; and *APRO Bulletin* (September 1975).

17. Kai Bird and Martin J. Sherwin, *American Prometheus: The Triumph and Tragedy of J. Robert Oppenheimer* (New York: Random House, Vintage Books, 2005), 388.

18. Ibid., 347.

19. Ibid., 390.

20. John E. Mack, *Abduction: Human Encounters with Aliens* (New York: Charles Scribner's Sons, 1994), 50.

21. John E. Mack, *Passport to the Cosmos: Human Transformation and Alien Encounters* (New York: Three Rivers Press, 1999), 94.

22. Albert Einstein and J. Robert Oppenheimer, "Relationships with Inhabitants of Celestial Bodies," in Paolo Leopizzi Harris, *UFOs,* 171.

23. See Websites for Stanton Friedman (*www.stantonfriedman.com*) and Steven Greer (*www.siriusdisclosure.com*).

24. Steven M. Greer, *Disclosure: Military and Government Witnesses Reveal the Greatest Secrets in Modern History* (Crozet, Va.: Crossing Point, 2001), 21.

25. Ibid., 19.

26. Leopizzi Harris, *UFOs,* xxvii.

27. Michael A. G. Michaud, "Negotiating with Other Worlds," *The Futurist* (1973): 71–77.

28. Ibid.

CHAPTER 3

1. Donald Keyhoe, *The Flying Saucers Are Real* (New York: Fawcett, 1950), 6.

2. Frank Scully, *Behind the Flying Saucers* (New York: Popular Library, 1951), 3.

3. Kal K. Korff, *The Roswell UFO Crash* (Buffalo, N.Y.: Prometheus Press, 1997). The most influential descriptions of the Roswell case

can be found in Charles Berlitz and William L. Moore's *The Roswell Incident* (New York: Grosset and Dunlap, 1980); Stanton T. Friedman and Don Berliner's *Crash at Corona* (New York: Paragon House, 1991); Kevin D. Randle and Donald R. Schmitt's, *The Truth about the UFO Crash at Roswell* (New York: Avon Books, 1992); and chapter 9 of Stanton T. Friedman's *Flying Saucers and Science: A Scientist Investigates the Mysteries of UFOs* (Franklin Lakes, N.J.: New Page Books, 2008). Note the dates of publication. These books were written three or more decades after the incident they describe. If one looks at newspaper articles published, such as the *Roswell Daily Record* for July 8 and 9, 1947, much of the story is already there and reported. For some reason beyond my comprehension, not much was made of the Roswell case at the time, but it became a worldwide public controversy by the time of its 50th anniversary in 1997.

4. Photocopies of the documents are provided by Stanton T. Friedman, *Top Secret/Majic* (New York: Marlow and Company, 1997), 224. cf. Ryan Roberts, "The Majestic Documents," *www.majesticdocuments.com*.

5. Ryan Roberts, "The Majestic Documents," *www.majesticdocuments.com/documents/intro.php*; Leopizzi Harris, *UFOs*, 166–172.

6. *The Roswell Report: Case Closed*, Headquarters of the United States Air Force, obtainable from the Superintendent of Documents, U.S. Government Printing Office, Washington D.C. 20402.

7. Kevin Randle, *Conspiracy of Silence* (New York: Avon, 1997), 7.

8. Ibid., 6.

9. Korff, *The Roswell UFO Crash*, 171.

10. Ibid., 185.

11. Ibid., 218.

12. Joe Nickel and James McGaha, "The Roswellian Syndrome: How Some UFO Myths Develop," *Skeptical Inquirer* 36, no. 3 (2012): 31.

13. Ibid., 32.

14. Ibid., 36. The public release of internal documents by the FBI dealing with the Roswell reports have gone viral, with the largest number of hits of any U.S. document. cf. *http://vault.fbi.gov/Roswell%20UFO/Roswell%20UFO%20Part%201%20of%201/view.*

15. Philip J. Corso with William J. Birnes, *The Day After Roswell* (New York: Pocket Books, 1997), 1.

16. Ibid., 115.

17. Ibid., 4–5.

18. Ibid., 46, 179.

19. Albert A. Harrison, *Starstruck: Cosmic Visions in Science, Religion, and Folklore* (New York and Oxford: Berghahn Books, 2007), 139.

20. Greer, *Disclosure*, 13.

21. Ibid., 562.

22. Ibid., 563–564.

23. Ibid., 13.

24. Ibid., 20.

CHAPTER 4

1. Hynek, *The UFO Experience*, 163.

2. Coral and Jim Lorenzen, *Encounters with UFO Occupants* (New York: Berkeley, 1974), 29–31

3. Ibid., 31.

4. Ibid., 133–136.

5. David Webb, *1973—Year of the Humanoids, 2nd ed.* (Evanston, Ill.: Center for UFO Studies, May 1976), 19.

6. Ted Bloecher, "The Stonehenge Incidents of January 1975," *Flying Saucer Review* 22, no. 3 and 4 (1976).

7. John G. Fuller, *The Interrupted Journey* (New York: Dial Press, 1966, and Berkeley Medallion edition, 1974). Jacques Vallée claims to have uncovered a detail of which John Fuller was unaware: The object seen by the Hills had been detected by military

radar. He cites a document in the files of the 100th Bomb Wing of the Strategic Air Command at Pease Air Force Base in New Hampshire in Jaques Vallee's *Dimensions,* 117f.

8. Hynek, *The UFO Experience,* 179n.

9. Budd Hopkins, *Intruders: The Incredible Visitations at Copley Woods* (New York: Ballantine, 1987), 115.

10. Gwen Farrell, "Function of Memory in Abduction-Contact Experiences," *MUFON UFO Journal* 544 (2013): 6. Neuroscientists are finding that physical stimulation of the brain can actually impart memories of events that never happened. Helen Shen, "US brain project puts focus on ethics," *Nature* 500, no. 7462 (2013): 261–262.

11. Lorenzen, *Encounters with UFO Occupants,* 267.

12. Mack, *Abduction,* 14.

13. Terrence Dickensen, "The Zeta Reticuli Incident" *Astronomy* (December 1974).

14. Stanton T. Friedman and Kathleen Marden, *Captured! The Betty and Barney Hill UFO Experience* (Pompton Plains, N.J.: New Page Books, 2007). On page 20, Kathleen Marden, the niece of Betty Hill and a UFO investigator, remarks about John Fuller's treatment: "Some of his facts were inaccurate, and the hypnosis transcripts were incomplete."

15. Lorenzen, *Encounters with UFO Occupants,* 97.

16. October 1973 was a period of flap in North America. John Ventre cites seven cases between October 1 and 17 alone in "Looking Back 40 Years: UFO Wave Spreads Across Country During 1973," *MUFON UFO Journal* 544 (2013): 7.

17. For a complete account see Charles Hickson and William Mendez, *UFO Contact at Pascagoula* (Tucson, Ariz.: Wendell C. Stevens, 1983).

18. Philip J. Klass, *UFOs Explained* (New York: Random House, 1974). Another assessment of the Pascagoula abduction is offered by Joe Eszterhas, "Claw Men from the Outer Space," *Rolling*

Stone (January 1974). However, Hickson told Elder and me that Eszterhas never interviewed either him or Parker.

19. *Skylook* (March 1976) 11.
20. Jerome Clark, "A UFO Abduction Case and Its Implications," address to the 1976 MUFON Symposium, Ann Arbor, Michigan, June 12, 1976.
21. Lowell Cauffiel, "It's Incredible! Tales of UFO Abductions on Upswing," *Detroit News,* (February 1976), 3A.
22. UPI report in *Skylook* (March 1976) 11.
23. Steven M. Greer, "Testimony of Dr. Richard Haines," in *Disclosure: Military and Government Witnesses Reveal the Greatest Secrets in Modern History* (Crozet, Va.: Crossing Point, 2001), 131.
24. Jan C. Harzan, "MUFON: For the Benefit of Humanity," *MUFON UFO Journal,* 537 (2013): 1.
25. Hopkins, *Intruders,* 6–7.
26. Ibid., 115.
27. Ibid., 281–283.
28. Ibid., 277. My criticism of Hopkins finds a partial parallel in that of Vallée, who identifies UFO abduction cases with medieval reports of abductions of humans by elves and fairies. Fairy tales, argues Vallée, include breeding experiments that fit exactly with what Hopkins is ascribing to extraterrestrials. The upshot of this observation is that we must go beyond the model of the Research Scientist and into the realm of ritual abuse or even more generic religion if we are to apprehend what the UFO phenomenon is really about. For more information, you can refer to Vallée's *Dimensions: A Casebook of Alien Contact* (New York: Ballantine Books, 1989), 267–268.
29. The most frequent criticism leveled against Hopkins' approach is different from what I have said here. Critics usually suspect that the method of hypnotic regression is faulty. Whitley Strieber, for example, says that "too many UFO researchers believe the Budd

Hopkins abduction scenario...[but] I believe that much abduction research is actually unintentional brainwashing and accidental imposition of narratives on hypnosis. Its effect is to leave already troubled people in much worse shape. I feel that it's only a matter of time before somebody is hurt, either driven psychotic or to suicide, and I feel that is very unfortunate." From "A Response to Critics," *MUFON UFO Journal* 242 (1988): 7.

CHAPTER 5

1. Franklin Roach, "Astronomers' Views on UFOs," in *UFOs—A Scientific Debate*, ed. Carl Sagan and Thorton Page (Ithaca, N.Y.: Cornell University Press, 1972), 32.

2. David Michael Jacobs, *The UFO Controversy in America* (Bloomington, Ind.: University of Indiana Press, 1975).

3. Jacob Bronowski, *Science and Human Values* (New York: Harper, 1965), 5.

4. Condon, *Final Report*, viii.

5. Ibid., 1.

6. J. Allen Hynek, "The Condon Report and UFOs," *Bulletin of Atomic Scientists* (April 1969) 39–42; Hynek, *The UFO Experience*, chapter 12.

7. Condon, *Final Report*, 2–3.

8. Ibid., 13.

9. Ibid., 14.

10. Ibid., vii.

11. Jacobs, *UFO Controversy in America*, 257.

12. Donald H. Menzel, "UFOs—The Modern Myth," in *UFOs—A Scientific Debate*, ed. Carl Sagan and Thorton Page (Ithaca, N.Y.: Cornell University Press, 1972), 125, 145.

13. Jacobs, *UFO Controversy in America*, 250.

14. Condon, *Final Report*, vi.

15. William K. Hartmann, "Historical Perspectives: Photos of UFO's," in *UFOs—A Scientific Debate*, ed. Carl Sagan and Thorton Page (Ithaca, N.Y.: Cornell University Press, 1972), 20.
16. Menzel, "UFOs—The Modern Myth," 126, 136–137.
17. James E. McDonald, *Unidentified Flying Objects: Greatest Scientific Problem of Our Times* (Washington, D.C.: Pittsburgh Subcommittee of NICAP, 1967), 17.
18. Menzel, "UFOs—The Modern Myth," 135.
19. Jacobs, *UFO Controversy in America*, 260–262.
20. Vallée, *Anatomy of a Phenomenon*, 88.
21. *Flying Saucer Review,* 21, no. 5 (1976): 2.
22. Menzel, "UFOs—The Modern Myth," 144.
23. Jacobs, *The UFO Controversy in America*, 227.
24. Keyhoe, *Flying Saucers From Outer Space*, 124.
25. Jacobs, *The UFO Controversy in America*, 228.
26. Ibid.
27. Keyhoe, *Flying Saucers from Outer Space*, chapter 8.
28. Condon, *Final Report*, 10; Jacobs, *The UFO Controversy in America*, 229; Keyhoe, *Flying Saucers from Outer Space*, 125.
29. Condon, *Final Report*, 14.
30. David Jacobs, *Secret Life: First Hand Documented Accounts of UFO Abductions* (New York: Simon and Schuster, 1992), 38.
31. Thomas E. Bullard, "UFOs: Lost in the Myths," in *UFOs and Abductions,* ed. by David M. Jacobs (Lawrence, Ken.: University of Kansas Press, 2000), 190.
32. Condon, *Final Report*, 5–6.
33. Ibid., 44.
34. Ibid.
35. Jacobs, *UFO Controversy in America*, 252.
36. Ibid.

CHAPTER 6

1. "The World of Mysteries of Erich von Däniken," *www.daniken.com*.
2. Erich von Däniken, *History Is Wrong* (Franklin Lakes, N.J.: New Page Books, 2009), 50–51.
3. Erich von Däniken, *The Gold of the Gods* (New York: Bantam, 1972), 212–216; Erich von Däniken, *Gods from Outer Space* (New York: Bantam, 1972).
4. von Däniken, *Gold of the Gods*, 212–216.
5. Erich von Däniken, *Chariots of the Gods?* (New York: Bantam, 1970), 26.
6. von Däniken, *Chariots of the Gods?* 37–39; *Gold of the Gods*, 216–221.
7. von Däniken, *Chariots of the Gods?*, 57; *Gods from Outer Space*, 126–127; *Gold of the Gods*, 36, 161–162.
8. von Däniken, *Chariots of the Gods?*, 74–75, 97.
9. Ibid.; *Gods from Outer Space*, 114–116.
10. von Däniken, *Chariots of the Gods?*, 22–23.
11. Ibid., 28.
12. von Däniken, *Gods From Outer Space*, 158, 162.
13. von Däniken, *Chariots of the Gods?*, 34.
14. von Däniken, *Gold of the Gods*, 229.
15. von Däniken, *Gods From Outer Space*, 143–145.
16. Ibid., 155–156.
17. Ibid., 156.
18. von Däniken, *Gold of the Gods*, 229.
19. Martin Gardner, *Fads and Fallacies in the Name of Science* (New York: Dover, 1957), 8–14.
20. von Däniken, *Chariots of the Gods?*, 13–14; 83.
21. Ibid., 29, 61, 80, 107, 122.
22. Ibid., 42.
23. Ibid., 28, 73.
24. Ibid., 32.

25. Ibid., 144.
26. Ibid., 50.
27. cf. Ted Peters, *Science, Theology, and Ethics* (Aldershot, U.K.: Ashgate, 2003); Ted Peters, ed., *Science and Theology: The New Consonance* (Boulder, Colo.: Westview, 1998); Ted Peters, Robert John Russell, and Michael Welker, eds., *Resurrection: Theological and Scientific Assessments* (Grand Rapids, Mich.: Wm. B. Eerdmans, 2002).
28. von Däniken, *Chariots of the Gods?*, 29.
29. von Däniken, *Gods from Outer Space*, 2.
30. von Däniken, *Chariots of the Gods?*, 6, 29–30, 68; von Däniken, *Gods From Outer Space*, 1–3.
31. von Däniken, *Chariots of the Gods?*, 90–96.
32. von Däniken, *Gold of the Gods*, 71.
33. Thor Hyerdahl, *Aku-Aku, the Secret of Easter Island* (Chicago: Rand-McNally, 1958); Clifford Wilson, *Crash Go the Chariots* (New York: Lancer Books, 1972), 19–24; Ronald Story, *The Space-Gods Revealed* (New York: Harper, 1976).
34. von Däniken, *Chariots of the Gods?*, 28, 73.
35. Wilson, *Crash Go the Chariots*, 88.
36. von Däniken, *Chariots of the Gods?*, 76–77.
37. Gardner, *Fads and Fallacies*, 179.
38. von Däniken, *Chariots of the Gods?*, 40.
39. Reece, *UFO Religion*, 201.

CHAPTER 7
1. *www.history.com/shows/ancient-aliens*.
2. Scott Alan Roberts, "Race Interrupted: Ancient Aliens and the Evolution of Humanity," in *Lost Civilizations and Secrets of the Past*, ed. by Michael Pye and Kirsten Dalley (Pompton Plains, N.J.: New Page Books, 2012), 156.
3. Coppens, *Ancient Alien Question*, 288.

4. See the Zecharia Sitchin Website, *www.sitchin.com*. Might the ancient astronaut theory gain confirmation through contemporary contact? Donald Zygutis, independent SETI researcher, claims to have identified just such a confirmatory signal on *www.xseti.org*: "The putative signal is a series of 46 previously unknown triadic sequences located in the Old Testament that exhibit a level of symmetry so unique and sophisticated that it is clearly suggestive of a higher intelligence." Preliminary testing and analysis by credible scholars, including a probability analysis, supports Zygutis's sensational claim. XSETI is convinced that these sequences are smoking gun evidence.

5. R.L. Dione, *God Drives a Flying Saucer* (New York: Bantam, 1969); R.L. Dione, *Is God Supernatural? The 4,000 Year Misunderstanding* (New York: Bantam, 1976).

6. Dione, *God Drives a Flying Saucer*, vii-viii.

7. Ibid., viii, 44–45.

8. Dione, *Is God Supernatural?*, 7.

9. Downing, *Bible and Flying Saucers*, 17–18.

10. Ibid., 76.

11. Ibid., 106.

12. Ibid., 126.

13. Ibid., 178.

14. Barry H. Downing, "The Bible and UFO Abductions," in *MUFON UFO Journal* 357 (1998): 3.

15. Ibid., 5.

16. Barry H. Downing, "The God Hypothesis," in *MUFON UFO Journal* 246 (1988): 12.

17. Barry H. Downing, "UFOs and Religion: Were the Ancient Astronauts Mistaken as Gods?" in *Ancient Astronauts* 3, no. 2 (1977): 51.

18. Downing, *Bible and Flying Saucers*, 24.

19. Ibid., 59.

Notes

20. William Bramley, "UFO Cults: A Brief History of Religion," in *Lost Civilizations and Secrets of the Past,* eds. Michael Pye and Kirsten Dalley (Pompton Plains, N.J.: New Page Books, 2012), 213.
21. Kenneth L. Feder, "Help! I'm Being Followed by Ancient Aliens!" in *Skeptical Inquirer* 37, no. 2 (2013): 55.
22. Michael Shermer, "Gods of the Gaps: Arguments of divine intervention—alien or otherwise—start with ignorance," in *Scientific American* 309 no. 1 (2013): 92.
23. Vallee, *Dimensions,* 284–285. Vallee's use of the term *multiverse,* indicating contemporary parallel universes, is partially consonant with the use of this term among physical cosmologists such as Stephen Hawking, whose M-Theory "predicts that a great many universes were created out of nothing...[and that] these multiple universes arise naturally from physical laws." Stephen Hawking and Leonard Mlodinow, *The Grand Design* (New York: Bantam, 2010), 8–9. Each universe has a separate history, and Hawking does not foresee openings to connect one universe with another as Vallée seems to do.
24. Vallée, *Dimensions,* 166.
25. Ibid., 221.
26. In Downing's astute review of *Dimensions,* he congratulates Vallée for showing that religion belongs "right at the heart of the mystery." Yet he criticizes Vallée for his poor use of biblical material and for failing to recognize that the deceivers behind the UFO phenomenon "...are God, or as god as we've got." Barry H. Downing, "UFOs & Religion: The French Connections," in *MU-FON UFO Journal* 242 (1988): 18–19.
27. Jacques Vallée, *Messengers of Deception* (Berkeley, Calif.: And/Or Press, 1979).
28. Vallée, *Dimensions,* 180.
29. This is also the position entertained by Whitley Strieber, who wrote the Forcword for Vallée's *Dimensions.* In his own book,

Communion, Strieber tips toward the advocates "seeking toward higher consciousness" in hope that we might find "that to know the mind is to know the universe." *Communion* (New York: Doubleday, 1980), 313.

30. See Sagan's position statement in *The Encyclopedia of UFOs,* ed. by Ronald D. Story (New York: Doubleday, 1980), 313.

31. Paul Kurtz, *Transcendental Temptation: A Critique of Religion and the Paranormal* (Buffalo, N.Y.: Prometheus Books, 1986). 443; cf. Vallee, *Dimensions,* 164–165; 215–216.

CHAPTER 8

1. Jim Morony, "An Alien Intervention," in *UFOs and Aliens: Is There Anybody Out There?* ed. Michael Pye and Kirsten Dalley (Pompton Plains, N.J.: New Page Books, 2011), 59–80.

2. Mack, *Abduction,* 181–182.

3. Robert N. Bellah, *Religion in Human Evolution from the Paleolithic to the Axial Age* (Cambridge, Mass.: Harvard University Press, 2011), 45.

4. Steven J. Dick and James E. Strick, *The Living Universe: NASA and the Development of Astrobiology* (New Brunswick, N.J.: Rutgers University Press, 2005), 9.

5. Edna Devore, "Voyages Through Time," *SETI Institute News,* 12, no. 1 (2003): 7.

6. Herbert Spencer, *The Data of Ethics* (New York: A.L. Burt Company, 1879), 28–29.

7. James A. Herrick uses the phrase "the Myth of the Extraterrestrials" to refer to "the idea that intelligent extraterrestrials exist and that interaction with them will inaugurate a new era in human existence." From *Scientific Mythologies: How Science and Science Fiction Forge New Religious Beliefs* (Downers Grove, Ill.: IVP Academic, 2008), 51.

8. Albert R. Harrison, *After Contact: The Human Response to Extraterrestrial Life* (New York and London: Plenum Press, 1997), 312.

9. Huston Smith, *Why Religion Matters* (New York: Harper, 2001), 30.

10. Carl Sagan and Frank Drake, "The Search for Extraterrestrial Intelligence, *Scientific American* 232 (1975): 80–89.

11. Carl Sagan, *Pale Blue Dot: A Vision of the Human Future in Space* (New York: Random House, 1994), 33. In the same book, on page 353, Sagan speculates not only about the scientific advances of ETI, but also wonders what might happen if visiting ETI would find human beings delicious to eat. "Why transport large numbers of us to alien restaurants? The freightage is enormous. Wouldn't it be better just to steal a few humans, sequence our amino acids or whatever else is the source of our delectability, and then just synthesize the identical food product from scratch?"

12. Ernst Mayr, "The probability of extraterrestrial intelligent life," in *Extraterrestrials: Science and Alien Intelligence,* ed. by Edward Regis, Jr. (Cambridge, U.K.: Cambridge University Press, 1985), 27.

13. Paul Davies, *Are We Alone? Implications of the Discovery of Extraterrestrial Life?* (New York: Penguin Books, 1995), 32–33

14. Ibid., 33.

15. Simon Young, "Introduction," in *Designer Evolution: A Transhumanist Manifesto,* ed. by Simon Young (Amherst, N.Y.: Prometheus Books, 2006), 16.

16. Michael Shermer, *How We Believe: The Search for God in an Age of Science* (New York: W.H. Freeman and Co., 2000), 61.

17. Douglas A. Vakoch and Albert A. Harrison, ed., *Civilizations Beyond Earth: Extraterrestrial Life and Society* (New York and Oxford, 2011), 10.

18. Langdon Gilkey, *Naming the Whirlwind: The Renewal of God-Language* (Indianapolis and New York: Bobbs-Merrill, 1969), 234.

19. Ibid., 260.

20. Bullard, "UFOs: Lost in the Myths," 143.

21. Thompson, *Angels and Aliens*, 92–93.

22. Raymond E. Fowler, *The Andreasson Affair* (New York: Bantam, 1979), 13.

23. Elsewhere we find that the spacelings are able to transcend time as we know it, so that they already know our future. They are virtually omniscient. Fowler, *Andreasson Affair*, 136–138.

24. At this point the response of Ray Fowler and another UFO investigator, Dr. Harold Edelstein, is instructive. They are baffled by the overtly religious nature of Betty's encounter. It does not fit. "At this juncture, a religious connotation caused great consternation among us. It somehow seemed completely out of place." Fowler, *Andreasson Affair*, 86. Later Fowler writes, "...the phoenix episode was difficult to accept as a physical experience." Fowler, *Andreasson Affair*, 181. These UFO investigators were working from within Model II and were dumbfounded when they found themselves in Model III.

25. Fowler, *Andreasson Affair*, 92. The suggestion that the giant bird might be the phoenix comes from Betty herself, although it appears that neither she nor her interviewers know much about the phoenix legend.

26. Fowler, *Andreasson Affair*, 91; cf. 209.

27. Ibid.

28. Toward the end of his first book on this case, Fowler shows considerable self-insight on this tricky matter of investigative interpretation. He writes, "Our present interpretation of such events might be purely mechanistic. We would probably accept the possibility of the visitors, but would filter out purported religious messages as irrelevant. Such was certainly the case during portions of our investigation of the Andreasson Affair." Fowler, *Andreasson Affair*, 201. By introducing the Celestial Savior or Religious model here, I am attempting to move UFO investigation beyond its present limitations. Religious messages are relevant!

We need to see them as such. The very task of *UFOs: God's Chariots?* is to expand our investigative conceptual set, which has been too governed by the mechanistic view that presumes the UFO to be only a nuts-and-bolts machine.

29. Raymond E. Fowler, *The Andreasson Affair, Phase Two* (Englewood Cliffs, N.J.: Prentice-Hall, 1982), 196; Raymond E. Fowler, *The Andreasson Legacy* (Englewood Cliffs, N.J.: Prentice-Hall, 1997).

30. Fowler, *Andreasson Affair, Phase Two*, 197.

31. Fowler should be commended for publishing all relevant types of evidence, even when it may not fit neatly into a preset scheme. The kind of criticism to which the Andreasson affair is usually subjected is aimed not at the bias of the investigators. Rather, it is aimed at the reliance upon testimony gained from hypnosis. The problem in general, according to critics, is that under hypnosis we cannot discriminate well between what is fact and what is imaginary. More specifically, critic Ernest Taves attacks the Fowler account for not recognizing the implicit sexual symbolism in what Betty Andreasson has said, suggesting that her UFO account amounts to a sexual fantasy. "Betty Through the Looking Glass," *Skeptical Enquirer* (1979–1980): 88–95. It is my judgment that sexual symbolism may be present, to be sure. Her report of being enclosed and immersed in warm liquid, for example, seems to connote a return to the security of her mother's womb. Fowler, *The Andreasson Affair, Phase Two*, 178. Yet I hesitate to reduce the entire Andreasson affair to sublimated sexual projection.

32. Fowler, *Andreasson Affair*, 110–111, 200.

33. Ibid., 138ff.

34. Ibid., 132.

35. Fowler, *Andreasson Affair, Phase Two*, 258.

36. Fowler, *Andreasson Affair*, 153.

37. Ibid., 134.

CHAPTER 9

1. I first introduced this fourfold structure in "UFOs: The Religious Dimension," *Cross Currents* XXVII, no. 3 (1977): 261–278; "UFO's and Modern Religion," *America* 138, no. 14 (1978): 30–38; "The Religious Dimension to the UFO Phenomenon," MUFON UFO Symposium Proceedings (1979).

2. Mircea Eliade, *Patterns in Comparative Religion* (New York: Meridian Books, 1963), 39; cf. Mircea Eliade, *The Sacred and the Profane* (New York: Harcourt, Brace and World, 1959), 118–119.

3. Jenny Randles, "Do We Now Have Two Ufologies?" MUFON UFO Journal 240 (1988).

4. Fowler, *Andreasson Affair*, 138.

5. Mack, *Abduction*, 52.

6. Ibid., 103.

7. Ibid., 134.

8. Strieber, *Communion*, 106.

9. Jacobs, *Secret Life*, 106.

10. Fowler, *Andreasson Affair*, 29.

11. Fowler, *Andreasson Affair*, 40, 113.

12. Fowler, *Andreasson Affair*, 1, 55.

13. Vallee, *Dimensions*, 42, 131f, 140, 287.

14. Strieber, *Communion*, 107.

15. Dione, *God Drives a Flying Saucer*, viii.

16. Robert Ellwood, *Religious and Spiritual Groups in Modern America* (Englewood Cliffs, N.J.: Prentice-Hall, 1973), 5–11.

17. Monsignor Corrado Balducci in Greer, *Disclosure*, 67.

CHAPTER 10

1. Carl Jung, *Flying Saucers. A Modern Myth of Things Seen in the Skies,* tr. R.F.C. Hull (London: Routledge and Kegan Paul, 1959), chapter 1.

2. Ibid., ix, xiv, 146–147, 149–150.

Notes

3. Ibid., 8. This collective psychic cause may precipitate seeing things that are physically unreal: "Even people who are entirely *compos mentis* and in full possession of their senses can sometimes see things that do not exist." Ibid., 2.
4. Ibid., 15.
5. Ibid., 21.
6. Lester Grinspoon and Alan D. Persky, "Psychiatry and UFO Reports," in *UFOs: A Scientific Debate*, ed. Carl Sagan and Thorton Page (Ithaca, N.Y.: Cornell University Press, 1972), 235.
7. J.A.M. Meerloo, "The Flying Saucer Syndrome and the Need for Miracles," *Journal of the American Medical Association* 203 (1968): 170.
8. In the contactee accounts of the 1950s we find the clearest examples of the nascent UFO myth. At first it may appear that things are more complicated in the 1980s and 1990s because of the growing tie between UFOs and New Age Gnosticism, but a close look at the philosophies of the early generation of contactees will show that the precedents had already been set, even for the importation of Asian doctrines such as reincarnation.
9. Jacobs, *UFO Controversy,* 115. In his book, *Extraterrestrials and the American Zeitgeist,* historian Aaron John Gulyas tries to place Adamski and the other contactees within the context of the Cold War of the 1950s. This is on target. However, Gulyas does not emphasize the tension between the scientific and religious dimensions that we will pursue here.
10. George Adamski and Desmond Leslie, *Flying Saucers Have Landed* (New York: British Book Centre, 1953), 195.
11. Ibid., 198
12. George Adamski, *Inside the Spaceships* (New York: Abelard-Schuman, 1955), 88, 91.
13. Ibid., 169.
14. Truman Bethurum, *Aboard a Flying Saucer* (Los Angeles: DeVorss and Co., 1954), 40.

15. Ibid., 43.

16. Ibid., 146.

17. Ibid., 144.

18. Ibid., 124.

19. Howard Menger, *From Outer Space* (New York: Pyramid, 1959), 111.

20. Daniel Fry, *The White Sands Incident* (Louisville: Best Books, 1966).

21. Ibid., 28.

22. Ellwood, *Religious and Spiritual Groups*, 144.

23. Fry, *White Sands Incident*, 92.

24. Charles Abrahamson, "Introduction to the Author" in *The Day the Gods Came*, George King (Hollywood, Calif.: The Aetherius Society, 1965).

25. King, *Day the Gods Came*, 7.

26. Ibid., 69.

27. J.A. Jackson and Patrick Moore, "Flying Saucers," *Man, Myth and Magic*, ed. Richard Cavendish 8, no. 24 (1970): 1404. cf. Ellwood, *Religious and Spiritual Groups*, 150–156.

28. Jacobs, *Secret Life*, 34.

29. Ibid., 284.

30. Unarius Academy of Science, *www.unarius.org*.

31. John A. Saliba, "UFOs and Religion: A Case Study of Unarius Academy of Science," in *UFO Religions*, ed. James R. Lewis (Buffalo, N.Y.: Prometheus Books, 2003), 192.

32. Ibid., 194.

33. Ibid., 197.

34. Susan Palmer, "The Raelian Apocalypse: Playing with Prophecy, Appeasing the Aliens, or Pleasing the Public?" in *UFO Religions*, James R. Lewis, 271.

35. Ibid., 264.

36. Robert Ellwood, "Contact, Religion, and the Human Future," in *UFO Religions*, James R. Lewis, 378.

Notes

37. Mack, *Abduction,* 390.
38. Ibid., 408.
39. Mack, *Passport to the Cosmos,* 300.
40. For the role of UFOs in spirituality, see Ted Peters, *The Cosmic Self: A Penetrating Look at Today's New Age Movements* (New York: Harper, 1991), 35–38.
41. Fry, *White Sands Incident,* 74.
42. Diana Tumminia, "From Rumor to Postmodern Myth: A Sociological Study of the Transformation of Flying Saucer Rumor," in *Encyclopedic Sourcebook of UFO Religions,* ed. James R. Lewis (Amherst, N.Y.: Prometheus Books, 2003), 103.

CHAPTER 11

1. C.D.B. Bryan, *Close Encounters of the Fourth Kind: Alien Abduction, UFOs, and the Conference at M.I.T.* (New York: Alfred Knopf, 1995), 9.
2. Hopkins, *Intruders,* 118.
3. Robert Sheaffer, *UFO Sightings: The Evidence* (Buffalo, N.Y.: Prometheus Books, 1998), 76.
4. Hopkins, *Intruders,* 36.
5. Moheb Costandi, "Corrupted Memory," *Nature* 500, no. 7462 (2013): 268–270.
6. Strieber, *Communion,* 100, 224.
7. Thompson, *Angels and Aliens,* 209.
8. Hopkins, *Intruders,* 186–187.
9. Ibid., 71.
10. 10. Ibid., 277.
11. Ibid., 118.
12. Ibid., 208.
13. Ibid., 149.
14. Thompson, *Angels and Aliens,* 168–169.
15. The International Center for Abduction Research, *www.ufoabduction.com.*

16. Jerome Clark, "UFO Abductions," *New Age Encyclopedia,* ed. J. Gordon Melton (New York: Gale Research Inc., 1990), 474.

17. Jacobs, *Secret Life,* 46.

18. Ibid., 91.

19. Ibid., 97.

20. Jacobs, *Secret Life,* 133.

21. David Jacobs, "Science, UFOs and the Search for ETI Hybrids," 2013 MUFON Symposium proceedings (B-W Graphics, Inc., 101 Westview Drive, Versailles, Miss.), 132.

22. David Jacobs, *The Threat: Revealing the Secret Alien Agenda* (New York: Simon and Schuster, 1998), 20.

23. Thompson, *Angels and Aliens,* 227.

24. Jacobs, *Secret Life,* 256.

25. Mack, *Abduction,* 39.

26. Ibid., 186.

27. Ibid., 43.

28. Ibid., 398.

29. Ibid., 399.

30. Ibid., 102.

31. Ibid., 8.

32. Ibid., 47.

33. Mack, *Passport to the Cosmos,* 18.

34. Mack, *Abduction,* 66.

35. Ibid., 412.

36. Kathleen Marden, "Alien Abduction: Fact or Fiction?" in *UFOs and Aliens: Is There Anybody Out There?* ed. Michael Pye and Kirsten Dalley (Pompton Plains, N.J.: New Page Books 2011), 101.

37. Kathleen Marden, "Abduction Study Complete," *MUFON UFO Journal* 536 (2012): 1–6. What Marden may be overlooking is that UFO abductions occurred before 1947. In previous centuries a form of literature appeared (the fantastic voyage novel), and this genre included reports of contact with beings living on

the Moon, Mars, and Venus. These overtly gnostic accounts referenced occult beliefs in astral travel, telepathy, and metaphysics. The only new item in the 1950s was the addition of the flying saucer as a travel machine. J. Gordon Melton, an expert in new religious movements, contends that "the flying saucer movement is in effect a new branch of occult religion" from ("The Contactees: A Survey," *Gods Have Landed,* 10). This suggests that selectively disregarding the occult traits of a UFO abduction report on behalf of the nuts-and-bolts elements within the report might be less scientific rather than more scientific.

38. Ibid.
39. Ibid.
40. Ibid.
41. Ibid.
42. Mack, *Abduction,* 24, emphasis in the original.
43. Stanton T. Friedman and Kathleen Marden, *Science Was Wrong* (Pompton Plains, N.J.: New Page Books, 2010), 198–199.
44. Carol Rainy, "The Priests of High Strangeness: The Co-Creation of the Alien Abduction Phenomenon," *Paratopia* 1, no. 1 (2011): *www.paratopia.net/paratopia_magazine/mag_preview_final.pdf.*
45. Ted Peters, *Sin: Radical Evil in Soul and Society* (Grand Rapids, Mich.: Wm. B. Eerdmans, 1994), 244–245.
46. David G. Bromley, "Satanism: The New Cult Scare," in *The Satanism Scare,* ed. by James T. Richardson, Joel Best, and David G. Bromley (New York: Aldine de Gruyter, 1991), 49–72. Bromley coined the term *anti-Satanism.* I added the triumvirate: *Satanism, anti-Satanism,* and *anti-anti-Satanism.*
47. Jacobs, *Secret Life*, 285.
48. Ibid.
49. Ibid.
50. Ibid., 291.
51. Jacobs, *Threat*, 155.
52. Thompson, *Angels and Aliens*, 231.

CHAPTER 12

1. Ted Peters, "Astrotheology," in *The Routledge Companion to Modern Christian Thought*, ed. by Chad Meister and James Beilby (London: Routledge, 2013). With or without this term, numerous theologians are seeing the need to consider the entire cosmos as God's creation; cf. Thomas F. O'Meara, *Vast Universe: Extraterrestrials and Christian Revelation* (Collegeville, Minn.: Liturgical Press, 2012); David Wilkinson, *Science, Religion, and the Search for Extraterrestrial Intelligence* (Oxford and New York: Oxford University Press, 2013); John Hart, *Cosmic Commons: Spirit, Science, and Space* (Eugene, Oreg.: Cascade, 2014).

2. Because, allegedly, Pagan astrology preceded Christianity, and because Christianity incorporated the very Astrotheology it rejected, Christianity is *de facto* a form of paganism. "The knowledge about Astrotheology would reveal the Christians' own religion to be Pagan in virtually every significant aspect, constituting a remake of the ancient religion." D.M. Murdock, "Astrotheology and the Ancients." *http://stellarhousepublishing.com/astrotheology.html#.UMjbpHecmIU*. cf. Michael Tsarion, "Astro-Theology and Siderial Mythology," *www.astrotheology.com/astrotheology1.html*; Craig Lyons, "Bet Emet Ministries," *http://jesusastrotheology.com*.

3. Acharya S., *www.youtube.com/watch?v=YKW9sbJ3v2we&feature=plcp*.

4. For an example of the theology of nature, see Robert John Russell, "Special Providence and Genetic Mutation: A New Defense of Theistic Evolution," in EMB, 196. The concept of creative mutual interaction, or CMI, is the contribution of Robert John Russell. See: *God's Action in Nature's World: Essays in Honor of Robert John Russell*, ed. Ted Peters and Nathan Hallanger (Aldershot, U.K.: Ashgate, 2006), 8–9.

Notes

5. Paul Davies, *God and the New Physics* (New York: Simon and Schuster, 1983), 71.

6. Paul Davies, *The Eerie Silence: Renewing Our Search for Alien Intelligence* (Boston and New York: Houghton Mifflin Harcourt, 2010), 188.

7. This data is drawn from Ted Peters and Julie Louise Froehlig, "Peters ETI Religious Crisis Survey" *www.counterbalance.org/search/search.php?query=Peters+Religious+Crisis+Survey&search=1.* This chapter is a revision and update of Ted Peters, "Astrotheology and the ETI Myth," *Theology and Science*, 7, no. 1 (2009): 3–30; Ted Peters, "Would the Discovery of ETI Provoke a Religious Crisis?" *Astrobiology, History, and Society: Life Beyond Earth and the Impact of Discovery*, ed. by Douglas A. Vakoch (Heidelberg: Springer, 2013), 341–355. The Peters ETI Religious Crisis Survey refines an excellent predecessor survey; see: Victoria Alexander, "Extraterrestrial Life and Religion," *Encyclopedic Sourcebook of UFO Religions*, ed. by James R. Lewis (Buffalo, N.Y.: Prometheus Books, 2003), 360.

8. Troy Matthew interviwed by Alejandro Rojas, *Open Minds*, February 7, 2013, *www.educatinghumanity.com/2013/09/ufo-poll-results-2013.html.*

9. Glenn McWane and David Graham, *The New UFO Sightings* (New York: Warner Books, 1974), 114.

10. Ibid.

11. John S. Dryzek, Richard B. Norgaard, David Schlosberg, "Climate Change and Society: Approaches and Responses," in *The Oxford Hanbook of Climate Change and Society*, ed. by John S. Dryzek, Richard B. Norgaard, David Schlosberg (Oxford: Oxford University Press, 2011).

12. Hart, *Cosmic Commons*.

Index

Index

Index

Index

Index

religious dimension of, 175 (*see also* Celestial Savior Model)

religious symbolism as belonging to, 185

symbolic discourse in the, 189, 191-205

triangular controversy regarding the, 42 (*see also* Keith Thompson)

reports,

  government debunking of, 41

  four families of symbolic meaning in, 191-205

sightings, political tensions and, 208

theology, 187-188

  religious questions and, 159

"true believers," 111, 112

UFOs

  as "natural" phenomena, 107-108

  as a substitute for the divine, 30

  as an escape from the constrictions of scientism, 204

  as fantasies, 209

  engaging in soil sampling and rock collecting, 80-84

  in schools, question of discussion of, 118-124

  possible reasons for, 81, 82

UFOs,

  author's course on, 122-123, 124

  author's four models to interpret, 31, 37

  importance of using, 38

  political implications of, 53

  political significance of, 33

  relatively close sightings of, 35-36

  relatively distant sightings of, 35

  religious valence of, 20

  spiritual sensibilities and, 22

  student interest in, author's suggestions regarding, 121-122

  technological advances influenced by, 70-71

  threat of ecological disaster and, 201

  two questions that orient most discussion of, 105

UFO Controversy in America, The, 106

ufology

  as an expression of religious feelings, 207

  in higher education, place of, 120-124

"ufolatry," 204, 262

Unarians, 226-227

Unarius Society, *see* Unarians

Understanding International, Inc., 219

Unidentified Flying Objects: Greatest Scientific Problem of Our Time, 113

United States Air Force

  and the Roswell crash, 63, 66, 68

  as a player in the triangular controversy, 42

  as denying the existence of flying saucers, 60

  MUFON and the, 118

UNUFO, 33

U.S. government, ufologists' denunciation of, 66-67

utopia, 24

Vakoch, Douglas, 175

Vallée, Jacques, 36-37

  extra-dimensional hypothesis of, 160-164, 194

  opinion on UFO-ETH of, 115

Van Tassell, George, 210

Vandenburg, Hoyt S., 63, 64

Von Däniken, Erich, 120

  ancient alien theology of, 142

  author's conclusion regarding the scholarship of, 141-142

  establishment science's reaction to, 125

  hermeneutical method of, 126

  inconsistencies in the argument of, 130

  religious doubts of, 143-144

  theory of,

    author's evaluation of, 122-123, 125-142

    author's evaluation of scientific proof of, 133-137

  writing style of, 135

About the Author

Ted Peters has been investigating UFOs for four decades, previous serving as the Louisiana State Director of the Mutual UFO Network (MUFON). He is currently Emeritus Professor of Systematic Theology and Ethics at Pacific Lutheran Theological Seminary and the Graduate Theological Union in Berkeley, California. He co-edits *Theology and Science* at the Center for Theology and the Natural Sciences. He has authored and edited more than two dozen books in theology as well as the dialogue between faith and science. See his Web page and blog, "Ted's Timely Take" at *tedstimelytake.com.*